Francophone African Poetry and Drama

ALSO EDITED BY RICHARD J. GRAY II

*The Performance Identities of Lady Gaga:
Critical Essays* (McFarland, 2012)

*The 21st Century Superhero: Essays on
Gender, Genre and Globalization in Film*
(coeditor, with Kaklamanidou, McFarland, 2011)

Francophone African Poetry and Drama

A Cultural History Since the 1960s

RICHARD J. GRAY II

McFarland & Company, Inc., Publishers
Jefferson, North Carolina

LIBRARY OF CONGRESS CATALOGUING-IN-PUBLICATION DATA

Gray, Richard J., 1971– author.
 Francophone African poetry and drama : a cultural history since the 1960s / Richard J. Gray II.
  p.   cm.
 Includes bibliographical references and index.

 ISBN 978-0-7864-7558-2 (softcover : acid free paper) ∞
 ISBN 978-1-4766-1705-3 (ebook)

 1. African poetry (French)—20th century—History and criticism.   2. African poetry (French)—21st century—History and criticism.   3. African drama (French)—20th century—History and criticism.   4. African drama (French)—21st century—History and criticism.   I. Title.
 PQ3982.G73 2014
 841.00996—dc23   2014029929

BRITISH LIBRARY CATALOGUING DATA ARE AVAILABLE

© 2014 Richard J. Gray II. All rights reserved

No part of this book may be reproduced or transmitted in any form or by any means, electronic or mechanical, including photocopying or recording, or by any information storage and retrieval system, without permission in writing from the publisher.

On the cover: antique map of Africa © Comstock/Thinkstock

Printed in the United States of America

McFarland & Company, Inc., Publishers
 Box 611, Jefferson, North Carolina 28640
  www.mcfarlandpub.com

Table of Contents

Preface	1
Introduction	5
1. The Black Man's Burden and the Struggle for Independence	31
2. Oral Societies and Writing in the Language of the Oppressed	58
3. Francophone African Poetry in the Modern World	84
4. Histories, Legends and Myths in Francophone African Theatre	106
5. Writing the Female Body in Francophone African Women's Poetry and Theatre	135
Conclusion	165
Appendix I: Transcript of Barack Obama's Speech at Nelson Mandela's Memorial	173
Appendix II: Recently Published Works by Francophone Women Writers	177
Chapter Notes	181
Works Cited	189
Index	201

Preface

Literature is the lifeblood of a people. Literary works contain all of the "trappings" and "underpinnings" that make culture and civilization understandable and transmittable. Whether in oral or in written form, it relates a civilization's past, its present, and its future. It encompasses the hopes and fears of a people. But the study of literature cannot limit itself to the study of literary forms such as the novel, poetry, or theatre. It must also include a perspective on what shapes those literary forms. It must examine culture. For writer and former president of Senegal Léopold Sédar Senghor, culture is "la symbiose des influences de la géographie et de l'histoire, de la race et de l'ethnie"/"the symbiosis of influences of geography and history, race and ethnicity" (Nadjo 1). We could also define culture as a specific way of being particular to a certain people that governs aspects of daily life and, as a result, that explains the values that this people holds. In short, culture *is* identity. Senghor inquires,

> Le fait pour lui de s'exprimer en français, c'est-à-dire dans une langue étrangère, radicalement différente des langues négro-africaines, permet-il ou non au Noir d'Afrique francophone de rester fidèle à son identité culturelle? Autrement dit, peut-il, tout en s'exprimant en français, rester essentiellement nègre[1] [Nadjo 1].
>
> Does the fact that an African expresses himself in French, that is to say a colonial or foreign language that is radically different from Negro-African languages, allow Francophone sub–Saharan Africa to remain faithful to its cultural identity? In other words, can he remain essentially Negro while expressing himself in French?

Senghor's question is an interesting one that forces us to think about how culture is acquired and how it is transmitted to other individuals.

The book that I started to write more than one year ago and the one that the reader now has in hand are two completely different projects. When I began my research and set my fingers to the keyboard for the first time, I had in my mind the idea of almost exclusively discussing the sociocultural elements of Francophone African "poetic literature," a term that I had fashioned specifically to describe the poetry and theatre of Africa written in French since the 1960s, the decade in which the nations of this particular geographic region began to gain their independence. What I discovered both during my data collection and during my reflections on my findings in an attempt to reach this specific and well-defined end, however, was that in setting this region apart geographically and by limiting it linguistically (*littérature d'expression française*), I risked both marginalizing and portraying inaccurately the very cultures to which I had originally sought to pay tribute. This contradiction is called "the historian's paradox." In his book of similar name entitled *The Historians' Paradox: The Study of History in Our Time*, Peter Hoffer states that "perhaps we should just embrace the paradox that we historians cannot know what we proclaim to know. After all, a paradox is an educated person's delight. It frames humor and inspires wonder" (x). Hoffer's words underscore the reality that history is impossible yet necessary at the same time. Thus, I fell into history's trap. In an attempt to recreate cultural history, I found myself initially caught in labyrinth of analyzing the study of history itself. To extend the notion of the "historian's paradox" further, it also refers to the historian's overall conundrum of revealing any information that s/he has discovered. To explain this scenario in concrete terms, it is like discovering a precious natural resource like gold or diamonds, but then quickly realizing that as soon as you reveal your discovery to the rest of the world, poachers and pillagers will descend on your findings and they will exploit these resources to exhaustion. The "poachers and pillagers" analogy is completely appropriate to describe the history of the continent of Africa, particularly since its division and redistribution in 1885.

In addition, my overall perspective on the nature of the project itself evolved during the course of my work, in part, because as I advanced through the research and inquiry necessary to make this book possible, I realized that although I must provide specific examples to describe the landscape of Francophone African poetic literature that I am considering here, I must also exercise care that I should not extend too far any generalities that I create. It is for this particular reason that my work sometimes includes observations and perspectives, rather than exclusively "hard facts." By connecting my work on Francophone African poetic literature to a larger "World" context, I believe that I have overcome some of the problems associated with establishing generalizations. In the chapters that follow, I have included discussions of themes that might initially appear to the reader to be outside of the general scope of this book that might lead one to ask the question, "What does this have to do with Francophone African poetic literature?" Themes include the "Myth of Shaka," a discussion of the South African warrior king Shaka Zulu,[2] a section dedicated to a discussion of Nelson Mandela, the former president of South Africa, and a section devoted to a discussion of the work of Josephine Baker, the black American dancer who set Parisian stages on fire in the 1920s. Toward the end of the completion of this book, it became clear to me that building bridges between various African cultures both within and outside of the continent of Africa itself had become a driving motivation of my work. A discussion of the "Myth of Shaka" allows me to thematically connect Francophone Africa to the rest of the continent. The section devoted to the life and work of Nelson Mandela and the Francophone African poetic literature that Mandela inspired thus permit me to build a bridge between Francophone Africa, the African continent, and the rest of the world. The section dedicated to Josephine Baker builds bridges between the Americas, France, and Africa, and it allows me to discuss the complexities of the perception of Francophone African women by white audiences. Therefore, my intent is not to create a static portrait of Francophone African poetic literature by showing the reader how it "is," but rather my goal here is to paint a picture of the cultural structures that have brought this literature into "being" from a theoretical perspective. In short, this book uses the lens of critical cultural discourse that according to Cynthia Lewis is "both a theory and a method that examines how social and power relations, identities and knowledge are constructed through written, visual, and spoken text and their production and consumption" (374) as the epistemological framework for examining the development of Francophone African theatre and poetry.

As I began to see the light at the end of the tunnel signaling that the completion of this book was, indeed, on the horizon, a significant world event occurred that both derailed my train of thought and culturally enriched my understanding of both my writing and Francophone African poetic literature: the death of the former president of South Africa, Nelson Mandela on December 5, 2013. Although I had already planned to discuss the figure of Mandela through the anthology of poetry collected by the Cameroonian poet Paul Dakeyo, Mandela's passing or "transition," as the South Africans call it, brought greater meaning both to Dakeyo's poetry collection and to the cultural and historical significance of its subject matter. The poems included in Dakeyo's collection deserve further examination outside of the context of this book. In a Facebook status on the day of Mandela's death, U.S. President Barack Obama summed up in excellent fashion the significance of this world figure: "Let us pause and give thanks for the fact that Nelson Mandela lived—a man who took history in his hands and bent the arc of the moral universe toward justice."[3] Mandela's memorial service witnessed the gathering of ninety-one heads of state and was broadcast worldwide in five languages. Although it is difficult to fully gauge Mandela's impact on our planet, journalists and writers throughout the world have linked his contribution to those of Gandhi and Dr. Martin Luther King, Jr., ranking Mandela among the most influential world figures of the 20th century. The fact that African writers choose to write about him in French underscores the reality that these writers consider the nations of Francophone Africa to belong to the "larger picture" of geocultural history. The nations of French-speaking Africa have both impacted and been impacted by world cultural and historic events.

I would be negligent if I did not acknowledge the individuals who have supported me throughout the research and writing phases of this book. Thank you to the staff at the Musée du Quai Branly in Paris who illuminated my experience during my visit in 2012. The vast collection of African art objects held there served as the inspiration for my research. I would like to thank my departmental colleagues Jen, Bill, Barb, Mary, and Lina for respecting the time restrictions under which this project had placed me. Thank you to my students who helped me to develop my ideas in the courses that I taught in French and Francophone literature and culture in the Spring 2013 and Fall 2013 semesters at Denison University and at Ashland University. Thank you to my close friend and colleague, Mike, who has always pushed me to research and to write even when I have been under the yoke of a heavy teaching load. Thank you to my parents, my in-laws, my sister and her family. You have helped me in more ways that you will ever know. My most heartfelt thanks go to my wife, Andrea, and to my four children, Geneviève, Madeleine, Catherine, and RJ. Andrea, you have provided continuous support for my teaching and scholarship and have helped me to navigate the road of life. Geneviève, Madeleine, Catherine, and RJ, you are the future of this planet. I sincerely hope that one day you will inherit the world that Nelson Mandela had envisioned; one that is full of peace, hope, and love.

Introduction

> Your joy is very often our anger, and your despair our hope. Most of us came here in chains, and many of you came here to escape your chains. Your freedom was our slavery, and therein lies the very difference in the way we look at life.
> —*Killens 15–6*

The citation that opens this book presents a perspective on slave life in the United States. It shows that when it is a matter of perspective, the point of view of the colonizer and that of the slave are often vastly different. From the beginning of the Atlantic slave trade in the 17th century, the "Dark Continent" opened itself up to the world. Frequently called "The Cradle of Mankind," Africa remains one of the most troubled areas on the planet. The economic, social, and political issues present within her fifty-four official countries are continually newsworthy.[1] Famine, disease, political instability, and civil warfare plague the Dark Continent. Impacted by the colonial enterprises of the 19th and 20th centuries and even after she gained her independence, the nations of what is arguably the world's most diverse continent face continued and often insurmountable obstacles. The challenges within these nations resound throughout the literary creations of their artists. Their voices—whether in drama or in poetry—resonate the obstacles, opinions, and viewpoints not only of their creators, but also of the diverse peoples for whom these literary artisans penned their works. In Francophone Africa, in particular, an area in which oral literature has always been the cultural lifeblood of the people, viewpoints on the colonized experience, suffering, and liberation flow like a river through poetic verses. The mother tongue of the colonizer, the French language became a mantel worn by the colonized that he could use for self-expression and liberation. Showcasing the juxtaposition of the development of Francophone African poetic literature (poetry and theatre) with an analysis based on French critical theory and an understanding of local anthropology and socioculturalism, this book offers a multidisciplinary perspective on Francophone African poetic texts representing the diverse nations of French-speaking Africa (including Benin, Burkina Faso, Cameroon, Côte d'Ivoire, Democratic Republic of the Congo, Guinea, Mali, Senegal, Togo). By exploring the principle themes of Francophone African society of the 20th century such as the gaining of independence, socio-political relations, gender equilibrium, and globalization, my work invites readers to examine the poetic texts of some of the most influential writers of the age including Sony Labou Tansi, Senouvo Agbota Zinsou, Léopold Sédar Senghor, David Diop, Gérald-Félix Tchicaya (Tchicaya U Tam'si),[2] Paul Dakeyo, Bernard Dadié,[3] and Werewere Liking Gnepo. The 21st century—The Internet Age—is an age of increasing globalization in which Francophone African literature enjoys a state of connectedness that it has never before known. Historically relegated to the margins of literary composition, Francophone literature has been a subject of study for the past fifty years. Marginality, quite literally, refers to the spatial property of a location in which something is situated. Figuratively speaking, marginality suggests something that is on the edges or at the outer limits of social acceptability. Recently, however, scholars of both continental France and of the former French colonies have begun to question whether or not to continue to study Francophone literature as a *œuvre à part* or to include Francophone literature within the larger category of literature composed in the French language. This book explores this particular question in detail.

Foregrounded in an analysis of the significant social and political events of both pre-independence and post-independence Francophone Africa, the Introduction pours the cultural and historical foundation for an examination of the creation and the impact of the poetic literature of the most significant Francophone African writers of the 20th century and beyond. Throughout this book, the reader should understand the term "poetic literature" as literary creations—traditional poems, stage plays, or other dramatic works—that follow relatively standard norms of poetic expression such as the use of rhyme and meter, but which also distinguish themselves from literary genres such as the novel and the short story inasmuch as the works in question here tend to operate with a limited number of characters (if any) and voices. It is important to also underscore the fact that the writers examined here all write in French, even though the author of this book recognizes the fact that there are other world (colonial) languages as well as indigenous languages used for self-expression within Francophone Africa. Therefore, use of the phrases "Francophone Africa"/"French-speaking Africa" or "Francophone African"/"French-speaking African" is intended to refer to those geographic areas and those writers impacted by French colonialism (not including the Maghreb,

Egypt, or Madagascar). Writing in a language that was, quite literally, forced on Francophone African peoples, these African writers *d'expression française* forged their own means of self-expression. Communicating both the unique identities of their peoples and the struggles endured throughout centuries of colonization, in particular, during the time and after the time of French colonization of the so-called "Dark Continent," through their poetry and through their drama, Francophone African writers sought to create new resounding voices.

The 1960s and 1970s, in particular, witnessed the emergence of a new kind of nationalist and post-nationalist poetic literature. Among the nationalist literature of the age included the reinvention of African myths such as seen in Léopold Sédar Senghor's *Chaka* (1956), Seydou Badian Kouyaté's *La Mort de Chaka* (1962), and Jean Pliya's[4] *Kondo le requin* (1966). The post-nationalist works that followed, though recognizing their forefathers, contained a distinctly militant component evidenced in the writings of Werewere Liking Gnepo (Senegal), Sony Labou Tansi[5] (Republic of Congo), and Senouvo Agbota Zinsou (Togo). The shared characteristic of these writers and others of this generation was the desire to create a new means of poetic expression—both in poetry and in drama—which, although recognizing the oral literature of their peoples' past, also employed a new means of self-expression. *Francophone African Poetry and Drama: A Cultural History Since the 1960s* focuses essentially on works of poetry and drama created and performed during the post-independence era, that is to say, from the 1960s until the present day. The contextual framework under investigation in this book is the one informed by the most noteworthy sociocultural and sociopolitical events of the age as they occurred in each of the countries under examination in this work. This Introduction, therefore, seeks to provide an engagement with the theoretical significance of these events, and subsequent chapters will explore their practical implications in the works of individual poets and dramatists. The Conclusion extends this analysis further by providing an overview of Francophone African poetic literature in the New Millennium, and it will suggest several new and exciting challenges that contemporary works provide to both readers and critics. As we will see, the work of the poets and dramatists on whom we will focus our examination inscribes itself into a long history of a dialectic that has been in continuous operation since the time that French colonists first set foot on the continent of Africa. In short, the works examined here underscore the realities of the contemporary Francophone world in which these authors, paradoxically, seek to explain the experiences of their peoples through a literature that by its very nature calls itself "French-speaking." It is for this reason that some Francophone authors have recently begun to abandon the Francophone categorization in favor of that of "World Literature in French," for this new classification brings Francophone writers into the fold of all writers who, whether because of the fact that they were born on French soil or because of their colonized past, chose to express themselves in the French language. Thus, for the purposes of this book, the term "Francophone African" or "French-speaking African" must be understood as a geographic limiter and not as a marginalizing label.

Chapter 1, "The Black Man's Burden and the Struggle for Independence," focuses on the conditions of the Francophone African individual whose nation is gaining independence. He is the direct recipient of the French cultural product first brought to the continent in the 19th century. The mission to civilize the African continent has historically been referred to as the "White Man's Burden." In homage to the Rudyard Kipling poem by the same name, this term refers to the presumed responsibility of white Europeans to govern and to bring their assumedly superior civilizations and cultures to African peoples. Throughout the centuries of the colonization of Africa, it was a slogan that served to validate European imperialism. In its sociological form, the "White Man's Burden" became the duty, obligation, and responsibility of every white man to ensure that his culture was bestowed on the pre–Enlightenment tribes of Africa. In its political form, the "White Man's Burden" was both a means to install foreign political systems within Africa and a way to relocate tribes of various ethnic groups in order to keep the latter under control. The African continent became a place of tremendous discovery for the white settler, a landscape that he must tame and cultivate. The "Black Man's Burden" formed the counterpoint. It was the African response to colonization. It was the black voice speaking out against invasion, a voice crying out against a foreign people who had used the reason of their inherent superiority over the black man as a means to subjugate an entire continent. In French-speaking Africa, in particular, the cry appeared in the poetic voices of its writers, its poets and dramatists who through descriptions of the scourges of colonization sought to reclaim their rightful place among the civilized and cultivated peoples of the modern world.

Thus, Chapter 1 examines the "Black Man's Burden" and the move toward independence reflected in the poetic literature of the period. Through an exploration of the works of writers including Léopold Sédar Senghor (Senegal), Guillaume Oyônô-Mbia (Cameroon), and Senouvo Agbota Zinsou (Togo), it explores the struggles of the French-speaking peoples of Sub-Saharan Africa as depicted in the poetry and the theatre of the era. These literary works cast a light on the difficulties of gaining independence in an age in which corruption became a defining characteristic of the African elite.[6] "The Black Man's

Burden and the Struggle for Independence" analyzes the social structures (political, familial, etc.) and their implications within Francophone African poetic literature. At the Council of Berlin of 1884–1885, the great nations of Western Europe convened to determine how to divide the African continent. No African nations were invited to this assembly. The result of this gathering was not only the division and reallocation of the continent of Africa, but also the redistribution of African tribes. To this effect, these African tribes, many of which had traditionally been warring adversaries were now placed *côte-à-côte* in "nations" created by white Europeans thousands of miles away the vast majority of whom had never set foot on African soil. The "Scramble for Africa" had begun with European nations sending hordes of white settlers to the Dark Continent in the hopes of bringing civilization to this unenlightened corner of the globe. The "White Man's Burden," God's will for the people of Africa that they should be subjugated to white external domination, became the driving principle of colonization.

In Chapter 2, "Oral Societies and Writing in the Language of the Oppressed," the exploration of Francophone poetic literature in this chapter discusses the role that the French language plays in the literary compositions of the authors examined. Language has the power both to unite people as well as to divide people. When the French language arrived in Africa with the first colonists, it already had not only a vast number of speakers, but also a well-defined, uniform, and highly-governed system of writing with the *Académie Française* responsible for language oversight. Francophone African nations, however, lacked both the volume of speakers, a written language (for the most part), and the financial capital necessary to ensure the propagation of their indigenous languages. When French settlers first cast an anchor on the continent of Africa, traditional African languages numbered in the hundreds. Multiple languages were necessary among a single-speaker, for these languages each served a different purpose. In the West African nation of Burkina Faso, for example, an inhabitant most likely already spoke at least two languages (a tribal language such as *mooré* and a language of business and trade like *dioula*). The large numbers of tribes combined with the need to conduct trade with neighbors created the necessity for a polyglottal society. With the arrival of the French language, however, the linguistic situation in Francophone Africa became very dicey. The French language carried with it all of the "organizations" of the motherland, that is to say that it also brought with it the governmental administrations, the educational structures, and the political systems of France. For a Francophone African—regardless of his ethnicity or his nation of origin—to write in French became an inherent irony. The French language (with its associated culture) was a foreign tongue containing structures and concepts that were strange to the African. Paradoxically, the French language afforded the Francophone African a linguistic vehicle through which he could comment on the colonial system. Through an analysis of literary works by authors such as Anchou Thiam, Haja M'Bana Diop (both of Senegal), and Manthia Diawara (Mali), and critical theories put forth by Édouard Glissant and Jacques Derrida, this chapter explores the use of the "language of the oppressed" as a means to express the African condition to a wide audience. As we will see, the title of this chapter is a play-on-words, for it expresses both the language used (French) as well as the thoughts, sentiments, and emotions of the colonized individual.

It is impossible for multiple languages to interact without some transference—cultural, linguistic, etc.—between the languages in question. Chapter 2 considers the notion of hybridity in Francophone African poetic texts. In its most concrete terms, hybridity signifies the blending of races, the result of which—as some scholars have suggested—is the dilution of both races. For the purposes of this chapter, the term "hybridity" must be understood within the context of postcolonial studies, namely through the definition proposed by leading theorists such as Homi Bhabha. In *The Location of Culture* (1994), Bhabha examined the liminality of hybridity as a paradigm of colonial anxiety. He maintained that colonial hybridity created ambivalence in the colonial masters and as such altered the authority of power. This postcolonial theory serves to better explain the dialectic existing between colonizers and colonized. Other postcolonial theorists such as Frantz Fanon and Edward Said provided complimentary theories to that of Homi Bhabha. Fanon's work examined the nature of colonialism and the detrimental effects of European colonialism on the mental health of black peoples who had been subjugated into economic colonies (Africa, the Caribbean).

For Fanon, colonialism was a source of physical and mental violence that must be resisted by the colonized peoples. As such, Fanon advocated that violent resistance to colonialism was a mentally cathartic practice that cleansed the psyche and restored the self-respect (identity) of those citizens whose political oppression and economic subjugation was established and achieved through the dehumanizing institutional violence (social, economic, cultural, etc.) of the colonial power. For his part, Said examined the subjugated people as the "Other," fashioned and forged by the West in order to create a hierarchical structure that would eventually self-perpetuate. His concept of "Orientalism" outlined in a book by the same name was an examination of the binary social relationship of the colonizer/colonized based on the notion that "knowledge is power." Europeans (obviously) had the knowledge as it was through this knowledge that they would be able to control the peoples of the world. Chapter 2 serves to illustrate the mixture of traditional and external forms of written expression of Francophone African poetic literature by asking questions such as: Where is the intersection of indigenous and foreign forms of written expression? What is the effect of hybridity? Is the hybrid creation a "watered-down" product or does the intersection of two different means of expression enhance the final product? Does hybridic writing evidence a failure on the part of traditional writers to resist external influences, or is it, rather, a reflection of the writers' ability to harness all of the tools that are available?

In Chapter 3, "Francophone African Poetry in the Modern World," I explore the Francophone African writer's attempt to convey his/her historic, literary, and cultural essence. Regardless of the level of assimilation present within a colonial system, even after years of colonization, there are still verifiable traces of the indigenous culture. There are certain characteristics of the Francophone African mindset that will never be fully replaced no matter the level of colonial or neocolonial influence. One such characteristic outlined here is the oral quality of the literature in question. For the purposes of this chapter, without prejudice I refer to this oral quality as the "native voice." Thus, Chapter 3 represents both a cultural and an ethnographic study of poetry. By exploring the poetic works of authors including Léopold Sédar Senghor (Senegal), David Diop (born in France, but of Senegalese/Cameroonian origin), M'Bana Diop (Senegambia), and Paul Dakeyo (Cameroon), this chapter seeks to understand the *africanité* of Francophone African poetic literature by asking questions such as: What traces of Africa are found in this literature? What literary styles serve as vehicles for traditional African self-expression? How are the local colors and traditions painted and described in this literature? How do African authors of French expression resist colonization through their writings? The "native voice" reflects the words, sounds, and music of Africa's traditional cultural past. Absent a written language in some cases, it is that which traces its origins to nations whose histories were transmitted from generation to generation by African oral poets (*griots*). These storytellers occupy a prominent place in traditional Francophone African societies. The "native voice" articulated in traditional French-language writings initially inscribed themselves in a literary movement called "Négritude." Coined by Martinican poet Aimé Césaire, the Négritude movement found solidarity in a common black identity as a means of rejecting the identity placed on Africans as a result of the colonial enterprise. This shared black heritage became a weapon used against French political and intellectual hegemony.

Chapter 4, "Histories, Legends and Myths in Francophone African Theatre," examines myth criticism, African national theatre, and the incorporation and development of the myth of Shaka Zulu within the theatre of French-speaking Africa. In *The Power of Myth* (1988), Joseph Campbell, the literary scholar who outlined a hero archetype from the mythology of many cultures, described a hero as "someone who has given his or her life to something bigger than oneself" (151). In his influential text entitled *The Hero with a Thousand Faces* (1949), Campbell defined the monomyth,[7] or the "quest of the hero" motif, a definition illuminating the development of the hero within the genre of the novel, in particular. The motif often showcases a conflict between the protagonist and contemporary traditions in which the protagonist slowly accepts the values of his society finally leading to his own acceptance within that particular civilization. Like the myriad cultures of French-speaking Africa, the world to which Campbell refers is steeped in myth. Myth criticism aids the reader to understand more fully the development of the "heroic" narrator. As a critical approach, myth criticism considers literary texts as time-honored, widely shared myths such as the Creation or the "hero's quest." The myth is a traditional narrative typically involving mystical persons embodying popular ideas on natural or social phenomena. As Claude Lévi-Strauss stated in *Myth and Meaning* (1978), "Mythology is static, we find the same mythical elements combined over and over again..." (17). This fact is particularly true within Francophone Africa, a region in which many myths circulate in both oral and written literatures. All myths contain heroes represented as protagonists. They are conflicted and flawed. These "hero myths" use symbolic language to tell stories that teach us how to overcome obstacles that we encounter either in the world or within ourselves.

African national theatre is steeped in notions of performance and focused on the traditional theatre play or the "pièce de théâtre." The Francophone African "theatre space," however, is not something that we can easily categorize. African national theatre is always the juxtaposition of the "performance" aspect and the "reception" aspect of theatre combined with the developing of relationships between the performers and the audience who are sometimes not that greatly distanced within the scenic space. With the arrival of the New Millennium, we must reconsider how we view Francophone African theatre by moving beyond examining traditional theatrical forms to look at new forms. More importantly, we must explore the cultural foundation that gives rise to these forms. Therefore, now is the time to investigate both how Francophone African theatre emerges from a larger theatrical tradition at the same time as it exhibits its own unique features. The sociocultural characteristics of Francophone African theatre combined with its historical aspects form African theatre aesthetics. Like that exhibited in traditional Greek theatre, one of the most important features of African aesthetics is its function of transgression. As we will see later in the case of the myth of Shaka, transgression is realized

Introduction 13

in the cathartic moment. The term "transgression" itself, however, holds a dual-meaning, for it also indicates a deviation from the standards of the traditional law. Thus, in a society in which established authorities are challenged, such confrontation is met with excessively severe punishment such as assassination or imprisonment. Chapter 4 explores the Myth of Shaka Zulu in Francophone African theatre, a legend that holds widespread appeal throughout the continent. There are many questions with regard to why this particular heroic myth has spread so widely throughout Africa. Is it because Shaka, the Zulu warrior-king, was the true savior that his people needed to escape troubled times? Or does Shaka somehow embody the classical mythical hero who, although great in many respects, will never be able to escape his tragic flaw, which is an ever-consuming hubris?

In Chapter 5, "Writing the Female Body in Francophone African Women's Poetry and Theatre," I examine the question of how Francophone African women write both *with* and *against* the female body. On the European continent itself, gender subjugation was also an important subject of debate. On April 21, 1944, the Republic of France granted French women the right to vote. Although feminism in France had certainly sprung up from the time of the Revolution, it was not until the close of World War II that French women were able to cast a vote. In reality, however, it was not before the events of May 1968 and the founding of the *Mouvement de libération des femmes* that French women fully participated in the French political system. In a very real sense, French women's struggles for political independence mirrored that of Francophone African citizens of the period. In French-speaking Africa itself, men and women had never been "equal." Each had served traditional family roles with women bearing the lion's share of domestic responsibilities. As part of the polygamist system, African men could choose multiple wives and multiple families. These wives would each take care of the home, but they would also labor innumerable hours in the fields. Until the publication of Jeanine Moulin's *Huit siècles de poésie féminine* (1975), women's poetry in the French and Francophone traditions had gone unnoticed. In 1984, French critic Jacques Chevrier stated that it was too soon to speak of the presence of Francophone women's writing in Africa. In the 1990s, however, significant critical works on Francophone Africa women's writing appeared including Irène Assiba d'Almeida's book entitled *Francophone African Women Writers: Destroying the Emptiness of Silence* (1994) and Odile Cazenave's *Femmes rebelles: Naissance d'un nouveau roman africain au féminin* (1996) that began to critically explore the cultural and literary significance of women's writing in the French-speaking world.

Chapter 5 of this book is devoted to women's writing in Francophone

Africa. By including a separate chapter on women's writing I do not intend to marginalize it, but rather to showcase the contribution of female writing to the body of writing produced in French-speaking Africa. This chapter explores themes including female subjecthood, feminine space, sexual politics, feminist theory as it relates to the continent of Africa, the "male gaze," the suppression of women's writing in Francophone Africa as a whole, the image of the African woman produced both within Africa and beyond, general representations of African women in literature, and lastly, "The Josephine Baker effect." In a way, literary movements such as Négritude, while promoting both the revitalization and a new understanding of African cultural, historical, and literary thought, for the most part, have continued to marginalize women. It is for this reason that the canon of poetic texts written by Francophone African women remains restricted. How can it be that John Conteh-Morgan's *Theatre and Drama in Francophone Africa: A Critical Introduction* contains only one Francophone women playwright (Werewere Liking Gnepo)? Do Francophone women not write plays? In addition, producing a list of Francophone female poets remains rather difficult. Does this suggest, then, that women do not engage in what I call "poetic literature," or is there another explanation for the lack of plays and poems *d'expression française féminine* in French-speaking Africa?

Throughout the Introduction and its five chapters, this book discusses several general themes including the role of sociopolitical relations in the development of the poetic literature of the period. I ask questions such as: How do the conflicts present in the social and political relations of the day resonate in poetry and theatre before, during, and after the coming of independence? What role does poetic literature serve in either helping or hindering Francophone African nations as they endeavor to work together (sometimes) with other African nations in the years following independence? What is the effect of neocolonialism in Francophone Africa and how does it perpetuate itself in the administrative, educational, and political systems after independence? This book also serves to examine gender (in)equalities within the traditional Francophone African family by asking the following questions: How are family roles portrayed in Francophone African poetic literature? Is there a struggle for power indicated in the literature? Is there any attempt to resolve these struggles or are they left to perpetuate in the future?

The 21st century is an age of increasing globalization. Francophone Africa plays a role in the current geo-cultural market. If the Council of Berlin of 1884–1885 served to divide Africa among the Western European nations, it also put Africa "on the map." Since independence, the countries of Francophone Africa have become part of a much larger sociocultural, socioeconomic, and sociopolitical system. The cultures, economies, and political systems of the region are tightly linked to such an extent that understanding the role of each individual country within the geopolitical system has become increasingly more difficult. For the purposes of this book, globalization refers to the role that Francophone African countries play within the geopolitical system, not necessarily what they contribute to that system, but often the subordinate role that they play in it. Suffice it to say, Africa as a continent consumes much of the world's resources in matters of relief, as the famines, wars, military coups, and genocide have turned the region into the poorest and most unstable part of the world. One could argue that the redistribution of Africa in the 19th century created the economic and political instabilities of the 20th century. Such a statement, however, assumes that Africa on the whole suffered no adversities prior to colonization. This assumption would be nearly impossible to verify. Nonetheless, it is safe to say that the challenges of Africa—in particular, those of French-speaking Africa—are more pronounced and are more greatly defined than those of preceding centuries. As globalization continues in the 21st century, the countries of Francophone Africa continue to adapt to the need to become a larger part of the geopolitical and geoeconomic systems.

Working across the genres of poetry and theatre, this book takes up the question of how Francophone African literature written in French is not only a cultural product, but also a reflection of the various cultures in which it originates. This book also focuses on new ways of understanding Francophone African literature and its multiple voices, such as the diversification of the processes of identity formation with and belonging to the African continent, the different means of resistance to former notions of literary composition as art, a remapping of themes of social responsibility and diversity, and finally the impact of globalization both of Francophone Africans' understanding of themselves as well as their ability to participate in geoeconomics, geopolitics, and geoculture. By looking at Francophone African literature from yesterday to today, this book hopes to highlight the possible canonization of contemporary Francophone works. I argue that the aesthetic as well as the political issues at play underscore this apparent dialogue as writers and critics increasingly acknowledge the validity of Francophone African writing. I wish to make it clear, however, that this book does not intend to be a literary analysis of Francophone African writing nor does it claim to present a comprehensive accounting of literary texts composed in the region of French-speaking Africa. As a result, I fully acknowledge the limitations of my writing. Given its grounding in cultural history, this book presents an overview of the sociocultural "inner workings" of literary texts created in Francophone Africa during the period under consideration.

As I write this book in the post–9/11 era, and age in which it always seems that we are heading from one crisis to another, both postcolonial and "Négritude" theories, two of the dominant analytical tools used to examine such literature, are at a crossroads. As noted by David Jafferess, Julie McGonegal, and Sabine Milz in "The Politics of Postcoloniality" in *Postcolonial Text* (2006), "Postcolonial theory has provided a valuable critique of the discourses that underwrote the colonial project and that continue to inform neo-liberal imaginings of a unified world (market), including 'civilization and progress'" (2). Postcolonial studies brings to bear a wide range of fields of inquiry including diaspora studies, ethnic studies, and globalization studies. We must acknowledge that such theoretical frameworks though necessary to form some point of entry to the study of a cultural product are also somewhat limiting. We could claim that postcolonial theory is nothing more than a capitalist product used not only to explain the postcolonial world, but also to perpetuate a Western capitalistic work. It is for this reason that many current scholars openly reject the notion of postcolonialism. As Terry Engleton wrote in *Sweet Violence: The Idea of the Tragic* (2003), "A faith in plurality, plasticity, dismantling, destabilizing, the power of endless self-invention—all this, while undoubtedly radical in some contexts, also smacks of a distinctively Western culture and an advanced capitalistic world" (xi). Through both recognizing and using postcolonial theory, one of the main goals of this book is to attempt to work against it so that the understanding conveyed within the Francophone African poetic literature discussed here is a reflection of the essence of the works examined rather than a reflection of the outside world. This endeavor presents a great challenge. Furthermore, in *Désir d'Afrique* (2002), Boniface Mongo-Mboussa discusses the idea that, by definition, postcolonialism is an entanglement for African writers that forces them into expressing their essence through a means that it entirely foreign to the African continent. He suggests the notion that "Francophone African literature's organic 'expansion' has wrongly been evaluated by critics as a series of ruptures, thereby preventing a full understanding of the field" (Cazenave 5). In short, he puts forth an entire re-evaluation of the idea of literary tradition. In a sense, this is one of the primary goals of this book. The notion of a Francophone African literary tradition should not restrict the range of possible interpretive responsibilities. In a sense, this book sets out to follow the central thesis of Ngũgĩ wa Thiong'o's *Decolonizing the Mind* (1986), an essay in which the Kenyan author argued for African writers to express themselves in their native languages, rather than in European (colonial) languages, in order to renounce neocolonialism.

When I began to think about writing a book on Francophone African literature, I had intended to focus on the development of Francophone African theatre since independence. Considering poetry and theatre both as "performance arts" and the voices that make up poetry and theatre as a component of that performance, I became interested in the diverse performative voices present within poetic literature itself through the framework of performance studies that had a clearly-defined anthropological component. In his book entitled *The Future of Ritual*, anthropologist Richard Schechner wrote that "performance's subject [is] transformation: the startling ability of human beings to create themselves, to change, to become—for worse or better—what they ordinarily are not" (1). Additionally, in *Between Theater and Anthropology*, Schechner commented on the characteristics that these two disciplines share such as containing the idea of a transformative act, notions of liminality, and the interaction between performer and spectator. Liminal spaces typically appear as places of birth, re-birth and renewal, and a loss of liminality leads to a loss of strength in the protagonist. Poetry itself constitutes a dramatic performance. Through performance, human beings move through the life cycle: birth, transformation, death. Fellow anthropologist Victor Turner noted that these performances seemed to occur in a liminal space of heightened intensity separate from routine life, much like a dramatic theatre performance. If Shakespeare is correct in claiming that "All the world is a stage," then it is our duty to see how these stage performances "play out" the cultural realities of the place and time in question.

Finally, this book initiates a conversation on the importance of Francophone African poetic literature today, more than fifty years after the French-speaking nations of Africa gained independence. Further, I intend here to argue that Francophone African poetic literature should not be understood as separated from the rest of the continent of Africa, nor should we consider it as separate from world literature as a whole. In my view, the originality of my work is found not only in the historical analysis of cultural events but also in my re-evaluation of the responsibility of writers to form our understanding of the very writing in which they are engaged. My decision to focus on poetic works is fully intentional. These particular works contain both the cohesion and the efficiency necessary for this type of examination. My work concerns African writers *d'expression française* that neither suggests nor implies that the writers selected agree with the politics of *La Francophonie*, but rather that they themselves are cultural products of the environment in which they write that includes the reality that they tend to use the French language to express themselves. I also acknowledge the possible connotative problems concerning the term "Francophone," a term that risks turning Africa into an artificial cultural and political minefield. Finally, rather than limiting my work to a few specific writers and their poetics texts, I have chosen to discuss theoretical issues across a variety of nations and perspectives and have largely steered away from entering into protracted literary analyses. Though I risk developing generalizations in my examinations, creating an anthology of plays and poems from French-speaking Africa was never my intention as such collections already exist in satisfactory number.

Toward a Definition of Poetic Literature and Cultural History

In the pages found between the covers of this book, I construct a cultural history of French-speaking Africa. To make this goal possible, I explore the poetic literature of Francophone Africa as it relates to the region, to the continent of Africa, and to the rest of the planet within the framework of cultural historical investigation. As John Ellis writes in *The Theory of Literary Criticism: A Logical Analysis*, "Whether we look at theory or practice, literary history always entails seeking both cause and meaning of literary texts in their local circumstances of origin" (225). It is this "cause" and "meaning" to which Ellis refers that I have attempted to highlight. For this reason, thus, the title of this book will necessitate an explanation of the term "cultural history." It is also essential to establish a basis for understanding the critical framework employed in this book brought about through the term "cultural history." "Cultural history" is a relatively new field of study. In the last two decades, cultural history has emerged in France with properties that have created new ways of examining both cultural production and cultural products. Using philosophical and historical analysis as a backdrop in addition to interdisciplinary interventions in historical research and scholarship, as Jean-Pierre V.M. Hérubel explains in "Observations of an Emergent Specialization: Contemporary French Cultural History," modern French cultural history centers on the "history of publishing, scholarship, mass media and spectacles, libraries, and museums, as well as opera and music. Not confined to these, contemporary French cultural history privileges specialization in nineteenth- and twentieth-century French phenomena..." (216). Historical scholarship intends to contain both the exploration of the past, including an assessment of the political, economic, and social structures present there-within as well as any other events and happenings that may have occurred in the development of a particular society. Among these political, economic, and social structures, cultural scholars are most interested in cultural objects loosely defined as an object made by humans for a practical or spiritual purpose. Cultural objects include art, books, pop culture, television programs, stage plays, etc. As our professional academic history has changed, so also our interest in cultural institutions has changed such that the inclusion of archives (Archives Nationales in Paris), museums (Le Louvre, Le Musée du Quai Branly), theatres (Théâtre des Champs-Elysées), etc., have now become significant storehouses of cultural objects from throughout the world. Accordingly, for the very reason that cultural objects are never truly separated from the *milieux* from which they emerge, cultural activities and products have become appropriate objects of critical examination. Our discussion of cultural objects moves quickly to a discussion of cultural activities such as theatre through which an understanding of the cultural processes of any given culture is both mediated and mitigated. For the purposes of this particular work, cultural historians sit on the fence between traditional historical writing and literary analysis the goal of which is to more fully understand the cultural processes at play in the construction of literary works. Among the contributors in contemporary French cultural history, historians are working to define theoretical scholarship. Trained in historical studies, by combining their work with perspectives from other fields such as anthropology, sociology or ethnomusicology, for example, they show the importance of transforming their traditional work into an interdisciplinary endeavor that reaches a much wider audience. Within the last twenty years, cultural historians have focused on both traditional and developing forms of communication such as digital and social media (Facebook and Twitter). From an analysis of news information, to coverage of world events, to an examination of identity, media brings together new ideas and perspectives reflecting the wider sociological and cultural contexts.

The term "cultural history" is used today to indicate a particular approach to history and is "mainly concerned with the sense men and women from the past gave to the world they lived in" (Arcangeli i). This approach distinguishes itself from a traditional historical approach in which current historians evaluate the work of past individuals. Cultural history paints a picture of the most significant cultural components of a given society, including gender, sexuality, family structure, capitalism and consumerism, and the media. As a field of critical inquiry, cultural history has witnessed a number of important developments. During the last several years, numerous books have appeared containing the label of cultural history. I would like to suggest, however, that even given the vast number of books on this subject that have been published over the last several years, cultural history is not a "fly by night" endeavor. And, although cultural history is still working to gain greater credibility within the academy, in many countries it has not yet reached the level of being called an academic discipline. Further, although the field of historical studies has, itself, experienced a Renaissance in the form of "New History" led, in part, by historians such as David McCullough, author of the books entitled *1776* (2005) and *The Greater Journey: Americans in Paris* (2011), who have served to popularize the study of history in the United States, cultural history has yet to reach a "critical mass."

In the New Millennium, cultural history is working to position itself in contrast to but not in conflict with more traditional forms of historical inquiry. The French language itself that is the linguistic vehicle through which the thoughts and visions of the poetic writers of the present study are conveyed comprises its own interesting definitions vis-à-vis "culture," "civilization," and "society." The French term, "civilisation," created in the 18th century, is a semantically-charged term containing two contradictory notions explained extensively in Peter Burke's book *A New Kind of History from the Writings of Lefebvre*, published in 1973:

> In the first case civilization simply refers to all the features that can be observed in the collective life of one human group, embracing their material, intellectual, moral and political life and, there is unfortunately no other word for it, their social life. It has been suggested that this should be called the "ethnographic" conception of civilization.... In the second case, when we are talking about the progress, failures, greatness and weakness of civilization we do have a value judgment in mind. We have the idea that the civilization we are talking about—ours—is in itself something great and beautiful; something to which is nobler, more comfortable and better, both morally and materially speaking than anything outside of it—savagery, barbarity or semi-civilization. Finally, we are confident that such civilization, in which we participate, which we propagate, benefit from and popularize, bestows on us all a certain value, prestige, and dignity. For it is a collective asset enjoyed by all civilized societies. It is also a privilege which each of us proudly boasts that he possesses [220].

Although we might reach an initial understanding of terms such as "culture" and "civilization," static definitions of cultural history as a field of inquiry do not yet exist. In this work, I have no intention of creating a static definition of cultural history. That would be a futile pursuit. I prefer to show the flexibility of the field itself through its application on literary studies. To the best of my knowledge, this type of application is rare in contemporary scholarship and has never been applied specifically to the study of Francophone African poetic literature. An understanding of its application forces a distinction between "cultural history" and the "history of culture." The latter looks at objects of interest. The former speaks to what kind of history is being examined. Although this detail might seem to be a minute one, it is an important distinction to make here. In brief, "cultural history" is as a product of the "history of culture" itself and the "history of culture" is the birthing parent of "cultural history." Nevertheless, when we use terms such as "culture," "civilization," and "society," sometimes the waters that we endeavor to clarify become increasingly murkier.

Peter Burke's work in the second half of the 20th century evidences the ever-shifting state of cultural history as we understand it today. In *History and Social Theory* (2005), Burke redefined the relationships between history and the social sciences that moved from a state in which both fields found themselves at polar opposites to a state in which the two disciplines ultimately converged. New points of interdisciplinary exploration could be explored. Within the French tradition, 20th century French culture became a place of unequivocal conflict between history and the social sciences. There was certainly some question regarding whether or not historical studies could be considered a science in the same way as sociology or anthropology. To be considered a science, a field of inquiry must contain a "method" that could be applied and reproduced without bias. Anthropology had clear methods of observation that serve the study of culture well. Among the anthropology methods relevant to the field of cultural studies include André Burguière's *anthropologie historique* detailed in an entry by the same name in the *Dictionnaire des sciences historiques* (1986). Burguière, a specialist in the history of family structures, divided his categories into material and biological anthropology, economic anthropology, social anthropology, and cultural and political anthropology (56–7). His groupings examined attitudes toward sex, food consumption, social, ethical or religious goals, family demographics, and the social and political hierarchy. What was significant to Burguière was the "history of behavior and habits" (54) in contrast to a more traditional historical framework involving an attempt to understand the "how" and "why" behind certain historical events. Here, it is not the "how" and "why" behind historical events that is of primary importance, but rather the social response to historical events that takes first interest. Like Burguière, other Frenchmen worked to cultivate the relationships between history and anthropology. Illustrated through his work in the 1960s, Claude Lévi-Strauss, the renowned structural anthropologist, openly objected to the traditional method of historical writing called "serial history" that functioned superficially. "Serial history" consisted largely of simply recounting historical events in succession without exploring the reasons for which these historical events emerged in the first place. "Serial history" serves little purpose here. The mantel of French cultural history has been taken up in subsequent years by Roger Chartier at the *École des Hautes Études en Sciences Sociales* who, in the 1990s and 2000s, has penned numerous books and articles on "l'histoire culturelle" including *The Cultural Origins of the French Revolution* (1991), *Inscription and Erasure: Literature and Written Culture from the Eleventh to the Eighteenth Century* (2007), and *Author's Hand and the Printer's Mind: Transformations of the Written Word in Early Modern Europe* (2013). Because of its freshness, the anthropological framework for the study of cultural history developed by Roger Chartier could hold great value in the study of Francophone African poetic literature.

Africa Between Millennia: A Word on Colonization[8]

Conducting cultural history requires a periodic stoppage to perform a self-evaluation. The framework of cultural history necessitates reflection on where we have come from, on where we stand at present, and on the direction in which we are likely headed. "The starting-point of a critical elaboration," writes Antonio Gramsci, "is the consciousness of that which really is, that is to say a 'knowing of yourself' as a product of the process of history that has unfolded thus far and has left in you, yourself, an infinity of traces collected without the benefit of an inventory" (1376). In this chapter, I undertake this general task for the important purpose of better situating the Francophone African poetic texts created at the arrival of independence within an appropriate cultural context. Among my primary questions of inquiry include analyzing in some detail the African postcolonial condition. In examining this particular question, I intend to seek out sources of failure in the traces of the colonial past that have continued to present themselves during the period of independence in order to suggest possible solutions for the future of Francophone Africa. 19th and 20th century European colonialism operated and forced its legitimacy through the subjugation of non–European peoples that foreign invaders characterized as primitive and uncivilized. For their own welfare, indigenous peoples of the continent of Africa received the glimmers of European enlightenment.

Paradox entered Africa in the form of violent benefactors who saw their *raison d'être* as the bearers of the lights of cultural truth. It was believed–at least by those from outside of Africa–that the White Europeans both carried the Truth and that they had also created the ideal system of social organization. This group also felt itself to have been summoned to civilize the rest of the world, even if civilization, as it were, must be made possible through the explicit use of force. In other words, as Placide Tempels stated, "It has been said that our civilizing mission alone can justify our occupation of the lands of uncivilized peoples" (171-2). The phrase "Might Makes Right" was born. As Edward Said explained:

> But what distinguishes earlier empires, like the Roman or the Spanish or the Arabs, from the modern [colonial] empires, of which the British and French were the great ones in the nineteenth century, is the fact that the latter ones are systematic enterprises, constantly reinvested. They're not simply arriving in a coun-

try, looting it and then leaving when the loot is exhausted. And modern empire requires, as Conrad said, an idea of service, an idea of sacrifice, an idea of redemption. Out of this you get these great, massively reinforced notions of, for example, in the case of France, the "mission civilisatrice." That we're not there to benefit ourselves, we're there for the sake of the natives [*The Pen and the Sword* 66].

In globalizing itself, as Said further underscored, Europe liberally used force, "but much more important ... than force ... was the idea inculcated in the minds of the people being colonized that it was their destiny to be ruled by the West" (68). By the end of the 19th century, the division and redistribution of Africa was complete. The seeds of a new mindset had been sown on the soils of Africa. The goal of restoring Africa as the "Cradle of Mankind," a sort of Garden of Eden or terrestrial paradise became evident. Over the course of the centuries, Africa had become a dystopia, a failure of the utopia that had originally taken root there. If Manifest Destiny was the unwritten 19th-century doctrine that justified the expansion of the United States throughout the American continent, then the "civilizing mission" played the same role in Africa in the 20th century. Social strata were forged, creating both higher and lower levels of humanity. The effect of force was proof in itself that inferior forms of humanity were in need of being subjugated both for their own good as well as for their own protection. If missionaries and explorers left Europe to follow their destinies, then it was the destiny of Africa to have to endure great struggles as a result of their presence.

Throughout the period of colonial rule, violence perpetuated itself. A European Africa was created, one that infused traditional (indigenous) customs with modern European ones. Europe convinced the peoples of Africa that the subjugation of the latter was both natural (fated) and necessary if the Dark Continent was going to be successful in bringing about progress. Civilization was a key term. Thus, a colonist Europe became rooted in the identity of a Westernized Africa. The dialect between colonizer/colonized, civilized/uncivilized was forged. This new dichotomy affected every aspect of African culture. As Basil Davidson indicated in *Africa in Modern History*, "Africans in Western-educated groups ... held to the liberal Victorian vision of civilization kindling its light from one new nation to the next" (82). As such, by outsiders it appears largely uncontested that pre-colonial Africa was shrouded in a veil of darkness. Removal of this veil formed the pretext of colonization and served as a means to advance European rule in a continent rich in both natural and human resources. The colonial conquest was justified, in part, by the fact that those who were colonized accepted this pretext. Said referred to the acceptance of the pretext as the "ideological pacification of the colonized" (*Pen and the*

Sword 67). Nevertheless, we must not blame the victim here, for no matter what theoretical premise we might successfully establish that permitted colonial rule to take a foothold in Africa, it remains clear that the peoples of the continent found themselves playing the role of an immovable obstacle met with an irresistible force with the latter defeating the former. European colonial rule in Africa emerged with the belief that the so-called superior White race was the chosen race that bore the responsibility of civilizing those races deemed less civilized. Said's seed of "ideological pacification" slowly germinated within the minds of subjugated African peoples who in time began to believe that their suppression was mandated by a higher order. It became their destiny that imprisoned them both physically and psychologically. In *Les damnés de la terre*, Martinican author and psychologist Frantz Fanon wrote extensively about the colonized personality. According to Fanon, "Dans le contexte colonial, le colon ne s'arrête dans son travail d'éreintement du colonisé que lorsque ce dernier a reconnu à haute et intelligible voix la suprématie des valeurs blanches"/"Within the colonial context, the colonist only stops his work of exhausting the colonized when the latter has recognized out loud and with a loud voice the superiority of white values" (9). Even after the fall of colonization, the *éreintement* to which Fanon referred manifests itself continually. The Francophone African postcolonial condition is thus one that has been consistently and continually subjected to this form of mind altercation.[9] Like thoroughbreds that needed to be broken, French colonists shattered the traditional "unbridled spirit" of the tribal peoples of Africa.

What remains incontrovertible is the fact that the fractured African psyche of which Fanon spoke has become a part of the cultural legacy of colonialism that has forged and fabricated a model of human existence serving as a cornerstone in the building of a Modern Africa. Thus, the Francophone Africa to which I refer throughout the course of this book has risen for the most part out of the ashes of the former colonial enterprise. Instead of looking to indigenous ways, African leaders, in their effort to rebuild their fatherlands, often used colonial models to bring about rebirth the results of which have not always been positive. The traces of a colonial presence remain in the new incarnations of Africa. Well-known Francophone African writer and statesman Léopold Sédar Senghor stated in his work entitled *On African Socialism*: "Let us stop denouncing colonialism and Europe.... To be sure, conquerors sow ruin in their wake, but they also sow ideas and techniques that germinate and blossom into new harvests" (80). Senghor's words suggest both that it would be unsuitable and that it would be completely unrealistic to fully reject Francophone Africa's colonial heritage. Although scholars might suggest that Senghor's concept of "Négritude" unquestionably creates of itself a label that could be used to further subject the peoples of Francophone Africa to colonial rule even after independence, Senghor remained firm in his convictions of the liberating power of the movement:

> When placed again in context, colonization will appear to us as a necessary evil, a historical necessity whence good will emerge, but on the sole condition that we, the colonized of yesterday, become conscious and that we will it. Slavery, feudalism, capitalism, and colonialism are the successive parturitions of History, painful like all parturitions. With the difference that here the child suffers more than the mother. That does not matter. If we are fully conscious of the scope of the Advent, we shall ... be more attentive to contributions than defects, to possibilities of rebirth rather than to death and destruction. Without ... European depredations, no doubt ... Negro Africans ... would by now have created more ripe and more succulent fruits. I doubt that they would have caught up so soon with the advances caused in Europe by the Renaissance. The evil of colonization is less these ruptures than that we were deprived of the freedom to choose those European contributions most appropriate to our spirit [82].

Although we could argue that the only way through which the dominated peoples of Francophone Africa might achieve a psychological rehabilitation is through a reexamination of their colonial history. This technique is the one that Senghor proposed. As nature sometimes sets the fields on fire seemingly leaving them in ashes forever, she also has a way of bringing forth new life from those very ashes. Any rejection of the colonial past is a psychological impossibility. Nonetheless, Senghor's "No pain, no gain" infantilized worldview is fundamentally problematic. Although we might go too far to suggest that Senghor accepts the gift of European colonialism as a necessity in which "the medicine is hard, but the patient requires it,"[10] we must also recognize the fact that much of traditional Africa was lost in the fire that began at the Berlin Conference of 1884–5. Finally, we must avoid stating that the colonization of Africa was nothing more than the fatalistic fulfillment of her destiny. Colonialism devastated the landscape of Africa, and today parts of Africa are engaged in civil wars and disease spreads throughout the continent. Yet, much of Africa shows great promise. It is because of this reason that the world is now beginning to direct its attention toward this once-forsaken continent.

In 2009, U.S. President Barack Obama said, "The twenty-first century will be shaped by what happens not just in Moscow or Rome or Washington, but by what happens in Accra [Ghana] as well" (Office of the Press Secretary 2009). Although in the minds of most citizens Africa is nothing more than a remote no-man's-land ravished by famine and disease, she has played and continues to play an important role in world cultural history. Her role will only grow in importance in the coming decades. The United States has kept a close watch on Africa and has intervened when the government has deemed such intervention to be necessary (Rwanda, for example). Some Africanists, however, have been critical of U.S. intervention. In "A Perspective on Africa and the World," Tukufu Zuberi claims that American involvement in Africa has often been based on lack of knowledge of the complex African sociopolitical and sociocultural landscape:

> American-led humanitarian intervention has often been based on ignorance, as in the lack of understanding why two U.S. military Black Hawk helicopters were shot down during the October 3–4, 1993, battle between Somalia militia forces and the U.S. military. This ignorance was also shown in our response to the genocides in Rwanda and, more recently, in the Sudan. The problem with considering Africa as a far-off land of which the American people know little is that the world has flattened politically, an America cannot afford to be ignorant of African realities.... Understanding the reality of Africa in the 21st century requires viewing the continent within a broader context of recent world history [6].

Understanding the cultural, economic, social, and political climates of the continent of Africa is essential in the New Millennium. By looking at the continent both from a broader perspective and within a wider context of recent world events such as World War II, the end of Colonialism, and the new global interrelations, we can begin to understand how Africa is impacted as much by events occurring across the Atlantic and in continental Europe as by events happening within its own borders. In contrast, we only need to recall recent happenings in Libya, Egypt, Darfur, and Sudan to have a glimpse of how the rest of the world is shaped by events occurring on the continent of Africa. Africa can no longer remain a remote area of famine, warfare, and disease. We must attempt to comprehend Africa's place in our world in a new way.

Throughout history, Africa has been a place of discovery. The second largest continent, Africa is home to approximately 1 billion people living in 53 countries who speak more than 900 languages and dialects (Zuberi 7).[II] Stretching approximately 5,000 miles (8,000 kilometers) from north to south, its sheer enormity engulfs the combined masses of China, India, and the United States. As a unified geographical whole, the continent of Africa is more culturally, economically, and politically diverse than any of the other continents. It is for this reason that scholars often run into danger when they attempt to construct a single African perspective to represent an entire continent. My work likely falls into the trap of generalization as well, but this result should not deter the scholar from creating meaningful dialogue on the state and condition of Africa. Our goal here should be to shed the Cold War label of "Third World countries" that continues to be used to describe the nations of Africa. Perpetuation of the viewing of Africa through the lenses of poverty, warfare, and disease, combined with our failure to understand or general lack of awareness of events occurring in Africa impedes the ability of so-called "First World" countries to accurately estimate the importance of Africa on the world landscape. Once again, U.S. President Barack Obama during his visit to Ghana in 2009 summarized the mutual dependency of Africa and the United States as follows:

> This is the simple truth of a time when boundaries between people are overwhelmed by our connections. Your prosperity can expand America's prosperity. Your health and security can contribute to the world's health and security. And the strength of your democracy can help advance human rights for people everywhere. So, we do not see the countries and peoples of Africa as a world apart; we see Africa as a fundamental part of our interconnected world—as partners with America on behalf of the future we want for all of our children [Office of the Press Secretary 2009].

As President Obama's words accurately suggest, there is a definite interconnectedness between the United States and Africa. Obama himself is truly "African-American."[12] In addition, if we continue to marginalize the continent of Africa during the New Millennium—and the term "Third World" serves to marginalize her—Americans will suffer the consequences of this marginalization.

As we stand here having recently crossed the threshold of the New Millennium, we find ourselves in the opportune moment to (re-)examine the *idea* of Africa from a cultural and historical perspective. When you think today of the continent of Africa, what images come to mind? Are the images that are produced stereotypical in nature? Although stereotypes occasionally form a useful point of entry into the study of another culture, if we do not work to deconstruct these cultural stereotypes we risk further perpetuating them. In the words of Søren Kierkegaard, "Once you label me you negate me." Therefore, we must be careful that our writings and our evaluations of others' writings on Africa do not reduce her to a land of poor, naked heathens "longing to be civilized" that would further perpetuate 19th century ideas of Africa. In his book entitled *Reflections on Exile and Other Essays*, Said calls this "the epistemology of imperialism," a structure that systematically creates images of Africa and perpetuates her destiny through the creation of cultural stereotypes (376). It is primarily the work of Western philosophers such as Locke, Hume, and Hegel who have sealed the fate of the "epistemology of imperialism" with regard to the continent of Africa. Their philosophical musings essentially gave currency to the notion that Africa's destiny was written in the stars. And one simply cannot fight destiny. Further, in a vulgarization of a Voltairean "le meilleur des mondes possibles"/"the best of all possible worlds" which is that which we see before our very eyes, the Western philosophical perspective galvanizes the notion that a colonized Africa serves a purpose in creating the ideal world. Every nation has its place. And although we tend to think of Africa as a continent comprised of many distinct, diverse regions–the Maghreb, the Arab Peninsula, Sub-Saharan Africa, the former English colonies, South Africa, etc.—that have little in common with each other, the citizens of this vast territory actually have many shared experiences, a shared history, and, perhaps, even a shared future. Thus, many questions remain regarding an Africa that has recently crossed the threshold from one millennium to another. Is it possible now or will it ever be possible to exorcise the colonial presence from the African mind? How can a splendid purgation occur if African writers—even as they claim to express a mind free from colonialism—continue to dip their pens in colonial inkwells? As Tsenay Serequeberhan articulated well in his article entitled "Africa in a Changing World,"

> Colonization did not merely destroy the modes-of-life through which pre-colonial Africa lived its existence; in demolishing pre-colonial Africa, it constituted Africa as a dependent and servile appendage of the West.... And the daily news of Africa—genocide, man-made famine, corruption—in an ongoing manner substantiates this *idea* or image, of a continent wedded to perdition [33].

The African Diaspora has shown significant evidence that the French colonial presence in Africa has also impacted the colonial state as thousands upon thousands of Africans have immigrated to France over the last six decades bringing about numerous sociocultural consequences there as well. But, Africa also remains an intellectual extension of continental France. Colonization concretized the intellectual constraints in effect both in France as well as in the former colonies throughout the world.

In an article entitled "1960s Africa in Historical Perspective: An Introduction," Benjamin Talton states that "...historical analyses of the continent during the second half the 20th century and the first decade of the 21st have not seriously considered the varied, dynamic, and complex artistic and cultural factors that have shaped African experiences alongside the more easily discernable economic and political" (4). His perspective is informed by the fact that Africanists tend to view Africa primarily through its economic and political developments and develop conclusions related to her successes and failure almost entirely along these same lines. Talton advances his thesis by explaining that "Collapsing the history of African liberation as a singular process gives short shrift to the rich diversity of African political experiences and cultural, intellectual, and political production during the second half of the 20th century" (6). Therefore, to generalize on a post-independence Africa is to misrepresent Africa's diverse historical relationship with Europe and Africans' relationships with each other. African studies benefits from reflecting on such quandaries to articulate some of the factors and events that shape African societies and politics. It is best to explore the ways in which Africans have forged their own social realities, not only through politics but, perhaps more significantly, through culture–the arts, literature, and everyday sacred and temporal social interactions. African studies would benefit from less emphasis on, as Frederick Cooper describes, "a generic colonialism, capitalism, markets and governance or an 'African culture' and 'African thought' as generalizable constructs" in favor of the dynamism, variation, and transformation that has taken place since 1960 (185). The performing arts in Africa were transformed and elevated following independence. Poetry and theatre acted as a vehicle to forge and strengthen national cultural identities. Instead of making Africa a passive recipient of geoculture, scholars should clearly emphasize how the diverse nations of Africa have contributed to shaping geoculture over the last fifty years.

1
The Black Man's Burden and the Struggle for Independence

> Students of African Language literatures should ... be encouraged to take an intimate look at developments in neighboring literatures of the region and vice versa. The possibilities for comparison and cross-fecundation in the future are endless.
> —*Swanepoel 72*

The French settlement in Africa began in the 19th century. The decade of the 1880s formed a central turning point in the history of the African continent bringing much of the area both quickly and cruelly into the colonial period. French colonial presence in Africa, however, did not occur overnight. Beginning in 1854, the French military led by General Faidherbe began to install troops along the Senegalese coast. Military expansion continued east from the Senegalese coast to the western border of present-day Mali in the late 1850s. Until 1880, most French military campaigns had focused exclusively on the coastal areas of Senegal, Mauritania, Guinea, and South Benin (*A History of Sub-Saharan Africa* 7–22). In the 1880s, the process gained in intensity with a continual movement from Senegal to the northern sections of the Gold Coast (present-day Ghana) and movement from north-to-south toward the Ivory Coast (Côte d'Ivoire). In the next decade, French military forces expanded eastward from Mali toward Chad (Tchad) and southward toward Benin. French Africa began in 1895 and ended in 1960 with the start of independence. Francophone Africa forms a peninsula attached to the African mainland. It extends from the mountains of Cameroon toward the Gulf of Guinea and the Sahara and southward toward the Equator. This zone is characterized by distinct longitudinal climates. The Sahara, which is nearly as large as the United States, the savannah (the Sahel), and forests form the principle topographical regions.

At the turn of the 20th century, when French colonization of the region had gained full momentum, French Africa consisted of a territory of approximately 1.8 million square miles inhabited by around 12,000,000 people of rich racial, ethnic, and linguistic diversity. Census records of the period show that population density during this era was relatively low (fewer than 2 people per square mile).[1] In contrast to 21st-century Africa in which more than half of all continental citizens live in cities or metropolitan areas, at the beginning of the 19th century Francophone Africa consisted largely of small rural villages. The largest cities of the period were Saint-Louis (24,000), Dakar (18,400), in Senegal and Conakry, Guinea (8,200). Today, Saint-Louis boasts 176,000 citizens, Dakar has over 1 million citizens (with a metropolitan population exceeding 2.45 million), and Conakry enjoys more than 1.5 million residents (*A History of Sub-Saharan Africa* 40–2, 199). Most citizens followed an agrarian way of life with residents of coastal villages participating in the fishing industry. During the dry season, "backcountry" hunting was widespread, particularly in the savannah. Trade had always been common throughout Francophone Africa, and production of iron ore and cotton textiles increased at the beginning of the 20th century. Trade itself fostered the development of small towns from the edges of the Sahara southward toward Bobo-Dioulasso. Philip Curtin writes that in the period "internal trade was still far more important than trade with the world overseas, as it had been in the period of slave trade" (325). In countries within French West Africa such as Burkina Faso, Côte d'Ivoire, and Mali, Dioula was–and continues to be–a trade language spoken by millions of people. Islam was the religion of practice. Political organization largely consisted of rulers who claimed authority over subjects within a defined geographic territory. These geographic territories formed the African kingdoms. African anthropologists also define "lineage-based" or "decentralized" societies, "segmentary societies," and "autonomous local systems" (Morrison, Mitchell and Paden, 1989). There exists a third category corresponding to chiefdoms that were smaller political entities than kingdoms. The size of the political entity was not directly related to the size of its society (Morrison *et al.*, 1989).

Economic considerations motivated French settlers in Africa. These settlers can be divided into two principle groups: civil servants and private sector workers. Although there were colonial governors, administrators, and secretaries, the public sector formed a relatively small share of workers. The public sector included French teachers, inspectors, doctors, and nurses, as well as both agricultural and civil engineers. Within the private sector, import-export companies proliferated in Francophone Africa. Thus, the majority of French settlers working within the private sector were involved in trade companies. There were also few manufacturers. Between 1884 and 1885, a conference in Berlin set into motion what is commonly known today as the "Scramble for Africa," that is, the dividing into pieces of the continent to be shared among such colonizing countries as Belgium, France, and Britain. The French colonial experience in Africa–like those of Belgium and Britain–was based on a central paradox expressed in the following quotation by Lord Salisbury, British Prime Minister from 1885–1886: "We have been engaged in drawing lines upon maps where no white man's foot ever trod; we have been giving away mountains and rivers and lakes to each other, only hindered by the small impediment that we never knew exactly where the mountains and rivers and lakes were" (quoted in Ndulo, 330). If we choose to play the "blame game" with regard to the colonial enterprise, we need not start any further back in time than the onset of the slave trade on the continent of Africa. From the start, the colonial state acted with impunity in all aspects of daily African life. Colonial power was based on a violence that was often met with violence. As Fanon expressed well:

> Au niveau des individus, la violence désintoxique. Elle débarrasse le colonisé de son complexe d'infériorité, de ses attitudes contemplatives ou désespérées. Elle le rend intrépide, le réhabilite à ses propres yeux. Même si la lutte armée a été symbolique et même s'il est démobilisé par une décolonisation rapide, le peuple a le temps de se convaincre que la libération a été l'affaire de tous et de chacun, que le leader n'a pas de mérite spécial. La violence hisse le peuple à la hauteur du leader [*Les damnés de la terre* 90–1].
>
> At the individual level, violence is a cleansing force. It rids the colonized of their inferiority complex, of their passive and despairing attitude. It emboldens them, and restores their self-confidence. Even if the armed struggle has been symbolic, and even if they have been demobilized by rapid decolonization, the people have the time to realize that liberation was the achievement of one and all, and no special merit should go to the leader. Violence hoists the people up to the level of the leader.

The primary goal of the colonial powers (France, England, Germany, etc.) was to seize economic power of the colonies by taking over control of both raw materials and markets. Throughout the colonial world, the most essential commodity was African labor.

Colonialism is a civilizing enterprise based on domination. It is a political exploit in which a colonizing nation exports both its culture and a portion of its people to a foreign geographical setting. Colonialism has several subdivisions including "internal colonialism," a term describing the oppression and domination of minority groups within a given country by members of the same national culture. A second division is "neo-colonialism" that refers to a form of colonialism perpetuating the relation between colony and Mother Country under the guise of nationalism or independence.[2] Oppression is not as overt as in direct colonialism, but it is equally as powerful. The crossing of racial, ethnic or gender boundaries is one criterion by which one may define the presence of a colonial system. The colonial context is not limited to the crossing of geographic borders. The colony is both a place and a state of mind. Colonization arguably takes place largely within the psyche, for its effects remain long after the physical colonial administration has returned to its European homeland.

In French colonial history, one of the absolutes of the multi-layered civilizing mission was the notion of France as the transmitter of the "essence of French civilization, presumed to be the noblest in existence" (Confer 3). France's actions abroad were justified because of its "priceless" contribution to the world: French culture. That culture was enhanced by ideas of the French Revolution as expressed in the *Déclaration des Droits de l'Homme et du Citoyen* (1789). In its simplest terms, the ideas of *liberté, égalité, fraternité* of the Revolution formed an ideological as well as a humanitarian element of the civilizing mission. Ideology is most often politically or culturally defined. It can be used to justify *any* means used to attain *any* goal. It becomes a propagandistic weapon representing ideas and concepts that shape peoples' motivation for action. An ideology may be identifiable by its slogans (*"liberté, égalité, fraternité"*), or it may be hidden within society. The *mission civilisatrice* encompasses notions that are simultaneously contradictory. One such meaning refers to the colonial attitudes of the period in which the civilizing mission came into existence indicating the superiority and inferiority of certain human beings. A second meaning refers to the self-perception of France as an exceptionally rich culture with rights originating from the enlightened philosophers of the Eighteenth century (*Le Siècle des Lumières*) such as Voltaire, Rousseau, and Diderot. An additional assumption was that France, due to its status as an enlightened culture, had the responsibility of disseminating these new ideas to less fortunate cultures. The term commonly used by historians to describe this responsibility is the "White Man's Burden." The ideology of the *mission civilisatrice* combined with the concept of French nationalism formed a tool of propaganda. The *mission civilisatrice* cannot be interpreted without some difficulties. The philosophy underlying the *Déclaration des Droits de l'Homme et du Citoyen* was not intended to extend to *all* men. It neither implicitly nor explicitly specified rights for those who were now French citizens, male, Christian, or Caucasian. It must be noted that one hundred years after the *Déclaration*, a prime minister of France declared that it did not, in fact, apply to blacks, nor did it apply to North Africa's Muslims (Dumont 37). Immediately following the French Revolution, the slogan *liberté, égalité, fraternité* was fervently embraced in France's colonial escapades throughout Sub-Saharan Africa.

The motivation behind French colonization in Algeria was summed up in the ideology of the *mission civilisatrice* whose meaning finds its origin before the Algeria War in the 1950s. The civilizing mission came into full bloom in the 1870s when Algeria became a storehouse for French immigrants after the Franco-Prussian War. A contemporary view of the *mission civilisatrice* has been construed as exploitative with all developments serving to keep "the colonized peoples under their subjugation [so as] to be able to exploit the economic and natural resources of the countries they occupied" (Offiong 42–3). Among the most significant Francophone writers to examine the colonized mind was Martinican psychiatrist Frantz Fanon.

Fanon, the well-renowned author, centered his work on race and the effects of the French colonial experience. Fanon's racial theory aides in understanding the varying forms of colonialism and in analyzing the importance of nationalism and the use of propaganda in the French *mission civilisatrice* in Africa. The most characteristic feature of the colonial situation is racism; a process of dividing society into the binary opposites of "human beings" and "natives." One of the earliest attempts to understand colonial domination was racial theories that attributed human differences to the genetic inferiority of certain races. Nevertheless, the tragic flaw of this theory is the inability to confirm any such biological stereotypes. Although racism based on biological factors might seem extraordinary in light of our present-day perspective, one must acknowledge that racial hatred based of biology indeed continues to exist. In his text *Peau noire, masques blancs* (*Black Skin, White Masks*) published in 1952, Fanon points to this ideology in his assessment of the prejudice based on skin color: "Le préjugé de couleur n'est rien d'autre qu'une haine irraisonnée d'une race pour une autre, le mépris des peuples forts et riches pour ceux qu'ils considèrent comme inférieurs à eux-mêmes" (95)/"The prejudice of race is nothing other than an unreasonable hate of one race for another, the loathe of rich and powerful people for those that they consider inferior to themselves." The characteristic of skin color is not only biological, but is also inalienable and non-transformable. A second type of racial theory bases its discrimination on psychological predispositions that inhibit effective functioning of a given group within society. It concludes that there are certain groups that are inherently superior. Unlike the former theory in which inferiorities are physical, the present theory is based on deficiencies of the mind. A third type of theory bases inequalities on cultural traits, particular to a group of people that impedes them in comparison to other groups. This theory posits that defects of the individual emerge from the deficiencies of the entire cultural group. It centers on the notions of ethnicity and cultural weakness. Like any biological theories, this theory is not without its flaws, as Eduardo Ysern-

Borras explains in his text *The Colonized Personality: Frantz Fanon's Concept of the Psychology of People Living under Socio-Political Conditions of Colonialism*: "Ethnicity and natural culture are by themselves questionable concepts which mystify the subtle yet important subcultures and classes that comprise a nation" (13).[3]

Fanon's theory of human inequality does not fit easily within any of the above-mentioned theories, for it is a mélange of all of them. Of great importance in the case of Francophone Africa is that domination is not only a result of external or internal causes of oppression, but of the dialectic between the colonizer and the colonized. These are the binary opposites that are mutually dependent and are continuously at play. Fanon's words paint a picture of the French colonists' thoughts with regard to black inferiority based on biological factors: "Les nègres sont des sauvages, des abrutis, des analphabètes" (94)/"Negroes are savages, morons, illiterates"/"Le nègre, lui, est fixé au génital…. Le nègre représente le danger biologique…. Avoir du nègre, c'est avoir peur du biologique. Car le nègre n'est que biologique. Ce sont des bêtes" (134)/"The Negro is attached to the genital…. The Negro represents biological danger…. To have Negro is to have fear of the biological. For the Negro is only biology. They are animals." Represented as a sexual beast, in the eyes of the colonist, the black must also be psychologically inferior. He is therefore less intelligent, which explains why the colonizer must infantilize him: "…un Blanc s'adressant à un nègre se comporte exactement comme un adulte avec un gamin…" (24)/"…a white talking to a Negro behaves exactly like an adult with a child…." In a sense, the black must be "dummied down to." As Fanon indicates, it is under the guise of calming them: "Parler aux nègres de cette façon, c'est aller à eux, c'est les mettre à leur aise … c'est les rassurer…" (25)/"Speaking to Negroes in this way, it's going toward them, putting them at ease, reassuring them." *We* know that this notion is as ridiculous as it is degrading. In the eyes of the colonist, the black is also inferior because of the deficiencies of his entire cultural group. It would be better to state this idea in terms of the black's ethnic inferiority. To perceive blacks as a "cultural group" would give them credit for a culture which the French colonists say did not exist: "Dans le cas du Noir…. Il n'a pas de culture, pas de civilisation, pas ce long passé d'histoire" (27)/"In the case of the Black…. He has no culture, no civilization, not this long past of history." If the French were to acknowledge such a culture, the *mission civilisatrice* would have no apparent purpose. Finally, according to the colonizer, blacks' inferiority is seen in their function in Hegel's master-slave dialectic. Francophone Africa society had been divided into "human beings" and "natives," henceforth referred to as "colonizer" and "colonized." The success of the former was directly related to the exploitation of the latter in a cyclical system in which the act of domination must be continually reproduced. A dialectic of colonizer/colonized emerged.

The French colonization of the African continent occurred at an important moment in French history as France sought to restore her honor after suffering defeat in the Franco-Prussian War. The fact that the colonial state did not have the interest and needs of Africa in mind is evidenced by the artificial nature of its countries' borders. As Muna Ndulo writes,

> Colonial powers imposed unfavorable terms of trade and strongly skewed economic activities toward extractive industries and exportation of primary goods. These conditions stimulated little demand to improve skills and educational levels of the work force, a situation that continued into post independence states [320].

Not only did the borders not conform to traditional trading patterns within the continent, they also failed to respect the relations of traditional ethnic groups. As a result, various ethnic groups were divided between different countries such as the Somali who were in Djibouti, Ethiopia, Kenya, and Somalia. The colonial enterprise devastated the African landscape and its peoples. "The foremost act of disruption," continues Ndulo, "was the unification of ethnic communities, under the umbrella of sovereign states, created pursuant to the Berlin Conference of 1884..." (331). Camille Lefebvre in her article entitled "We Have Tailored Africa: French Colonialism and the 'Artificiality' of Africa's Borders in the Interwar Period" wrote that "African borders were drawn with rulers and colored pencils on inaccurate maps by diplomats intoxicated by their sense of superiority" (191). Indeed, since independence, the artificial nature of Africa's borders has become an axiomatic feature of any discussion on the continent. Such a discussion, however, was predicated on the notion that African state borders were merely the result of subjugation and that as such they were entirely imposed on African states. Rival ethnic groups were placed together in the name of the colonial state, which clustered tribes in urban areas. Christianity was favored over indigenous religions. Colonial rule was "philosophically and organizationally elitist" (Ndulo 331). Independence for African countries was a three-stage process: the first involved the physical removal of the colonial power from the African state, the second was the continuous fight against neocolonialism, and the last stage involved achieving economic independence. Nonetheless, true independence remained incomplete.

The 1950s and 1960s became a time of independence for many Francophone African nations. After a century of colonization, Africa was prepared to write a new chapter in her history. The mission to civilize the so-called

"Dark Continent" had traditionally been called the "White Man's Burden" and it was referred to in French as the "mission civilisatrice." In February 1899, British novelist and poet Rudyard Kipling wrote a poem entitled "The White Man's Burden: The United States and The Philippine Islands." In his poem, Kipling urged the U.S. to take up the "burden" of empire, as had Britain and other European nations. African Americans, among many others, objected to the notion of the "White Man's Burden." Among the dozens of replies to Kipling's poem was "The Black Man's Burden," written by African-American clergyman and editor H. T. Johnson and published in April 1899. A "Black Man's Burden Association" was even organized with the goal of demonstrating that mistreatment of brown people in the Philippines was an extension of the mistreatment of black Americans at home. The English-language slogan paid homage to the Rudyard Kipling poem by the same name and it expressed the assumed responsibility of white Europeans both to bring their superior civilization and culture to African peoples and to ultimately oversee those cultures. In a sense, this catchphrase served to validate European colonialism since it first began on the African continent. In its sociological form, the "White Man's Burden" encompassed the duty of every white European to bestow his cultural artifacts on pre–Enlightenment African peoples. As a political ideology, the "White Man's Burden" became both a vehicle for installing foreign political systems in Africa and a way to redraw the tribal map of Africa in order to exert control over diverse ethnic groups. The African continent became a place of tremendous discovery for the white settler, a landscape that he must tame and cultivate. "The Black Man's Burden" formed the African response or the counterpoint to European colonization. It consisted of a "black" voice speaking out against occupation, a voice crying out against a foreign people who had used the reason of their inherent biological superiority as a means to subdue an entire continent. In French-speaking Africa, especially, the cry emerged from the poetic voices of its poets and playwrights who through portrayals of the scourge of colonization endeavored to claim their rightful seat among the civilized peoples of the 20th century.

In *The Black Man's Burden*, originally published in 1920, Edmund Dene Morel (born Georges Eduard Pierre Achille Morel de Ville) responded to Kipling's poem. Morel (1873–1924), a French-born British journalist and socialist, brought attention to colonial exploitation and championed a campaign to end slavery in the Belgian Congo. While working for a Liverpool shipping company in Brussels, Morel noticed that the ships leaving Belgium for the Congo carried no commercial goods–only ammunition, guns, and chains–and that returning ships arriving from the Congo contained valuable products including ivory and rubber. This observation led Morel to conclude that Belgian King Leopold II's colony was not, in fact, a trading colony, but rather one whose natural resources were exploited through slave labor. Morel wrote,

> It is [the Africans] who carry the "Black man's burden." They have not withered away before the white man's occupation. Indeed ... Africa has ultimately absorbed within itself every Caucasian.... In hewing out for himself a fixed abode in Africa, the white man has massacred the African in heaps. The African has survived, and it is well for the white settlers that he has" [7].

Morel concluded that by attempting to subjugate the diverse peoples of Africa, the white man had spilled blood throughout the streets. The African had endured. He had persisted. For centuries, the white man captured and enslaved millions of Africans and transported the latter abroad. Africans had sold their own people to slavery. "The Black Man's Burden" was not simply a struggle against the White Man, it was a struggle against the very environment of Africa that had been transformed since the arrival of the first settlers. Imported diseases such as measles, smallpox, and syphilis impacted the African continent. Morel's account of European exploitation in Africa is clearly biased. In his chapter entitled "The Story of the Congo Free State," Morel writes: "I do not propose to narrate here the European history of the Congo Free State.... I shall confine myself as far as practicable to describing the system of exploitation set up in the Congo basin therein from 1891 to 1911; and its effects upon native life" (109). In the approximately forty pages that followed, Morel somewhat myopically explained how the presence of European settlers over a period of twenty years had significantly impacted both the social and the economic systems of the region. Through his colorful prose descriptions, Morel painted a formerly idyllic Congo whose society enjoyed "innumerable centres of population varying from 5,000 to 40,000; of settlements extending for hundreds of miles along the river banks; of communities of professional fishermen..." (114). He described the local agricultural products, the people who produced these products, and the means by which they distributed these products. Civilization was present within the Dark Continent. One French explorer noted that if civilization "were measured by the number of vegetable conquests, these people would rank among the most advanced in Africa" (114–5). Nonetheless, the peoples of the Congo River valley had an effective system of treaties and trade that extended one hundred fifty miles. It was a system that had served its peoples well for centuries. To argue that natives had rights to native lands, however, was futile.

World War II (1939–1945) significantly impacted the entire continent of Africa. Africans from French and British colonies fought for the allies in

Europe, Asia, and North Africa. In recruiting African soldiers, the British and the French had highlighted the fact that African soldiers would be fighting for a free Europe. At the end of the war, however, these African soldiers returned to their homeland to contemplate the irony that although they had fought for an independent Europe, they still lacked independence within their own nations. African citizens had been waging their own war against the colonial systems that had been exploiting their nations for generations. In the late 1940s and early 1950s, new political parties began to form in nearly every African colony that eventually disrupted the balance of power within African colonized nations. From the beginning of the 1950s, African nations began to gain independence. The first French-speaking Sub-Saharan nation to gain its own independence was the Republic of Guinea (October 2, 1958). Following Guinea's lead, a host of French-speaking Sub-Saharan African nations gained their independence from France.[4] The year 1960 was a tumultuous one to say the very least. While the movement to independence after World War II was quite rapid, it did not occur without challenges. It was also a time of self-discovery for many Africans. The yoke of colonial racism was cast aside and the feeling of liberation from the chains of colonial captivity became real. The period of post-independence centered on the notion that economic and political development would bring the African continent success. As Basil Davidson wrote in *The Black Man's Burden: Africa and the Curse of the Nation-State*, "this belief that 'development' was now at last possible ... may explain a good deal about the general conviction ... that rapid expansions of wealth and mass consumption were not only attainable but could be of an almost automatic nature" (199). But, one factor that was not initially considered was the reality that this type of speculation could engender corruption. Thus, "development" led to the idea of "modernization." For all intents and purposes, "modernization" consisted almost exclusively of importing ready-made non–African products and ideas. "Africa would prosper upon condition of rejecting itself," wrote Davidson (199). Although Francophone African writers certainly harken to the past as the means through which restoration will occur, the future of Africa would not be rooted in the past. It would not spring up from native roots. Rather, it would be grafted onto the African landscape from foreign skin. The slogan "Africa for Africans" circulated. Innovation soon came. The English and French languages spread throughout the continent. Cities in Africa began to resemble their European counterparts. Automobiles circulated on paved streets and highways. New goods and services appeared. The notion of an independent African capitalism seemed possible. Africans had been promised a New Africa and one began to emerge. But, what no one seemed to initially notice was how all of this prosperity might ultimately increase the divide between the so-called "haves" and "have-nots." Curiously, no one thought of or cared about how this prosperity might actually further perpetuate stereotypes of Africa that had existed since the arrival of French settlers there.

As Christophe Konkobo has stated well, "the idea of uncanny and inhuman Black creatures inhabiting Africa fed the Western popular imagination through various fictional and purportedly factual narratives long before the first encounter of the so-called 'Black Continent' with the West" (1095). Before European explorers first set foot in Africa in the 15th century, the notion of uncivilized African peoples already existed in Europe. If the European encompassed the ideal mind, then the African exemplified the physical form. The notion of the "Other" was born. According to Edward Said, father of the seminal postcolonial theoretical text entitled *Orientalism*, "modern thought and experience have taught us to be sensitive to what is involved in representation, in studying the Other, in racial thinking, in unthinking and uncritical acceptance of authority and authoritative ideas" (327). Said maintains that the "Orient" is a fictional construct fashioned and forged under an external Occidental optic, which serves as an initially fragmented or marginalized identity. Marginality refers to the spatial property of a location in which something is situated, but the term also suggests something that is positioned at the outer limits of social adequacy. The "Orient" is a forgery created by Westerners in an effort to objectify peoples during the colonial enterprise. It is a counterfeit that continued to perpetuate itself in the neocolonial period and that also continues to flourish in the 21st century (Ashcroft 193–200). Since independence, Africans have begun to more fully understand how the fragmented, marginalized identity continually works against the authentic identity in order to become progressively more capable of rejecting the stereotypes created by French society with the ultimate goal of forging one's own identity by rejecting the concept of the "Other."[5] Since the beginning of the French colonial experiment in the 19th century, a discourse emerged that endeavored to better understand the dichotomy that exists between the East and the West. Westerners continue to think of the East as the "Other" of the West, an untamed, exotic landscape. Literature, art, film, and political writings have perpetuated and disseminated stereotypes of Africans (Armes 3–20). Western culture has exploited these stereotypes and taken advantage of these falsifications both to increase its own political authority throughout the world as well as to keep its subjugated peoples under its continual cultural control. The media has propagated stereotypes of Africans. As Konkobo continues to explain, "a Western imagination thus established a hierarchy of values where Europe was viewed in rational and cognitive terms and its Other as abject bundles of muscles devoid of cognitive and spiritual capacities" (1095). Images of weak, helpless Africans have had a long history of circulation in Europe and beyond. Scattered and spontaneous early representations of the Dark Continent in narratives gradually gain momentum and culminate in the 19th century in an organized and sustained ideology that forcefully (re)invents Africa for the purpose of justifying colonial domination. The image of African tribes yielding to White intruders is a false one that continues to circulate in the New Millennium. In reality, when the French arrived in Africa they were greeted with fierce resistance, particularly in the West African kingdoms of Wasoulou (present-day Guinée) and Dahomey (Benin). King Gbehanzin of Dahomey and his army of female warriors fought the encroaching French. King Samory Touré (1830–1900) battled the French army for nearly two decades. The French army suffered great casualties at the hands of the *tirailleurs sénégalais* (Deroo 220).

The Cultural Backdrop of Francophone African Literature

After Africa's "discovery," European imperialists sought to colonize territories to gain exclusive rights on exploitation of natural resources and manpower. But the European nations confronted the necessity of justifying colonization to their own people. France, for example, could not promote its imperial mission to its citizens simply on the premises of achieving economic expansion. A more compelling reason, such as the moral need to civilize savages, became a more productive way to gain popular support for the Empire's cause. For that reason, a colonial machinery was brought together to effectively demonize the native Africans and therefore claim the need to save their souls by civilizing them. The church, the sciences, the army, and the government fully contributed expertise to effectively construct and convey images of the Black as evil, animal, and uncivilized. In *Théorie critique et modernité négro-africaine: De l'école de Francfort à la "Docta Spes Africana,"* Jean-Godefroy Bidima underscores that the colonial system established and thrived on three main pillars, "the administration, Christianity, and trading posts" (120). It is difficult to find a description of the development of early theatre that does not promote stereotypical definitions of Africa. Formalized Francophone African theatre debuted in the beginning of the 1930s in Senegal at the *École Normale d'Instituteurs de Saint-Louis* and in Côte d'Ivoire at the *École Primaire Supérieure de Bingerville*. In his book entitled *Le Théâtre en Afrique noire et à Madagascar*, Robert

Cornevin (1970) created an aesthetic and a historical account of the colonial and earlier post-independence Francophone African theatre that promoted the colonial stereotypical definition and support of that theatre. Cornevin suggested that African theatre was largely about Africans dancing around and singing, an opinion echoing that of Charles Béart, who had written in a 1937 issue of *L'Education Africaine* that "...it is mostly through tales, music, and dances, that the black soul expresses itself" (55). A competing view is that of John Conteh-Morgan, author of *Theatre and Drama in Francophone Africa: A Critical Introduction*, who argued that most dramatists "see history uniquely from the top: as the product, that is, of the actions of kings and queens. Such a perspective ... does not only distort the true picture ... but reveals the 'bourgeois,' 'elitist' or feudal orientation of the dramatists" (73). Thus, many Francophone African plays created after independence projected a stereotypical identity of *Négritude* to which many Africans no longer relate(d). In a sense, although the African body is immutable, that is, it cannot be physically rejected, seeking to create a discourse rooted in the African body has the effect of creating an African essence that is not unique. Suffice it to say, colonial stereotypes *vis-à-vis* African identity have become so concretized that even the most truthful evaluations of what is means to be an African do not risk to shatter them.

In their book entitled *Contemporary Francophone African Writers and the Burden of Commitment*, Odile Cazenave and Patricia Célérier highlight a significant hindrance to African writing, stating: "The critical understanding of francophone African literature's 'context' has been overly determined by its ties to engagement" (17). To claim that Francophone African writing is not a "littérature engagée" would be a misrepresentation as well. Yet, to state that all Francophone African writing is an act of engagement would be an untruth. To pigeonhole writing as engaged or militant can bring negative consequences. Let us consider as an example J.D. Salinger's 1951 novel *The Catcher in the Rye*. *The Catcher in the Rye* has earned the title of "the quintessential American anti-establishment novel." This classification caused Salinger to withdraw from writing to such an extent that he lived much of the last part of his life in seclusion. Although Francophone African literature must be both "for" and "about" something, the notion that it must be a committed literature continues to trouble the literature. It harkens back to the particular premise for the interpretation of Francophone African literature that consisted of "the aligning of the value of African writers and their production with the expression of progressive (or revolutionary) politics ... dominated by two historical movements, Négritude and Nationalism, both largely influenced by the ideas of Pan-Africanism" (Cazenave 19). Pan-Africanism refers specifically to both an ideology and movement promoting the solidarity of Africans worldwide that centers on the belief that solidarity is essential to the success of peoples of African descent (Frick 235). The notion of commitment has served as a prime foundational element of Francophone African literature both in the 20th and in the 21st centuries. Despite the fact that I would argue that not all Francophone African literature is steeped in diatribe and vitriol, it goes without saying that this particular literature does, indeed, contain "the history of a fighting Africa, the history of an African resistance against foreign domination and exploitation" (M'Bokolo 13). The cultural backdrop against which writers residing in the former French colonies penned their works was marked by the effects of war, colonization, and nationalism that ultimately gave rise to Francophone writers such as Aimé Césaire and Frantz Fanon. Nevertheless, the sum of the value and message of Francophone African literature, particularly its poetic literature, is found more in its ability to express the human condition than in its cry of revolt.

There is also some question regarding the continued need to marginalize *littérature d'expression française* by labeling it "Francophone Literature." In a manifesto published in *Le Monde* on March 19, 2007, forty-four prominent writers, including Édouard Glissant (Martinique), Jean-Marie Gustave Le Clézio (France, winner of the 2008 Nobel Prize in Literature), and Maryse Condé declared the death of francophone literature and the birth of "une littérature-monde en français."[6] This manifesto emerged at an important era in the history of French literature. In Fall 2006, five of the seven French literary prizes–the Goncourt, the Grand Prize for Novels of the Académie Française, the Renaudot, the Femina, and the Goncourt for High School Students–were awarded to foreign-born writers, the successes of whom suggested the death of "Francophone" literature and the birth of a "World Literature in French." For the first time in French literary history, a generation of emigrant writers had endeavored to develop a literature that drew from the well of their plural identities. This literary re-evaluation signaled an attempt to move francophone writers from the margins of literary composition to being truly "on the page." To cite the manifesto,

> Combien d'écrivains de langue française, pris eux aussi entre deux ou plusieurs cultures, se sont interrogés alors sur cette étrange disparité qui les reléguait sur les marges, eux "francophones," variante exotique tout juste tolérée? ... L'émergence d'une littérature-monde en langue française consciemment affirmée, ouverte sur le monde, transnationale, signe l'acte de décès de la francophonie. Personne ne parle le francophone, ni n'écrit en francophone. La francophonie est de la lumière d'étoile morte ["Pour une 'littérature-monde' en français"].
>
> How many writers of the French language caught between two or more cultures have not contemplated this strange incongruence that pushed them to the

margins, calling them "Francophones," a scarcely tolerated exotic variety? ... The emergence of a consciously affirmed, transnational world-literature in the French language, open to the world, signs the death certificate of so-called francophone literature. No one speaks or writes "Francophone." Francophone literature is a light from a dying star.

Though the idea of a "World Literature in French" might appear overly "politically correct" for some scholars, let us consider the notion that literatures in French around the world today are discernibly multiple, diverse, forming a vast ensemble, the implications of which link together five continents: Africa, Asia, Europe, North America, South America. Let us also understand the term "world literature" in the sense that all around us these literatures portray the world that is emerging right in front of us, and by doing so recover, after several decades, from what was "forbidden in fiction," what has always been the domain of artists, novelists, creators: the task of giving a voice and a face to the global unknown—and to the unknown in each and every one of us. We live in a new age. We live our lives with a Post–9/11 consciousness. The purpose of this book is to reveal the cultural foundation that brought great French-speaking writers in Africa to the forefront of literary expression. It is not to marginalize these same writers by relegating the latter to second-class citizenry. Nonetheless, the creation of a canon of Francophone African literature that does not risk simultaneously discounting and subjugating its writers to a larger order remains only a theoretical possibility.

In *Littérature et développement: Essai sur le statut, la fonction et la représentation de la littérature négro-africaine d'expression française*, Bernard Mouralis outlined the principle reasons for labeling Francophone African literature a "littérature engagée." Mouralis posits that the African historical context that forged this literature centered on three main factors: "The existence of an elite trained by the colonizer, the introduction and superior status of a European language making for an ambiguous relationship between the writer and his readers, and the lack of adequate structures to ensure a truly independent cultural existence, notably in the realm of information and publishing" (18–19). More specifically, the definition of Francophone African literature as a "littérature engagée" is based on the perception that all Francophone African literature must, for one reason or another, ascribe to the tenets of either the Négritude or Nationalist movements. As Odile Cazenave and Patricia Célérier explain, "Francophone African literature suffers from a burden of representation" (24), signifying that the classification of Francophone African literary texts by movements has effectively undermined these very texts.

African National Literature: From the Global to the Local

In the wake of a new-found independence, African nations inherited the Western notion of a "national literature," creating a strong connection between language, literature, and national identity. In West and Middle Africa, a written language and literature such as French offered evidence that Africa had finally become modern. Critics including Adrien Huannou perceived that the African continent was moving away from a traditional oral literature. As postcolonial nationalism spread throughout the continent, the process of establishing African national literatures was a particularly complex one that consisted, in part, of putting the pieces back together from colonized peoples that were now newly independent nations. The creation of national literary canons was inherently problematic as the hopes and ideals reflected in these now "modern" African nations were themselves inconsistent and sometimes contradictory. In *Postcolonial Criticism: History, Theory and the Work of Fiction*, Nicholas Harrison underscores the reality that there has been a general misunderstanding that postcolonial African writers are somehow representative of the nations in which they live. At best, these writers function as a spokesperson putting forth a particular, arguably biased, perspective of their nation's transition from colony to free state (92–111). Nonetheless, as Harrison correctly contends, the representative view of any given author usually is much less a matter of the nature of the literary work itself than the context in which a text is received. It is for this reason that the filter of cultural history could work to counter some of the bias created in reception provided that it does not contribute unnecessary bias at the production end. Francophone African literary works thus often find themselves caught in a paradoxical situation; they must find a way to describe the life of the nation in clear, unbiased ways, but their use of the French language to describe their unique indigenous cultural histories risks appearing profoundly misleading when it comes to embodying an authentic national identity. Whether in former French colonies or in former English colonies, this is the quandary of any so-called "national" literature that has taken root on the African continent since independence. Therefore, within the former French colonies, how can we call any literature in French a "national" literature at all when there remain large numbers of the populations of French-speaking nations who neither read nor write French? Is there any possible solution to this particular problem?

Noted Kenyan author Ngũgĩ wa Thiong'o has struggled to find an answer to this question throughout his career. Although working within the context of a different colonial language (English), the hypocrisy of attempting to authentically represent the people of Kenya through a "foreign" language is the same. Now a professor at the University of California at Irvine, in his novels, plays, short stories, and essays, Ngũgĩ wa Thiong'o expressed himself in the English language. His first novel, *Weep Not, Child* (1964), which he wrote while attending the University of Leeds in England, was the first novel in English to be published by a writer from East Africa. More recently, however, Ngũgĩ has begun to write in Gikuyu, a Bantu language spoken primarily by the Kikuyu people of Kenya that has approximately 6 million speakers. Ngũgĩ's decision to abandon English in order to write in Gikuyu was fully intentional. Inasmuch as it concerns the formation of a literary canon within his Kenyan homeland, he supports the development of national literatures in "indigenous" African languages over "elitist" European-language literatures such as English and French. For Francophone Africa, in particular, the use of indigenous languages over that of colonial languages is, once again, problematic. In Senegal, for example, the indigenous languages (Wolof, Pulaar, Sareer, etc.) did not have a standardized (formalized) written form until recent decades and, even today, literacy rates in these languages continue to remain relatively low. Although there are currently a number of publishers who produce texts in Wolof, Pulaar, and other Senegalese languages, their readership is limited. More significantly, Ngũgĩ's notion of the link between language and consciousness is somewhat self-fulfilling. As Jacques Derrida argued in *Le monolingualisme de l'autre* (1998), it is a fallacy both to suggest that languages "belong" to any particular people or that these same languages can be employed to express an "essential" identity that would otherwise be inexpressible in another language. The linguistic landscape of Senegal is representative of most African nations, particular those within Francophone Africa. We should point out that within 19th-century France, the advancement of a national literature frequently involved the marginalization of regional (indigenous) languages. More recently, however, the French government has begun to recognize the importance of regional languages such as Breton, Picard, and Alsatian.[7] This paradox likely contains no easy solution for any colonized individuals who see the light of independence. In the case of Senegal, in particular, the nation itself did not officially come into being until 1960. Therefore, to accept the notion that literature *d'expression française* embodies the peoples' cultural history suggests that Senegal had no history before 1960.[8]

One way through which the cultural historian might reconcile this apparent paradox is by recognizing the fact that the literary works produced both in Senegal and within other Francophone African nations are characteristically hybridic. Their hybrid nature as texts that contain indigenous elements mixed with French culture have now become the "industry standard." Embodying a "black soul" as Léopold Sédar Senghor, father of the "Négritude" movement had indicated, Senghor also supported the concept of "francité" ("Frenchness"), a way of seeing and conveying the world that he believed to be shared by all French-language speakers.[9] According to Senghor, Senegalese literature was characterized by its expression of both "Négritude" and "francité": it is black–African in terms of the values it expresses but nonetheless it maintains a certain sense of balance, which reveals the French influence (9). Throughout Africa, the French colonial enterprise created hybrid cultures mixing "Africanness" and "Frenchness" placing in juxtaposition African emotions and French reasoning. It is quite clear that Senghor's perspective on the relationship between language, literature and identity were influenced by French conceptions of national literature. For Senghor, only the French language had the ability to harness the hybrid consciousness created by the colonial experience.

The concept of hybridity itself is a tendentious one and forms an important subject of discussion within Postcolonial Studies. Among postcolonial critics, Homi Bhabha's writings have fueled debate about the colonial and postcolonial world for the greater part of the last two decades. Bhabha posited that hybridity is not simply the resolution of the tension between the cultures of the colonizer and the colonized, but rather that hybridity brings to the forefront the fact that the colonizer's authority is questionable. For Bhabha, colonial discourse is problematically uncertain: "[T]he colonial presence is always ambivalent, split between its appearance as original and authoritative and its articulation as repetition and difference" (107). Bhabha's phrasing suggests that colonialism created colonial indigenous imitators who challenged the very notion of colonial authority by responding to colonization with an indigenous version of the colonizer's discourse. Thus, although we recognize the fact that that French colonial policy was one of assimilation that had profound effects on Francophone African societies, we must acknowledge that the process of assimilation was met with resistance. Within Senegal, France's oldest colony in Africa going back to the 17th century, an "elite" emerged and, in 1871, was rewarded by being granted representation in the French parliament. François Manchuelle, Christophe Konkobo and others have challenged the historical vision of complete assimilation without resistance. Throughout the French colonial enterprise, stories of African peoples rejecting French culture remained widespread. Even from the early stages of French educational endeavors in Africa, Africans challenged the expression, "Nos ancêtres, les Gaulois." In *L'enseignement dans les territoires français de l'Afrique occidentale de 1817 à 1920: Mission civilisatrice ou formation d'une élite?*, Denise Bouche highlighted the fact that the reality of French education in the colonies never matched the total assimilation seen in colonial propaganda: "[It] was constantly adapting itself to the colonial situation on the ground" (895). In *Notre fille ne se mariera pas* (1969), a play by Cameroonian writer Guillaume Oyônô-Mbia, the dialogue between Colette and her son Jean-Pierre (note the assimilated French names) concerning a piece of camembert underscores the truth that, for some Africans, French culture was sometimes "difficult to swallow":

> COLETTE: C'est vrai que tu refuses de manger ton camembert, chéri?
> JEAN-PIERRE: Je n'aime pas le camembert!
> COLETTE: La question n'est pas là! Il ne s'agit pas d'aimer le camembert Il s'agit de le manger comme un bon petit garçon! (*L'entraînant de force vers la table*) Viens!...
> JEAN-PIERRE: (*pleurant toujours*) J'veux pas de camembert!
> COLETTE: (*toujours tendre et ferme*) Il faut vouloir le manger! C'est la culture!
> JEAN-PIERRE: (*obstiné*) J'veux pas manger la culture!
> COLETTE: Is it true that you refuse to eat your camembert, dear?
> JEAN-PIERRE: I don't like camembert!
> COLETTE: That's not the question! It's not about liking camembert: It's about eating it like a good little boy! (*Forcefully dragging him toward the table*) Come!...
> JEAN-PIERRE: (*still crying*) I don't want any camembert!
> COLETTE: (*still tender and firm*) You must want to eat it! It's culture!
> JEAN-PIERRE: (*stubborn*) I don't want to eat culture! [cited in *Mais Oui!* 191].

Oyônô-Mbia's words clearly challenge colonial authority, but at the same time they transform the colonized individual into something new; a dual identity steeped in both indigenous and French culture offering the individual a perspective on two different contradictory worlds. Resultantly, the Francophone African citizen is confronted with several challenges. He can champion the spread of indigenous languages at the same time as he reads and writes in French. He can look to France for advancements in science, technology, and agriculture while at the same time taking into consideration the real needs of his homeland. He must be careful, however, not to represent an idealized view of his country's future. Perhaps, he should describe his country's future as one that sees French nationalism as a partnership between Africa and the former colonizing nation. But, even this notion is risky. In short, even at the beginning of the New Millennium, the Francophone African still stands at the crossroads of cultural history that inevitably forces a complex reevaluation of postcolonial era texts in an effort to further deconstruct the boundaries between colonizer and colonized.

It is thus important to understand that the hybridity of African nations cannot be confined to the extent to which Africans adopted and transformed European models. As Aijaz Ahmad has already pointed out, "it is deeply misleading to read the history of formerly colonized "nations" purely through the prism of the colonial encounter, and in terms of European influences" (cited in Murphy 59). In addition, it would be yet another fallacy to assume that African culture even before the arrival of the colonial machines was not already hybridic. The number of racial, ethnic, linguistic, and religious cultural groups in Africa alone is astounding. Therefore, we should resist the temptation to turn Africa into a "Garden of Eden," an Abbaye de Thélème (to borrow a scene from François Rabelais), an idyllic environment that was contaminated by the arrival of European colonists.[10] Though the development of national literary canons in Africa that began to take place in the 1960s underscored a particular cultural shift, postcolonial critics should be careful to avoid overestimating that this fact somehow suggests that all post-independence literary texts were oriented in the same direction. As Harrison describes:

> [I]f one takes a skeptical, historicizing view of any "national" body of literature, or a body of literature in a given language, the particular significance of "sharing" the language and even the extent to which "it" is shared, both across time [...] and across the globe, come to seem far from clear, a matter of diverse overlapping histories rather than something that can be captured at the level of a general "identity" [109–10].

Thus the use of European languages within former colonies is an inevitable characteristic of Postcolonialism. Even within the same language within a given society, there have always been competing discourses. Language becomes one of the most marked visual and auditory remnants of the colonial system. As a cultural product, it exhibits a life of its own. Nonetheless, this linguistic and cultural hybridity cannot be separated from either the politics or the history that created them. In *Discours sur le colonialisme*, Aimé Césaire questioned whether or not colonialism itself was truly the best means to construct a cultural dialogue. In the New Millennium, we continue to ask ourselves the same question that Césaire asked himself.

Writing the Black Man's Burden: Senouvo Agbota Zinsou and the "Black Comedy"

In this chapter, I offer Senouvo Agbota Zinsou's "black comedy" including *Le club*, *On joue la comédie*, and *La tortue qui chante suivie de La femme du blanchisseur et de Yévi au pays des monstres* as prime examples of Francophone African theatre of the post-independence period. Zinsou is one of the most prolific and influential stage dramatists of Francophone Africa. Born in

Lorné, Zinsou studied in France where he earned degrees in theatre and communications. In 1968, after working with several student companies, he cofounded a university theatre company (Troupe Nationale du Togo). He began to receive attention outside Togo when his play *On joue la comédie* received first prize at the Radio France Internationale's 1972 "Festival of Black Arts and Culture" in Lagos, Nigeria. Zinsou directed a production of the same play that later toured France. Since 1978, Zinsou has been director of the Troupe Nationale du Togo, which is also a ballet and music company. He directs the company in productions of his own plays, including *L'Arc en Ciel* and *Le Club*. Zinsou premiered *La Tortue qui chante* in 1966 during the Francophone Summit in Lomé in a production that was later performed in France at the 1987 Limoges Festival. He is also a prize-winning short story writer whose fiction and plays are published in France by Hatier. *On joue la comédie* (1972) earned Zinsou both a first prize and a scholarship to study in Paris. In the French capital, he conducted graduate-level work in Theatre Studies at the *Institut des Études Théâtrales* at the *Université de Paris* where he wrote a thesis entitled "Éléments pour un théâtre national Togolais" directed by Jean Schérer. After returning to his native Togo, Zinsou was appointed to serve on the Ministry of Culture where he founded the National Company for the Performing Arts. He headed this organization until 1992 (Ricard 1987: 100–3). Zinsou's other published poetic works include *Yévi et L'éléphant chanteur* (2000) and *Le Médicament* (2003). *On joue la comédie*, which saw its first performance at the Pan-African Cultural Arts Festival in Lagos, Nigeria in 1977, has been produced in many African nations including Togo and Burundi. This initial performance brought Zinsou's talent for creating pioneering stage writing into the light and it also revealed a desire to showcase the popular aspect of contemporary Francophone African theatre. Avoiding the critical tone of Francophone African theatre of the period, *On joue la comédie* redefined theatre based on traditional Togolese forms, most notably, the "kantata," an oral, music-based popular theatrical genre. Zinsou writes: "In *On joue la comédie*, I've sought to adapt to the written theatre the techniques of popular forms which derive from an oral and improvised theatre. I've wanted, in so doing, to render a personal tribute to the popular actors of the concert party" (quoted in de Saivre 1982: 74–5). Instead of focusing on hammering home traditional themes such as heroism or nationalism, *On joue la comédie* plays with the very components of theatre itself: illusion, song, dance, and ritual performance. It is a "concert party" redefining theatre aesthetics of the period and of the area. It is Togolese "Black Comedy."

Like traditional theatre from other Francophone African countries, Togolese theatre is deeply-seated in cultural and religious ceremonies transformed into a spectacle and performed in front of an audience. As Alain Ricard notes, "le théâtre comme pratique sociale ou esthétique est le propre d'une société désacralisée: il repose sur des acteurs qui jouent ... sûrement pas pour des raisons rituelles"/"theater as social or esthetic practice is a feature of a desacralized society: it is based on actors who act ... certainly not for ritual reasons" (199). Subsequently, one cannot begin to examine African theatre without considering the influence of the numerous ritualistic, religious, and cultural events taking place at any point during the calendar year and how these events relate to a playwright's sociocultural framework. From this viewpoint, the dialogue between the structure of Zinsou's dramatic writing and that particular sociocultural exterior in which the playwright has evolved and that bears on his dramatic project is a mine to explore. Certainly, Zinsou's theatre has experienced other influences, in greater or lesser degrees, such as that of Samuel Beckett through his manipulations of sound and silence, but it remains deeply rooted in the notion of the concert party, the *Ewe* popular theatre whose first presentations, in Togo, take us back to 1929.[11] Furthermore, what is particular to Zinsou's theatre is the tendency of the performance to become autonomous, distanced from the writing, reduced most often to a basic theatrical framework. The performances are in fact molded in the aesthetic of the "kantata," a religious theater that is entirely sung that formed the bulk of Zinsou's early dramatic writing: "Les spectacles de mon père mêlaient le texte parlé au chant, à la danse, à la musique et c'est ce que je tente de faire. D'ailleurs mon père n'était-il pas influencé par une certaine culture artistique, celle de la kantata..."/"My father's spectacles mixed the written word with song, dance, and music, and that is what I try to do. Furthermore, my father was influenced by a certain artistic culture, that of the cantata..." (qtd. in Ricard 221). As a result, Zinsou's theatre is a combination of several oral artistic varieties that often skirt the line between literary text and spectacle. The "concert party" is his "Black Comedy." Within Togolese theatre tradition, the concert party shatters the fourth wall thus merging the actions of the spectators with those of the actors. It is a popular theatrical form that audiences continue to embrace. Zinsou's theatre translates the concert party into a new form of theatrical writing. Thus, his work is a matter of adapting an oral creation with its own unique aesthetics to written form. In principle, the concert party has no "text," so to speak. It is improvisational to the extent that it sees its genesis in the live performance of the actors combined with the receptive nature of the spectators. The actor who performs an improvisational text must continuously create the text. Therefore, from that reality results the difficult notion of writing a concert party. To script the improvised forms a paradox.

We should not underestimate either the contribution of African theatre to the world theatre scene nor should we fail to acknowledge the impact that other "theatres" have made on African theatre throughout the ages. Given the effect of globalization, theatrical forms throughout the world are in constant dialogue with each other. The "concert party" that we are addressing here has measurably altered the landscape of Francophone African theatre development. To divorce our understanding of the evolution of Zinsou's theatre from the cultural communication of the African peoples, particularly the *Ewe*–an indigenous people of French Togoland and the Volta region–would be another mistake. In order to fully understand the cultural relevance and "trappings" of Zinsou's theatre, we must examine the sociocultural status of his characters, his manipulation of language, and how he transforms the theatrical space specifically as the latter pertains to the relationship between the performers on stage and the viewing public. It is also important to understand that a characteristic of Zinsou's theatre is that is brings together two distinct African theatrical genres, the concert party, of which I have already written, and the traditional African (folk)tale. His stage plays incorporate the discourses of tales and of the concert party into a structured narrative.

More specifically, in its most essential form, the "concert party" represents spontaneous theatrical composition made possible, in part, through the immediate response of an audience. Unlike traditional (Western) theatre in which the fourth wall impedes spectators from fully interacting with the performers on stage, in the concert party the success of the dramatic performance is largely dependent on the audience's willingness and ability to become a part of the unfolding drama. To most Westerners, the notion of an interactive theatre is a bit disjointing, since the lion's share of performances that Westerners attend are traditionally "European" in nature. Nonetheless, the concert party structure becomes blurred in Zinsou's theatre at the point at which the theatrical composition ceases to be improvisational as spectators are recruited and trained for the parts that they will play. This technique risks creating a false reality in the theatre akin to the traditional theatre "plant," a phony spectator who deceives the spectators by participating with them. In Zinsou's theatre, the actors appear to be carrying out their daily lives rather than performing in front of an audience. In doing so, the playwright uses a large amount of characters (some anonymous) suggesting that he is holding up a mirror to everyday street life. In *La Tortue qui chante*, for example, the "Crowd" is an actual character playing a role in the play. The "Crowd" serves to advance the narrative, it pauses to comment on the action, but it does not alter the course of the story. The play's *didascalies* (stage directions) cautiously indicate the role of the "Crowd":

> Une foule bruyante entoure le fou
> La foule se tait...
> Progressivement
> Murmures de la foule... [5].
>
> A loud crowd surrounds the fool
> The crowd becomes quiet
> Progressively
> Murmurs from the crowd....

In *La femme du blanchisseur*, the collective now takes the form of "voisins," and in *Yévi au pays des monstres*, it is the plural "monstres" that refer to the reality of that anthropological anonymity already prefigured in Zinsou's first play, *On joue la comédie*. In point of fact, in the initials of pages of that particular work, the playwright writes:

> Une troupe de comédiens, la plus nombreuse possible puisque les acteurs devront interpréter différents rôles sur la scène et assumer dans la salle des interventions de supposés spectateurs. Parmi les rôles principaux:
>
> —Le présentateur (qui interprète le rôle de Chaka)[12]
> —Deux policiers blancs
> —N'Koulou-Nkoulou (Dieu des Zoulou)
> —Plusieurs anciens détenus
> —Un gardien de prison
> —Un travesti jouant la femme de Chaka
> —Le Commandant président à l'exécution
> —Un spectateur contestataire
> —ETC... [*La tortue* 5].

> A group of actors, as many as possible since the actors must play different roles on the stage and assure the interventions by supposed spectators in the room. Among the principal roles:
>
> —The presenter (who plays the role of Chaka)
> —Two white detectives
> —N'koulou-Nkoulou (God of the Zulus)
> —Several former detainees
> —A prison guard
> —A male actor playing the role of Chaka's wife
> —The Commander presiding at the execution
> —An anti-establishment spectator
> —ETC....

As noted in the previous examples, the characters presented here lack a true identity outside of their social status. Their function in the concert party is important only to the extent that they illustrate the role that these particular characters play within society. The concert party is not concerned with the individual, but rather with the collective culture. Chaka's words at the end of *On joue la comédie* summarize this notion well:

> Mesdames, Messieurs, pour ce soir, notre jeu va prendre fin. Mais n'oubliez pas que ... [c]ette histoire si gaie en apparence, que nous avons eu à la fois le plaisir et la peine de bâtir devant vous sur cette scène, comme un de ces gratte-ciel de Johannesbourg, de Salisbury ou même de New York, Londres et Paris, n'est pas faite de rire bon marché [61].
>
> Ladies and Gentlemen, for this evening, our play will come to an end. But do not forget that ... this story, so gay in appearance, which we have had both the pleasure and the pain of putting together before you on this stage, like one of those skyscrapers in Johannesburg, Salisbury, or even New York, London and Paris, is not made of cheap laughter.

The richness of Zinsou's plays is in their organic composition that by its very essence produces a different text at each performance. His works require a mutual cultural exchange between the actors and the audience. John Conteh-Morgan states that to Zinsou "the theatre should stimulate the audience into a critical judgment and appraisal both of the action represented and its mode of representation" (194). In other words, the audience should not be reduced to the level of a passive theatre consumer. Rather, it should become engaged in the production of the play. In *On joue la comédie*, Zinsou illustrates the process of dramatic composition rather than a packaged theatrical product.

Divided into a prologue and four acts, *On joue la comédie* opens in the streets of Johannesburg, South Africa where a band of street performers decide to create a play about apartheid. Just when the play is about to begin, two police officers enter the stage, interrupting the performance by conducting a background check on the actors to see if they are terrorists. The action is interrupted a second time, not by the police, but by an aging spectator who wishes to participate in the drama. A self-proclaimed minister, he gives a sermon about a messiah named Chaka who will deliver the blacks of South Africa from their troubles. While the impatient actors try to push the minister off the stage, two spectators begin to argue over the relevance of the sermon that the minister delivered. The two cannot agree on whether or not the audience should see another escapist, entertaining play, or whether they should see one that treats the challenges of postcolonial South African society. Towards the end of the prologue, it is agreed that the actors will perform a play entitled "Chaka le Messie" that will be an improvised response to the minister's sermon. A general plot and story is created, roles are distributed, and the actors quickly work to begin the performance.

Entirely aware of the reality that they are creating a play-within-a-play, Act One of *On joue la comédie* coincides with the opening of the improvised play entitled "Chaka le Messie." It is a play, however, that will never be performed, for just when the presenter (Xuma) agrees to play the title role, a group of street actors who were not present when the decision to improvise a new play was made are confused to see Xuma ready to perform in a different play. Further, they are also surprised to see the police arrest "Chaka" and his men, for the police are convinced that these are the terrorists that they were seeking. Chaos ensues. By this time, the actors have abandoned any notion of staging a play and, now confirming that they are, in fact, the terrorists that the police were looking for in Act II for the former attack the prison holding African revolutionaries. In Act III, Chaka finds himself sitting in a jail cell. He has been sentenced to death. In Act IV, Chaka talks about what he wants to do before his sentence is fully carried out. His last wish is to perform a one-man play called "The President of Repression." With just moments to spare before his hanging, Chaka's friends break him out of prison. The message of *On joue la comédie* is strong. The play's failure to fully materialize speaks volumes on the inability to create social theatre (anti-apartheid theatre) in South Africa. At the same time that the spectator feels a sense of betrayal that he did not really see the performance of "Chaka le Messie," he has also played a role in the creation of *On joue la comédie*.

Zinsou's play exhibits an obvious Brechtian quality, in particular, in the way in which the drama shatters the illusion of reality through the constant interruption of planted actors. The very plot of *On joue la comédie* in which the creation of one play is abandoned in favor of another brought about by players who are not, in fact, part of the original "cast" shatters the notion of reality. While techniques such as this point toward European influences, the concert party of the Togolese theatrical tradition takes precedence over European theatre. The link between the concert party and *On joue la comédie* is inextricable. The very nature of the play's plot points to the concert party's characteristic of improvisation. Again like the characters in the concert party, those of *On joue la comédie* are of humble origin, forming a complete antithesis to the princely figures of traditional Francophone theatre such as in Aimé Césaire's *La tragédie du Roi Christophe*. Filled with mockery, mime, and self-deprecation, parody and satire, Zinsou's characters are like the court jester of a medieval fair. His "Black Comedy" not only criticizes apartheid and religion, but also traditional forms of Francophone dramatic literature. Another innovative feature of *On joue la comédie* is the use of stage space. The traditional proscenium arch with the fourth wall limiter is abandoned in favor of a stage space that encourages interaction between actor and spectator. The singing and dancing in which the audience is invited to participate no longer takes place within the traditional stage space, but rather throughout the entire auditorium. Zinsou's burden consists of redefining both the way that actors manipulate stage space as well as the way that spectators understand how that space can be used. His aesthetic of total participation of actors and spectators in the development of a play contains clear ideological implications. It was a metaphor for the construction of an independent Togo. In the same way in which the spectators could work together with the actors to produce a play, so also the people of Togo could work together to bring about political and social change (in the play, it was an end to apartheid). Zinsou's theatrical style is encouraging. It is a theatrical aesthetic in which the subject matter is constantly negotiated between those who have agency and those who are characteristically powerless. Certainly, both aesthetically and ideologically, Zinsou's theatre represents a radical divergence from traditional Francophone theatre embedded in an elitist postcolonial framework. It is for this reason that *On joue la comédie* was considered revolutionary in the 1970s, for it sought to encourage greater participation not only in dramatic creation, but also, more importantly, in social and political life.

2

Oral Societies and Writing in the Language of the Oppressed

> "Through language, we have what the past left us as a message and what the present prepares for us. It is language that connects us, and it is language that is the basis of our identity. It is an essential element and, without it, there is no culture. Language helps us to interpret.... We were the dominated, the colonized and language was for us an element of liberation."
> —*Seydou Badian Kouyaté*[1]

Given both the fact that printing as we know it did not come into being until the arrival of Gutenberg's printing press in 1436 and that the number of illiterate individuals throughout the world stands at approximately 800 million,[2] one could make the claim that the majority of world histories have been transmitted orally. Within the continent of Africa, in particular, history has been preserved throughout the ages primarily through the transmission of oral folktales. Orality has historically served as a vehicle for the transmission of culture and tradition. The Latin phrase for this concept is *translatio studii* referring to "the transfer of knowledge or learning." In a sense, the terminology itself speaks to the translatability of cultural elements, that is, the ability to transfer elements either within a given culture or from one culture to another. The spoken word is the carrier of these cultural elements. Through the spoken word, the customs and cultural modes of a particular social group are transmitted from one generation to the next. These cultural elements, therefore, form the glue that holds our societies together. If this glue is removed, we risk the distinction of our social groups. Oral culture makes an accounting of a cultural group's myths, legends, and histories. It takes stock of its proverbs, jokes, songs, dramas, and stories. The oral culture connects the present both to the past and to the future in an apparently seamless transition both backwards and forwards through time. The sum total of the cultural objects that a particular society deems important over time permits the given society to both define itself in comparison to other societies and it allows a particular society to set itself apart from other societies. It is from these same cultural elements that cultural identity formation originates. Thus, both the identity of a group of people with a dominant oral tradition and the historicity of a group of people is transmitted through speech (discourse) within a variety of specific contexts. One needs to look no further than the infamous newspaper headline "Dewey Defeats Truman" on the front page of the Chicago Tribune on November 3, 1948, the day after incumbent Harry S. Truman won an upset victory over Republican challenger and Governor of New York Thomas E. Dewey in the 1948 presidential election to find evidence that sometimes even written history makes mistakes. It is for this very reason that we should not underestimate the oral record.

Operating under the general assumption that few cultures are, in fact, truly one hundred percent isolated from the outside world, I underscore the fact that within any cultural system, the transmission of culture is codified through linguistic signs that are arbitrary in nature. In his *Cours de linguistique générale*, Swiss linguist and semiotician Ferdinand de Saussure poured the foundation for many developments both in linguistics and semiotics in the 20th century. For Ferdinand de Saussure, the linguistic unit is a double entity, one formed by the association of two terms: the "signifier" and the "signified." As Elisa Fiorio suggests in her article entitled "Orality and Cultural Identity: The Oral Tradition in Tupuri (Chad)," this linguistic unity formed by the signifier and the signified "preserves the ensemble of notions which are attributed to it to designate an element of the visible world, a social relationship, and so forth" (71). We should, therefore, not underestimate the value of the spoken word as part of this linguistic reality, for it is fundamental. As Fiorio further emphasizes, "Comprehension and transmission of the spoken word allows restitution of the profound, precise signification of the traditional way of thinking for the next generation" (71). In an age in which technological innovation commands "texting" or "tweeting" over traditional face-to-face voice communications, the study of the transmission of culture through oral discourse has gained greater importance. With the absence of written communication, the problem of the preservation and transmission of culture presents itself when the chain of orality is broken. What happens when the number of speakers of a language is severely diminished? What occurs when speakers start to communicate in a language that is not their native language (as is the case for some Francophone writers from Africa)?

Consequently, in light of the challenges that technology has placed on oral communications on the whole, a re-examination of oral tradition and its relation to modern Francophone African literature is of vital importance for any meaningful study of this particular literature. This re-examination fully acknowledges previous work on the subject of the study of oral tradition, including Ruth Finnegan's classic study entitled *Oral Literature in Africa* (1970). In her groundbreaking work, she argued that most Western scholars were completely unfamiliar with the notion of "oral literature":

> The concept of an oral literature is an unfamiliar one to most people brought up in cultures which, like those of contemporary Europe, lay stress on the idea of literacy and written tradition. In the popular view it seems to convey on the one hand the idea of mystery, on the other that of crude and artistically undeveloped formulations [1].

In her subsequent anthology of oral poetry, *The Penguin Book of Oral Poetry* (1978), Finnegan sought to argue that poetry itself was part of a universal oral tradition that had yet to be fully understood. Here she stated quite explicitly that oral literature was not unique to those produced on the continent of Africa, but rather that the oral tradition itself was "a universal phenomenon throughout the ages, and not something confined to Africa" (7). Research conducted on indigenous peoples throughout the Americas and Australia would most likely substantiate Finnegan's claim. In complement to Finnegan's research, Cora Agatucci suggests that this oral tradition still continues in contemporary African writings because "every human culture in the world seems to create stories (narratives) as a way of making sense of the world" (1).

Therefore, we cannot deny the fact that oral tradition is central in any attempt to understand the nature of Francophone African literature. If we are going to make the argument here that poetic literature itself is rooted in orality, we must certainly understand the nature of that rooting. As Richard Johnson has noted, "contemporary written literature in Africa continues to derive a great deal of its vitality from older traditions of verbal art" (s.a. 1). For the purpose of the present study, it is important to establish an appreciation for oral tradition as a cornerstone of African literature. By "literature," I fully intend both traditional canonical works and other works of a more popular nature. Literary works would include written texts, spontaneous poetic texts (slam poetry, in the American literary tradition), or dramatic works such as those produced during the "concert party." Through the African literary tradition, histories are created. Here, I offer several complementary working definitions of oral literature as relevant within the context of Francophone literature of Africa. *The Concise Oxford Dictionary of Literary Terms* (1990) defines "oral tradition" as "the passing on from one generation (and/or locality) to another of songs, chants, proverbs, and other verbal compositions within and between non-literate cultures; or the accumulated stock of works thus transmitted by word of mouth." However, we should point out that within the contemporary view oral literature can, in fact, include works presented in written form: "Strictly speaking, 'oral' means 'expressed in spoken words,' but oral literature now includes material in written form (as long as it was originally expressed orally)" (Lusweti 1). These definitions offer the scholar and the reader flexibility when approaching an oral text. In its simplest terms, oral literature is that which combines the three main characteristics of orality: oral composition, oral performance, and oral transmission/aural reception.

This said, pre-colonial traditional societies in Sub-Saharan Africa were mostly oral societies whose languages had yet to take written form. This fact is true despite Africa itself being one of the first regions on the planet in which written characters were used to express human thought. In the African context, specifically, the mostly oral traditions of tribal societies' languages were neither appreciated nor promoted as a means of communication or means of education by the colonizing Europeans. Due to their perceived "primitivity," African oral literatures were also not accepted as valid forms of social, cultural, or political expression. Consequently, for the European powers that controlled African life in the colonial hegemony, only literature written in colonial languages such as English and French was considered legitimate literature. Ngũgĩ wa Thiong'o observed this fact in his book entitled *Decolonizing the Mind: The Politics of Language in African Literature*:

> [It is the fact than otherwise] that the privileging of the written over the oral had roots in the relationship of power in society and history.... The dominant social forces had become identified with the civilized and the written. With colonization, the same binary opposition was exported to Africa, with the written and civilized being identified with Europe as a whole, the oral, and the historical being identified with Africa. The product of the oral no longer belonged to history because quite clearly, the colonizer did not want the colonized to have any claims to any history as the basis of his resistance and affirmation of his humanity [108].

Ngũgĩ wa Thiong'o's words suggest that written histories confirm cultural history. As Bogumil Andrzejewski suggested, "there is mounting evidence that the presence of literature is a universal characteristic of human society; [that is that] literature is an art which uses language as its medium irrespective of whether it is oral or written" (31). Although poets themselves have traditionally enjoyed some political power in many oral societies in Africa—we need to look no further than the *griot* to find evidence of this fact—narrative or good "old fashioned" storytelling also played an important role in traditional societies. Walter Ong stated that "although it is found in all cultures, narrative is certainly more widely functional in primary oral cultures than in others....

Most, if not all, oral cultures generate quite substantial narratives or a series of narratives" (140).

In storytelling, a widely used method of education in oral societies, famous storytellers are, in many cases, respected and referred to as "poets." Storytelling is an art that may come naturally to some, but in most cases it is an acquired skill. In many African societies, as Anne Pellowski stated:

> There is still a high priority assigned to family storytelling.... Some groups in Africa have special names to describe the storytelling events within the family circle. For the Edo of Benin, Nigeria, such a gathering is called an *ibota*. It includes the children, youth, wives, and the head of household in one compound. It usually takes place in the largest room, and it can celebrate anything from the successful sale of a crop to the visit of a relative, or just being in good mood [44–5].

As Gillian Brown has remarked, "one of the sources of risk in communication is that whereas speakers may think that what they have to say is sufficiently important to be paid attention to, listeners (even younger ones) may have other priorities and may not listen in detail but only partially, or perhaps not at all" (26). Like their European-language counterparts, African indigenous languages contained complex structures and specialized vocabulary that expressed both the individual and the collective experience. The African poet transmitted the histories of the people. As Elizabeth Drew stated:

> The poet's own immediate task is to bring all the depth and intensity of his own consciousness to a verbal surface: the reader starts from the surface, penetrates gradually to the full consciousness beneath. Poetry is thus both act and instrument. It is the poet's tongue, speaking a language of enticement to his fellow men and urging them, through a sharing of his speech, to share his own aftersight, foresight and insight [61].

Poetry, whether formalized or not, served as a vehicle for expressing the thoughts and actions of traditional African societies. With the arrival of white colonists, oral languages suffered an inevitable linguistic decay, with the written word grafting its own cultural values onto local languages. In the case of West and Middle Africa, French failed to recognize the importance of African oral languages as the carrying vessel of tribal social and cultural history. As Ashcroft, Griffiths, and Tiffin noted when discussing African oral art in their work, *The Empire Writes Back*:

> That African cultures had not ... developed writing beyond the earliest stages by the time of the colonial onslaught should not serve to obscure the fact that African oral art had developed forms at least as highly wrought and varied as those of European cultures. Recognition of this led critics to urge that the study of these forms should be removed from the limiting anthropological discourse

within which they were set and be recovered as a legitimate and distinctive enterprise for literary criticism [127].

It is, therefore, impossible to separate the practical and political implications of the arrival of written colonial languages within Africa. The colonial language—in our case, French—became instantly endowed with a political power that could both "make or break" its possessor. For a Cameroonian or Senegalese to speak French, for example, might allow him to acquire social and political status. As Mazrui and Mazrui (1998) have indicated, the impact of European colonization has been so extensive with the effect of leveling out African indigenous languages, in particular, that in the contemporary world "one out of every five blacks on earth has a European language for a mother tongue" (13). The subjugation of the peoples of Africa both physically and linguistically created a second citizenry on the continent. To learn the French language in Africa might suggest that you have forgotten your place of origin: Africa.

In addressing this particular issue within the context of his experiences in colonial Kenya, the renowned writer Ngũgĩ wa Thiong'o' in his book entitled *Moving the Centre: The Struggle for Cultural Freedoms*, wrote:

> Our Language gave us a view of the world.... Then I went to primary school and the bond was broken. The language of my education was no longer the language of my culture—it was a foreign language of domination, alienation and disenfranchisement. As a practice in colonial Kenya, anyone who was caught speaking the native language in the school vicinity was to be punished [11].

Accordingly, by going to the colonial school, his language was taken apart element by element. Such was the life experience of many indigenous populations living in Sub-Saharan Africa. Whether writing in the colonial English tradition or the colonial French tradition, this fact was not missed by a number of African writers who commented on the loss of culture that had taken place and the overall disruption of a locally sustainable Africa.

Lacking the essence of African cultures in both colonial and postcolonial development in Africa, economic and political inefficiency began to manifest themselves. In his book entitled *No Life Without Roots: Culture and Development*, Thierry Verhelst also asserts how development that is not both culturally based culturally responsive is not practical:

> Only the cultural dimension can give coherence and finality to development.... [Culture] is dynamic in that it evolves through needs, desires, and external contacts. Culture is holistic because it encompasses all aspects of life whether they be material or spiritual, symbolic or technical, economic or social. In short, the cultural approach is synonymous with the human approach in all its complexity and richness ... stressing the cultural dimension of development means placing human beings at the center of all analyses and initiatives [160].

In colonial relationships, the process of eroding traditional (indigenous) ways of expression and the general "way of doing things" served to undermine the cultural and historical achievements of traditional African peoples creating an image of Africa as an "underdeveloped" place. Walter Rodney explains this concept well in his work *How Europe Underdeveloped Africa* (1982) in which he comments on how the disempowerment of the African persona and the African community occurred through the creation of a series of imposed cultural identities that eventually enrooted itself to such an extent that the "new" African identity is the only one that could be seen from the outside. As Ahmed Sékou Touré, former President of the Republic of Guinea, stated in 1962: "The relation between the degree of destitution of peoples of Africa and the length and nature of the exploitation they had to endure is evident. Africa remains marked by the crimes of the slave-traders: up to now, her potentialities are restricted by under-population" (qtd. in Rodney, Chapter 4).

Even well-received writers such as Ngũgĩ wa Thiong'o who had stopped writing in English and began to write in Kikuyu, quickly abandoned the path of writing in an indigenous language. The reasons are multiply that include the reality that the African literary elite is not prepared to have their works read, analyzed, and circulated in a native language that are spoken by the uneducated, unworldly, and unknown lower classes. Ngũgĩ wa Thiong'o is probably one of the few writers to even attempt self-expression in a native tongue, for more than most African writers, he understands how the African citizen develops an understanding of the "self" through the language that he uses. Nevertheless, the acquisition of colonial languages is a present reality on the continent of Africa that is explained, in part, by its necessity. As Mazrui and Mazrui state:

> Africa is an acute case of linguistic dependence. Credentials for ruling an African country are disproportionately based on a command of a Euro-imperial language. In Africa South of the Sahara it has become almost impossible to become a member of parliament or president without being fluent in at least one of the relevant European languages [69].

But, as the case of Malian filmmaker and New York University professor will show later in this book, no matter the level of contact that Africans have with colonial languages, historically speaking, these languages will never be their own. To turn Edward Said's word on its head, they are the languages of the colonial "Other" imposed on the peoples of Africa that do not reflect an indigenous cultural perspective. It was Martinican writer Frantz Fanon who in *Peau noire, masques blancs* said that "Un homme qui possède le langage possède par contre le monde exprimé et impliqué par ce langage"/"a man who has a language consequently possesses the world expressed and implied by that language" (18). Furthermore, in his book in which he discusses the case of language-subject relationship and language and literature ownership entitled *Culture, Education and Development in South Africa: Historical and Contemporary Perspectives*, Ali Abdi wrote:

> And to the general question of whether a language belongs to all who use it, the answer, from my perspective, is a categorical NO. A Language, be it English, Kiswahili or Burmese has a history, it has also its value systems, moral sanctions, inherent emotional expressions, and special sentimental attachments. These all create a specialized and un-severable relationship between a language and the person who is native to that language [254].

The question of language ownership is certainly an interesting philosophical one. French philosopher Jean Hyppolite stated that "Language is the universal instrument of mutual recognition" (10). Therefore, by definition, language is a form of communication that exists in a shared community space. In that sense, it is more "on loan" by the individual speaker than it belongs to him.

The Characteristics of Poetic Literature: Sound Architecture, Listening and Narration

Poetic literature has several defining characteristics the most obvious of which is the presence of language. Languages themselves are based on the balanced juxtapositions of phonemes. Phonemes are distinct units of sound that permit the listener to distinguish between similar, though different, words. The poet and playwright use the sound palette to paint a picture of the scene within the minds of their audiences. One of the most recognizable sounds is the human voice. Voices are a composition of sounds that can exist either inside or outside of the speaking subject. Poetry and theatre have the capacity to take the speaking subject's internal monologue and, by use of the appropriate directions, it can present that speech in front of the ears of the entire audience. Whether in the context of the French *chanson de geste* or the Senegalese *griot*, poetry is also a performance genre. Theatre is characterized by the fact that there are essentially no written words except those in scripts memorized by actors. Sounds, dialogue, and music scroll by the audience's ears and quickly disappear into the ether. Actors and actresses memorize these sounds and bring them to life in front of a live audience. Many actors would agree that theatrical lines are easier to remember if the latter have an established rhyme and meter (thus a measurable "poetic" characteristic). Consider, for example, the closing monologue of Shakespeare's famous play, *A Midsummer Night's Dream*, first performed in 1595:

> *Robin.*
> If we shadowes haue offended,
> Thinke but this (and all is mended)
> That you haue but slumbred heere,
> While these Visions did appeare.
> And this weake and idle theame,
> No more yeelding but a dreame,
> Gentles, doe not reprehend.
> If you pardon, we will mend [159].³

The rhyme and meter both unquestionably aid the actor in memorizing Shakespeare's verses. Alliteration and assonance play key roles as well. Alliteration refers to the repetition of specific consonants used to create dramatic effect. Assonance, in comparison, refers to the repetition of vowel sounds. "The potent poison" of which Hamlet speaks in his death scene, for example, has both the aural effect of hammering the final nails into the tragic hero's coffin and of creating a vivid image for the spectator.

Since the 1950s, when television reached the masses and dethroned radio as the main form of home entertainment, society has depended on images created by others to define our world. In the wake of the flood of televised images that have pervaded our homes over the last sixty years, some theorists have rediscovered the role that the aural element plays in awakening the power of the imagination. The recipient of oral literature encounters a "text" that he must interpret aurally, and this differs from television, film, and even stage theatre where images explode in front of an audience. The oral poet/dramatist is a sound architect who structures sound and cultivates its unique properties in order to evoke emotions in the listener that permit visualization. Sound architecture consists of constructing meaning through aural imagery. The sound architect understands the uniqueness of audio design and endeavors to use its language to express ideas and feelings. He understands that audio is a process that moves from aural source to the listener and then back to the aural source. The listener distinguishes between the various aural input, the brain decodes the aural input, from which the listener produces meaning (Ferrington 61–7). Aural input includes speech, sound effects, music, and silence. The sound architect knows the limitations of aural imagery and works to facilitate the listener's capacity to interpret the aural input. Each listener individually negotiates meaning from the aural input that he receives and forms mental images of objects and events that he may not have experienced himself. As a result of the power of the imagination, the listener is able to smell, taste, hear, see and touch objects that are not physically present. The smell of a sugar maple, the taste of a warm strawberry, the crackling of a fire, a red sky at sunset, or the feel of the grip on a baseball bat are but a few of the possible experiences that may stimulate the mind. Sound defines space. Aural architecture increases human experience through the brain's capacity to create visual representations based on a composite of images produced by an individual's senses. In his article entitled "Cognitive Mapping and Radio Drama," Alan Beck underscores his particular theory that specifies that listening, in general, demands a competence in navigating or orienteering through the imaginary "scenery" via the model of cognitive mapping (1). The mapping to which Beck refers is a two-fold process. Cognitive mapping depends on the ability of the dramatist to construct links that will be perceived by the listener. The dramatist creates "scenery" and "movements" that form "a sort of abstract geometry of outlines and a flattening of perspective, and that time-space-motion is compressed" (1). The listener perceives these elements through a cognitive process and constructs a visual image of the play as it unfolds. Don Druker, in contrast, argues that "what we hear when we listen ... to sounds depends a great deal upon how these sounds are coded—and coding in this sense involves social, intellectual, geographic, and even physiological factors" (334). The oral poet/dramatist takes this factor into account when "coding" his works.

Beyond the use of sound, the poet and playwright also participate in the creation of narrative. As a writer's tool, the narrator is responsible for developing what Alan Peacock calls the "space of narration." According to Peacock, "the space of narration is the location of a semiotics of narration—the signs that indicate that a story is taking place (announcements, tone of voice, graphical style), the kind of story it is (genre), how it relates to the broader social world (parable, allegory, moral, simulation, exaggeration, etc.) (n. pag.)."[4] Narrative exists as a shared space, or *diegesis*, which is separate from but part of the social world. The storyteller and the listener meet in the "story world" (the diegetic level), inside the space of narration. The "story world" contains the sequence of events. The storyteller and the listener also meet at the extradiegetic level, which is the "social world." Similarly, in his chapter entitled "Discours du récit: essai de méthode," Gérard Genette outlined several narrative moods/voices that facilitate an understanding of diegesis that functions well within the context of poetic literature. His four general categorizations are as follows: distance (diégèse/diagesis, mimésis/rhesis), perspective (focalisation/focalization—interne/internal, externe/external), narrative levels (intradiégétique/intradiegetic, extradiégétique/extradiagetic), and persons (homodiégétique/homodiegetic, hétérodiégétique/heterodiegetic) (Genette 65–282). A writer might employ a narrative mood in which the narrator speaks (diegesis) that would function in contrast to the narrative mood in which the fictional character speaks (rhesis). In oral poetry or theatre, the listening audience embraces this narrative mode because they find a character-narrator who, in a sense, represents the audience within the text itself.[5]

The narrator may stand outside the action without being completely external from it (heterodiegetic narrator). The narrator's role transforms as soon as he begins to judge the characters or if he expresses his opinion of the events. Heterodiegetic narrators indicate the presence of the writer as a moderator of the action, actively interfering with the audience's interpretation of the story. The choice of narrative voice indicates at what level the writer wishes to mediate the action. If the heterodiegetic narrator does not represent the writer himself, it may become necessary to make the narrator a full part of the action of the story; a homodiegetic narrator. Narration in the form of a reporter or chronicler is not a new concept in the French literary tradition, or in any Western literature, for it has been employed since the Medieval period. Geoffroi de Villehardouin, participant of the 4th Crusade, and Jean de Joinville, participant of the 7th Crusade, created chronicles in prose outlining events of the Crusades to which they bore witness. Villehardouin's *La Conquête de Constantinople* (1203-1207) and Joinville's *Vie de Saint Louis* (1309) related eyewitness accounts of battles and depicted life in the East. Like the medieval chronicler, the reporter functions not only as an eyewitness to events, but also as an intermediary between the characters in the story and the audience, and finally, as a character within the actual story. In Francophone African theatre derived from an oral tradition, the reporter transitions from an observer to the main character, who ultimately guides the development of the drama, relates the principle themes to the audience, and creates the action of the story as he recounts it. The audience, for its part, shifts from passive spectator to active spectator in the drama.

The use of the reporter as narrator in Francophone African theatre parallels the narrator of Biblical narrative. Much Biblical narrative was presented through a trustworthy, omniscient narrator–Genette refers to the omniscient narrator as *focalisation zéro*—who created a world filled with characters, described their words and deeds, showed their hidden feelings, and yet separated himself from this world. The characters lived, breathed, and interacted with each other largely without the knowledge of the existence of the narrator. At the same time, through the mediation of the narrator, the words and feelings of these characters were addressed to the audience. This homodiegetic narrator walked the line between storyteller and participant in the action of the drama. If he failed to remain an observer, he would influence the events and transform their natural course. In a sense, the homodiegetic narrator is a cultural anthropologist who navigates the slippery slope of his field: he must observe a culture in order to understand it, but his observations must not be intrusive to the extent that they influence or contaminate the culture. In the absence of an omniscient narrator, the homodiegetic narrator is obliged to take control of recounting the story. His speech remains a commentary on the words of others as he transforms the characters into a reality for the audience.

On the level of discourse, we understand the homodiegetic narrator to be a component of the narrative (Culler 197–200). If the homodiegetic narrator recounts a story or directly quotes the speech of other characters, he simply fulfills his role as narrator. The liberty that he may exhibit as a privileged speaker within the world of the drama is offset by the fact that he is also a character created in someone else's discourse. The character that functions as narrator always exhibits a conflict between autonomy and dependence. The more authority an author gives to a homodiegetic narrator, the more self-effacing the homodiegetic narrator becomes, and the more we see the ultimate control of the author emphasized. The more a character holds the role of the narrator, the more he must take on a certain level of passivity, or anonymity, in the interest of objectively telling the story. Since the story told is not primarily the character's story, the narrator's story is ultimately an expression of his dependence on the author both for his knowledge and his point of view.

Having thus broadly defined both oral tradition and how oral composition is produced for and received by the listening public, I will now pay some attention to the contribution of oral literary tradition to a study of written literature. Without question, oral tradition has enriched literature on the whole in part because it is both a unique form of literature and a unique means of *translatio studii*. If we are to claim that this study centers on using cultural history as a framework for the study of Francophone African poetic literature, we cannot neglect continually underscoring the importance of oral tradition in that endeavor. As Nigerian novelist, and critic Isidore Okpewho has stated well:

> By a strange but happy coincidence, the recent boom in the publishing of contemporary African literature has occurred side by side with advances in the study of oral literature in Africa and the world at large. The two phenomena have been motivated by quite disparate circumstances, but their effects have clearly shed light on one another and together they promise to give us a better understanding of the nature of human culture in general [3].

If the goal then is to better understand "the nature of human culture in general," it is practical to start our journey of understanding on the continent of Africa, the so-called "Cradle of Mankind." In addition, due to its long history, the study of Africa oral literature is a reasonable place to start in working toward developing a better understanding of world literature.[6]

The Role of the Griot in Francophone African Society: A Cultural and Historical Perspective of Oral Poetics

It is virtually impossible to discuss the importance of oral literature within Africa without also discussing the role that the traditional African storyteller, the *griot*, plays in that literature. In addition, any study of the role of the *griot* in Francophone African literature must be comparative in nature. It must also have an ethnographic focus. The comparative nature to which I am referring here requires an examination of the role of the *griot* not only in the nations that make up Francophone Africa, but also in those nations throughout the continent of Africa that also have a long tradition of a *griot* presence. Within Senegal, in particular, the oral poet or *griot* is known by a variety of terms including *gewel*, *gawlo*, and *mabo*, and outside of West Africa, such as among the Xhosa in Southern Africa, the *griot* is called a *imbongi* (Kaschula "Imbongi and griot" 55–6). Due to the varying functions of the role of the *griot* within traditional African societies, the *griot* resists a static definition. Nonetheless, if we were to attempt to create a working definition of the *griot*, I would suggest the one provided by Eldridge Jones, Eustace Palmer, and Marjorie Jones in their book entitled *Oral and Written Poetry in African Literature Today* (1988). The *griot* is an artist who "was, and still is, observer, commentator or councillor on the past and passing scenes. He happily still survives in some parts of Africa, not only rehandling traditional material ... keeping the heroic feats of historical figures alive, but also commenting in traditional style on contemporary matters" (1). Moreover, the *griot* is a product of global culture that, quite literally, speaks to the cultural diversity of our planet. Exploring the cultural diversity of the world through an exploration of the oral poetry produced within the continent of Africa helps the world citizen to better understand our modern world. Ruth Finnegan explains this imperative as follows: "Oral poetry is not just something of far and away and long ago. In a sense it is all around us still..." (*Oral Poetry* 4). If the oral poet speaks not only to the past, but also to the current sociocultural reality, it behooves us to listen to what Finnegan has to say on the matter. Ethnographers continue to recognize the fact that these oral performances are the cultural product of their sociocultural *milieux*. Thus, oral poetry within Africa, in particular, is not a dish prepared exclusively for the upper crust of society, but rather an organic element of the pop culture. An understanding of the form and function of African oral poetry requires a complementary understanding of the cultural traditions that shaped this poetic form. We should be careful, however, that we do not paint an unrealistic view of the form's history. If there is one quality of African oral poetry that stands out as essential, it is its inherent flexibility. It is arguably because of the genre's ability to adapt to change that has assured its survival into the 21st century. When entering into a discussion of the importance of oral poetry within Francophone Africa, it is important to ask the question of the significance that the individual *griot* plays in delivering the message contained in the poetic composition. Thus, we must understand that within the *griot* tradition in Senegal, for example, Samba Diop suggests that "the person of the griot has more importance that the performance itself" (*The Oral History and Literature of the Wolof People* 246). Regrettably, Diop fails to acknowledge the larger role that the performance plays within the African oral poetic tradition. Taking into account the long history of oral poetry within the continent, the scholar begins to understand the function of the *griot* as social, political, and historical commentator. As Russell Kaschula states,

> On the one hand, the power of the tradition, which informs the function of the poet, does not only exist in relation to the performance, the performer or the text, but rather in relation to all of the above. On the other hand, power and function also exists in relation to those who are in control—there is a dependency relationship between the poet and those who hold power [Kaschula "Imbongi and griot" 60].

We could certainly argue that the relationship to which Kaschula refers is fluid, ever-changing. This relationship depends, in part, on the nature of the government in power and on how that government chooses to manipulate the cultural tradition. Does the government choose to seek glory in ages passed (Shaka Zulu) or does it wish to venerate a contemporary hero (Mandela)? No matter the perspective, the past and present functions of the *griot* remain significant.

In his essay entitled "Two Griots of Contemporary Senegambia," Edris Makward traced the traditional and the modern characteristics of the performances of two Wolof *griots*, Anchou Thiam and Haja M'Bana Diop, against the backdrop of sociocultural and sociopolitical change. Makward chose these two particular *griots* because they represented two opposite though complementary representations. Anchou Thiam represents the *griot* of "times gone by" who tells the traditional (folk)tales of West Africa. Haja M'Bana Diop, in contrast, represents the modern *griotte* who relates the telling of her tales to important cultural figures such as Léopold Sédar Senghor. The fact that these two storytellers are of different genders is an interesting detail that I will discuss later. Also interesting in Makward's comparison of these two oral poets is the fact that they were born and raised in the same part of Senegal, Richard-Toll, a city in the northern part of the country with a population of approximately 70,000 (Britannica). Traces of the two *griots*' small-town past spring from their respective poetic compositions. In Anchou's poem entitled

"Muse Fari Joop," the *griot* "concentrates on the bravery of a noble warrior of the past, who happens to be an ancestor of the late Lamine Gueye, the well-known Senegalese lawyer and politician" (Makward 35). The poem begins with references to Muse Joop's ancestral line:

> Jaajiri Awa Dembaane.
> Maa Joop Gandiool.
> Ranaan Joop Maar Sere.
> Njante Joop Maar Sere.
> Mbaas Joop Maar Sere.
> Maa Joop Gandioo.
> Muse Saar Fari Joop, le hero...
>   [cited in Kaschula "Imbongi and griot" 61].
> Jaajiri Awa Dembaane.
> Maa Joop Gandiool.
> Ranaan Joop Maar Sere.
> Njante Joop Maar Sere.
> Mbaas Joop Maar Sere.
> Maa Joop Gandioo.
> Muse Saar Fari Joop, the hero....

Anchou's reference to the historical past is incontrovertible, as his words recreate a genealogy of his people. M'Bana's poetry, in comparison, "deals more specifically with the actions and the events of her time, rather than with those of the past..." (Makward 29). As Georgina Collins states, as a modern-day *griotte*, M'Bana has a modern approach to orality, and while she may continue to perform songs that are traditionally female such as ceremonial wedding songs, she also recites a "chant du développement" (to enhance her country's development and government), as well as performing political songs formerly a male genre (Collins 353–4). Regardless of the gender of these *griots*, with regard to the contemporary sociocultural and sociopolitical contexts, these African oral poets are lured by a force that issues from the contemporary cultural events that they have set out to narrate in verse form. Though pioneering work in this particular area of study was already begun at the end of the 20th century, extensive analysis remains to be completed in researching the relationship between Francophone African oral poetry and gender studies. In speaking about the role that women have played in African oral performance, John Johnson, Thomas Hale, and Stephen Belcher stated, "Duran argues that women will sing an entire epic if no man is available for the task. Although no epic by a woman has appeared in print, Duran reports that some songs by women extend over long periods of time—as much as two hours—and contain in essence all of the elements of epic" (xviii).

As I have previously stated, it is impossible to divorce the study of Francophone African oral literature from its sociocultural and sociopolitical contexts. As Finnegan has articulated well in *Oral Literature in Africa*, "in the case of oral literature ... far more extremely than with written forms, the bare words can *not* be left to speak for themselves" (15). Within this context, the *griot* at the same time becomes both the storyteller and the interpreter of the story that he tells to the contemporary audience. Unlike a presentation in which the performance itself holds greater significance that the message that it communicates, within the setting that we are describing here, the message and its interpretation through the *griot* remains of prime importance. If we claim that Francophone African oral literature draws from the well of contemporary sociocultural and sociopolitical contexts, it should not be surprising that similar themes emerge throughout Francophone Africa such as heralding a particular nation's leader (Nelson Mandela). For that matter, if we have established well the fact that what takes place in terms of the organic composition of oral literature within French-speaking Africa also occurs throughout the entire continent, then it should not surprise us that other nations throughout Africa focus on similar (socio-) political themes such as the arrival of independence and (inter)national heroes.

The Language of the Oppressed: Using Jacques Derrida's Critical Texts to Understand Language

Using Derrida's text *Le monolingualisme de l'autre ou la prothèse d'origine* (1996) as a theoretical framework, this section serves to explore several concepts related to the notion of writing in the language of another culture. Information for use here is drawn from a session of the November 1997 annual conference of the American Council for the Teaching of Foreign Languages (ACTFL) during which three Francophone writers, Ahmadou Kourouma[7] (Côte d'Ivoire), Suzanne Dracius[8] (Martinique), and Barry Jean Ancelet[9] (Louisiana), openly discussed their respective experiences with regard to expressing themselves in a colonial language.[10] The individual perspectives indicated during the course of this conference session were particularly important because they reflected the cultural identity of three different parts of the Francophone world at the close of the first modern millennium. Our exploration of writing in the "language of the other" brings to the forefront Robert Phillipson's theory that he called "linguistic imperialism," a label used to explain the hegemonic domination of one culture over another through language (15). Phillipson had originally brought this concept to light in his 1992 book entitled *Linguistic Imperialism* and it is a concept that resurfaced in his 2010 redux entitled *Linguistic Imperialism Continued*. Although his work focuses primarily on the hegemonizing role played by English as a so-called "world language," we could reasonably argue that the effects of the French language as part of this notion of "linguistic imperialism" are analogous to those of the English colonial system. The reader should understand this concept as the transfer of a dominate language to another group of people that often occurs through force. The dominate language is considered dominant because it originates from a civilization that holds economic and/or military power. It is through the imposition of the dominate language that other cultural elements are also imposed.[11] Scholars must be careful, however, not to assume that all minority groups seek either cultural or linguistic assimilation. In addition, as I have indicated elsewhere in this book, we should also neither assume that the diverse tribes of Africa simply gave up their languages without a fight nor that these diverse groups no longer fight to preserve their traditional languages in the present day.[12]

Jacques Derrida (1930–2004) was a philosopher born in French Algeria. A major figure of Post-structuralism and Postmodern philosophy, Derrida is best known as the founding father of a form of semiotic analysis called "Deconstruction." Deconstruction is an attempt "to expose and undermine the binary oppositions, hierarchies, and paradoxes on which particular texts, philosophical and otherwise, are founded" (*Reader's Guide* 164–71). Derrida saw deconstruction as a challenge to unquestioned assumptions of the Western philosophical tradition. Thus, if structuralism serves "to 'construct' the system of logical relationships governing the disposition of individual elements in a text, deconstruction is, among other things, a critique of structuralism" (*Columbia Dictionary* 73). Derrida approached all texts as created around binary opposites that all speech must articulate if it intends to make itself understood. This approach to text, in a broad sense, emerges from semiology advanced by Ferdinand de Saussure whom literary scholars and applied linguists consider one of the fathers of structuralism. Ferdinand de Saussure posited that terms obtain their meaning in reciprocal determination with other terms inside language. Derrida also considered himself to be a historian.[13] His work has a striking interdisciplinary quality that is well noted by Raman Selden, Peter Widdowson, and Peter Booker:

> From the outset one of the difficulties of Derrida's work has been the way it has moved across philosophy, linguistics, psychoanalysis, literature, art, architecture and ethics, and thus evaded traditional discipline and subject boundaries. Not only does Derrida seem not to belong definitively to any one of these areas, his work persistently questions the assumptions and protocols on which they, or

their canonic representatives, depend. This is why, though it is common to term his work "poststructuralist" (and this does usefully signal an association with a broader intellectual trend), it is more accurate to describe it as "deconstruction," since the rigorous questioning of assumed binary divisions and supposed unities which characterizes this modus operandi describes the very relation Derrida has to those disciplines. As Derrida typically writes, "the task of deconstruction is to discover ... the 'other' of philosophy." The result is a questioning, now common practice in radical sections of the Humanities, of notions of identity, origin, intention, and the production of meaning [*Reader's Guide* 169].

It is for this reason that using Derrida's working to conduct cultural history is relevant within the present study. Derrida questioned assumptions of the Western philosophical tradition and also more broadly Western culture. By questioning the dominant discourses, and trying to modify them, he attempted to democratize the university scene and to politicize it. Particularly in his later writings, he frequently addressed ethical and political themes present in his work. These writings influenced various activists and political movements. Although his approach to philosophy and the notorious difficulty of his work made him controversial, Derrida became a well-known and influential public figure. As Gary Gutting states in *Thinking the Impossible: French Philosophy Since 1960*, "Derrida's central point ... is that there is no possibility of an expression of knowledge that is purified of the contingent and varying features of the signs needed to formulate it" (56–7).[14] Derrida's deconstructionist framework challenged the notion of "truth" as we perceive it. This aspect is particularly important within the study of writing itself. According to Derrida, "writing is a field of limitless play" (*Columbia Dictionary* 74). The notion of "text" itself becomes highly problematic. Poststructuralists would agree that narrative can never escape the discursive level. As has been demonstrated by Gérard Genette in his "Frontiers of Narrative" and by many others, the *histoire/discours* distinction is not logical. For Genette, in particular, there can never be a pure narrative that is devoid of "subjective" effect.

At the very core of research and debate on the use of a foreign language to express oneself, my goal here is to inquire specifically about how Derrida's life and work might be used to explain the use of the French language to express the lives and experiences of the diverse peoples of French-speaking Africa. Encouraged by Derrida's musings in *Le monolingualisme de l'autre ou la prothèse d'origine* of his particular life experience growing up in Algeria where he used French and Arabic in daily life and by his intent to explore the labyrinth of language, I wonder how taking on the language of the colonizer can serve the goals of colonized peoples who ultimately seek to develop their own forms of nationalism and self-identity. Derrida wrote, "Je n'ai qu'une langue et ce n'est pas la mienne, ma langue 'propre' m'est une langue inassimilable. Ma langue, la seule que je m'entende parler et m'entende à parler, c'est la langue de l'autre"/"I have only one language and it is not mine. My 'own' language is an inassimilable one. My language, the only one that I hear myself speak and hears me speak is the language of another" (*Monolingualisme* 13). Like Derrida, I also wonder if any attempt to go back to a "prior-to-the-first language" state in which postcolonial Francophone Africa returns to pre-colonial languages would work and if such an attempt is, in reality, possible. Finally, since the question of preserving indigenous languages now also occurs in the context of a rapidly-integrating France, what can we learn from reading *The Other Heading* (1992), one of Derrida's reflections of the phenomenon of Europe?[15] Is it possible to understand both the fate of the French language *and* the indigenous languages of Francophone Africa in terms of cultural fragmentation and centralization? Our understanding of the continued relationship between French and traditional indigenous languages throughout the former French colonies in Africa requires an understanding of the myriad roles of language itself.

Language exhibits both a unifying and a dividing property. Apart from an individual's physical appearance that might reveal specific characteristics related to national origin, language is a shared characteristic that can both immediately join or separate individuals. Language can also be a source of national pride. One needs only to think of certain island nations such as Japan or Iceland to call to mind geographic locations in which primarily one language is spoken there and, in the particular case of Iceland, for example, it is reasonable to assume that if one encounters a speaker of Icelandic, said speaker more than likely originated from Iceland. The loss of a language under the pressure and the violence of colonization produces alienation within one's own homeland, but also, it turns out, also produces alienation in the attempted restoration of the nearly extinct national language.[16] Researchers perceive the effects of linguistic alienation in countries such as Ireland and even in France in the current restoration of the Breton language. If those seeking to restore a national language couch their efforts in the appearance of the healing of an "illness," their efforts are more likely to engender negative effects rather than positive ones. As Derrida reminds us in *Le monolingualisme de l'autre*, together these alienations must direct us instead to the "abiding alienation that, like 'lack,' appears to be constitutive" (47). Derrida's words suggest that Africans themselves must be at the center of the restoration of indigenous languages. In addition, he hints at the notion of a "prior-to-first language" consciousness that is entirely relevant within Africa, "The Cradle of Mankind."

The concept of a "prior-to-first language" is of specific interest to the study of poetic literature within Francophone Africa. A "prior-to-first lan-

2. Oral Societies and Writing 77

guage" is inherently culturally pure because it contains the essence of the culture in question. But, how can a language be pure, and a "prior-to-first language," for that matter? Derrida writes:

> Inventée pour la généalogie de ce qui n'est pas arrivé et dont l'événement aura été absent, ne laissant que des traces négatives de lui-même dans ce qui fait l'histoire, telle avant-première langue n'existe pas. Ce n'est même pas une préface, "un foreword," une langue d'origine perdue. Elle ne peut être qu'une langue d'arrivée ou plutôt d'avenir, une phrase promise, une langue de l'autre, encore, mais tout autre que la langue de l'autre comme langue de maître ou du colon, encore que les deux puissent parfois annoncer entre elles, les entretenant en secret ou les gardant en réserve.... [*Le monolingualisme de l'autre* 118–119].
>
> Invented for the genealogy of what did not happen and whose event will have been absent, leaving only negative traces of itself in what makes history, such a prior to the first language does not exist. It is not even a preface, a "foreword," or some lost language of origin. It can only be a target language or, rather, a future language, a promised sentence, a language of the other, once again, but entirely other than the language of the master or colonist, even though, between them, the two may sometimes show so many unsettling resemblances maintained in secret or held in reserve.

The notion of a "prior-to-first language" suggests that during colonization, the peoples of Francophone Africa were estranged from their own languages. With the arrival of independence and the neocolonial system in the 1960s, a return to the former linguistic systems based on traditional indigenous languages remained fundamentally impossible. It was a desire, as Derrida writes, to invent

> une *première langue* qui serait plutôt une *avant-première langue* destine à traduire cette mémoire. Mais à traduire la mémoire de ce qui précisément n'a pas eu lieu, de ce qui, ayant été (l')interdit, a dû néanmoins laisser une trace, un spectre, le corps fantomatique, le membre-fantôme—sensible, douloureux, mais à peine lisible—de traces, de marques, de cicatrices [*Le monolingualisme de l'autre* 118].
>
> a *first language* that would be, rather, a *prior-to-the-first language* that would translate that memory. But to translate the memory of what, precisely, did not take place, of what having been forbidden, must nonetheless leave a trace, a specter, the haunting body, the ghost-member—sensitive, painful, but hardly readable—of traces, marks, and scars.

The "prior-to-first language" is always in danger of being "encore une langue du maître, parfois celle de nouveaux maîtres"/"again the master's language, sometimes that of new masters" (119), and this was a process framed and enforced by French administrators. The neocolonial system, with its continuation of "French" administrative and educative systems, assured this fate. The mistake, as Derrida indicated, is that:

> Car contrairement à ce qu'on est le plus souvent tenté de croire, le maître n'est rien. Et il n'a rien en propre. Parce que le maître ne possède pas en propre,

naturellement (italics in original text), ce qu'il appelle pourtant sa langue; parce que, quoi qu'il veuille ou fasse, il ne peut entretenir avec elle des rapports de propriété ou d'identité naturels, nationaux, congénitaux, ontologiques; parce qu'il ne peut accréditer et dire cette appropriation qu'au cours d'un procès non naturel de constructions politico-phantasmatiques; parce que la langue n'est pas son bien naturel, par cela même il peut historiquement, à travers le viol d'une usurpation culturelle, c'est-à-dire toujours d'essence coloniale, feindre de se l'approprier pour l'imposer comme "la sienne. " C'est là sa croyance, il veut la faire partager par la force ou par la ruse, il veut y faire croire, comme au miracle, par la rhétorique, l'école ou l'armée [*Le monolinguisme de l'autre* 45].

For contrary to what one is often most tempted to believe, the master is nothing. And he does not have exclusive possession of anything. Because the master does not possess exclusively, and *naturally*, what he calls his language, because, whatever he wants or does, he cannot maintain any relations of property or identity that are natural, national, congenital or ontological; Because he can only accreditate and tell this appropriation in the course of a non-natural process of political-phantasmic constructions. Because the language is not his natural possession, by that even he can historically, though the rape of cultural usurpation, that is to say the colonial essence, pretend to appropriate it in order to impose it as "his own." That is his belief; he wishes to make others share it through the use of force or cunning; he wants to make others believe it as they do a miracle, through rhetoric, the school, or the army.

Though transformational, the "rape" that Derrida describes here remains metaphorical. Nonetheless, according to Derrida, returning to a "prior-to-first language" stage is a two-step process. Firstly, the African citizen must recognize that the former colonizer actually holds no power over him. Secondly, he must seek this freedom through true independence. Derrida assures his reader that there is never any such thing as total appropriation or reappropriation of the language (and its culture), for language itself holds no natural properties (*Le monolinguisme de l'autre* 121). There is really no such thing as the ownership of a language. For all intents and purposes, we are more "sharers" or a language than we are "owners," for our languages form a sort of "community property" the governance of which is determined, in part, by those who share the language. To place Derrida's perspective in culturally relevant terms, it is the simultaneous fear that French culture will spread "in a dust of provinces, a multiplicity of enclaved idioms or jealous, untranslatable little nationalisms" (*The Other Heading* 41) and impose its authority as a cultural capital that will be commodified and traded by the peoples of French-speaking Africa.

Within the context of Francophone literature on the whole, our point of understanding begins with the particular form of colonial alienation described by Martinican writer, poet and literary critic Édouard Glissant in *Poétique de la relation* as the "non-mastery of an appropriated language" (132), which offers an excellent complement to Derrida's perspective. Within the

French colonial context, specifically, Glissant refers to a type of *diglossia* in which the citizens of a particular group either uses two distinct languages separately or in which speakers "code shift" between two different languages. Both forms are relevant within the context of this study. Glissant states, "Les rapports de langues ainsi constitués peuvent être de différents types: rapports 'de domination, de fascination, de multiplicité ou de contagion, de complaisance ou de dérision, de tangence, de subversion ou d'intolérance'"/"The relationships of language thus made can be of differing types: relationships 'of domination, of fascination, of multiplicity or of contagion, of indulgence or derision, of tangency, or subversion, or of intolerance'" (*Poétique de la relation* 118). There is no question that within Francophone Africa, Glissant's notion of diglossia clearly applies, in particular, when it pertains to matters of domination (linguistic or otherwise). As Glissant writes in *Le Discours antillais*, "Nous sommes collectivement parlés par nos mots bien plus que nous ne les pratiquons, que ces mots soient français ou créoles, et que chacun pour soi les manie à la perfection ou non..."/"We are collectively spoken by our words even more so than we practice them, whether or not these words be French or Créole, and each one for himself wields them to perfection or not..." (403). More specifically then, the diglossic relationship can be characterized as incongruence between the French terms "langue" and "langage" with the understanding that "langage" indicates "l'attitude collective vis-à-vis de la langue utilisée"/"the collective attitude regarding the language employed" (*Discours* 403). Diglossia is certainly not limited to the French colonial situation. In French colonial Africa, the reader might substitute Glissant's term "créole" with any of the indigenous languages spoken in the region. For Glissant, diglossia refers specifically to "la domination d'une langue sur une autre ou plusieurs autres, dans une même région"/"the domination of one language over another or several languages within the same region" (*Poétique* 132). What remains of particular interest and importance is that this diglossic environment fosters language hierarchies, language transference/interference, and risks pushing certain languages toward a path of extinction. Glissant continues,

> Il est vrai, tout de même qu'on se trouve malade de l'histoire qu'on ne fait pas, qu'on peut l'être d'une langue; en souffrir le manque, alors même qu'on la pratique et que l'on croit la fréquenter sans problème. Il me semble que c'est la situation de toute langue de compromis. (...) Il est patent que la langue de compromis est là pour remplacer dans une situation donnée deux langues impraticables quotidiennement. (...) Le patois ne pose pas problème à celui qui l'emploie dans un usage quotidien concurrent de l'usage de la langue véhiculaire. Mais une langue de compromis qui "patoise" manifeste de manière implicite la situation dangereuse (la menace d'imperceptibilité) de ses locuteurs [*Discours* 618, 619].
> It is true, nevertheless, that one becomes sick of the story that one does not

make, one can be it with a language, suffering a lack of it, even when we practice it and that we believe to use it without any problem. It seems to me that this is the situation any language of compromise. (...) It is clear that the language of compromise is there to replace in a given context two languages that are impractical on a daily basis. (...) The patois is not a problem to he who employs it in everyday use as a rival to the usage of the lingua franca. But a language of compromise that "patois" implicitly expresses the precarious situation (the threat of imperceptibility) of its speakers.

The diglossic environment can also promote what Glissant labels the "délire verbal coutumier"/"customary verbal delirium" that perpetuates itself in all forms of communication including poetry and theatre (*Discours* 651). It is important to note that "customary verbal delirium" creates a feeling of alienation for the speaker of the language of compromise who now judges the "foreign" language to be superior primarily because "les élites intellectuelles des pays en développement à l'usage révérencieux d'une langue de prestige dont on ne se servit que pour s'appauvrir"/"intellectual elites of developing countries have reverent use of a language of prestige that one only used to impoverish" (*Poétique* 119). Such language conflict can result in a measurable crisis of language conscience in the individual language speaker.

Glissant goes on to describe a condition that he calls "language torment" that emerges from having endured a particularly difficult linguistic situation. He defines this "condition" as a cultural and a historical one that is shared by all those individuals whose cultures are based on unequal language relationships. Glissant writes,

> Il y a une poétique forcée là où une nécessité d'expression confronte un impossible à exprimer. Il peut arriver que cette confrontation se noue dans une opposition entre le contenu exprimable et la langue suggérée ou imposée. C'est le cas dans les petites Antilles francophones où la langue maternelle, le créole, et la langue officielle, le français, entretiennent chez l'Antillais un même insoupçonné tourment [*Discours* 402].
>
> There is a forced poetic there in which necessity of expression confronts an impossibility to express it. It may happen that this confrontation is tied in an opposition between expressible content and the suggested or imposed language. This is the case in the lesser French Antilles where the native language, Creole, and the official language, French, hold in the Antillean the same unsuspected torment.

Derrida suggests that "Et même d'une terreur dans les langues (il y a, douce, discrète ou criante, une terreur dans les langues, c'est notre sujet)"/"And even a terror in languages (there is, soft, discreet or resounding, a terror in languages, that is our subject" (*Le monolingualisme de l'autre* 45), a perspective that certainly aligns well with the language perspective that Glissant expressed. The "tourment de langage" is a constant, even if it is not formally recognized by those whom it afflicts. Nonetheless, the indigenous language still contains some of its linguistic roots that are difficult for the colonizer to completely pull out. As both Derrida and Glissant articulate well, for those Africans who have a first language distinct from the language of their colonial masters, to be colonized means to live in a situation controlled almost exclusively through a language that will never entirely belong to them, and in which the acquisition of mastery in the language will always be scrutinized by the colonizer.[17] Language *is* power.

In expanding on the idea that the colonizer will always scrutinize the African individual's mastery of the French language which the former will always judge to be inferior, I cite a happening that occurred in 2010 during the "'France Noire/Black France' Film Festival" in Paris at the Forum des Images.[18] In the course of introducing his documentary film entitled *Rouch in Reverse* (1995), Manthia Diawara, a Malian writer, filmmaker, cultural theorist, and professor at New York University, recounted the experience that he had had with the French film board when he was attempting to seek the latter's "approval" of his film. *Rouch in Reverse* opens with an English-language narrator who continues to speak in English throughout the film. On hearing the English language spoken in the cinema hall, several spectators immediately left the screening. After the fifty-two minute film ended, Diawara presented himself in front of the audience to explain why the narrator had spoken in English. "Il est dommage que certaines personnes aient décidé de partir,"/It is a shame that some people decided to leave," he said. Diawara then recounted an anecdote describing the film board's outright refusal to allow the film to "pass muster" unless he removed his own French-language narrative voiceover, replacing it with a French speaker whose speech did not include traces of any "foreign" accent. Diawara explained the cultural and linguistic crisis in which he had instantly and surprisingly found himself: "Je suis malien. Je suis français. Je suis américain"/"I am Malian. I am French. I am American." Diawara holds three cultural identities at the same time: The first cultural identity is a result of his birthplace in Bamako, Mali; the second cultural identity comes from the fact that he was only seven years old when Mali gained its independence; the third cultural identity is a result of the decades that he has spent in the United States as a student and a professor.[19] As Diawara revealed to the spectators who remained in the cinema hall that day, he would have rather changed languages and used his own voice than to yield in front of the film board to a voice in French that was not his own. Both linguistic identity and cultural identity are significant components of the African experience.

As previously stated, language is a "shared" cultural experience. In "Treatise on the Origin of Language," Johann Gottfried Herder called language 'the conservation reserve and the depot for experience and knowledge of past generations, like the means of transmission of this same knowledge to future generations, which will thus receive all past experiences" (67). His viewpoint reflects the notion that the spirit of a people is closely associated with the language that a people speaks. It is confirmed by the bi-directional notion that language defines the way people speech as much as people define the ways in which language develops. Thus, language "constitutes" the people, since it forms both the building blocks of their civilization and a collective way of thinking. A living language is an heirloom that is passed from generation to generation. Whether in spoken or in written form, language represents bi-directional communication. It has meaning and nuance. Language can be manipulated for any endgame. Therefore, language itself plays an essential role in the development of this form of knowledge comprising the interpretation of common meanings, elaborated and shared by members of a common social or cultural group. As Fabienne Leconte writes, "Les individus construisent leur identité à travers et par les systèmes linguistiques dans lesquels ils sont socialisés. C'est la langue qui attache les individus à un groupe enthno-culturel traditionnel..."/"Individuals construct their identity through and by the linguistic systems in which they are socialized. It is language that binds individuals to a traditional ethno-cultural group..." (164).

The study of language can be ethnographic or sociolinguistic. As George Bernard Shaw suggested in his play *Pygmalion* (1912), the ways in which individuals use their language—accent, diction, lexical choices, etc.—indicate their position on the socioeconomic ladder. Africa is a linguistic cornucopia containing seven of the sixteen linguistic families registered by ethnologists as studied by Jacques Leclerc. The diversity of languages in Africa cannot be sufficiently appreciated so long as efforts at studying African linguistic heritage rest on the latter's phonetic consistency more so than its ideological, political, and spatial consistency and worldview. Moreover, African languages have a long history marked by three factors: orality, colonization and the slave trade, and writing.[20] Orality has constituted the principal character of the development and vitality of African languages for millennia. Language was the first means of communication and spreading of culture in Africa. This is seen in the considerable social role of *griots* who functioned as tribal cantors. Language was also a function of connection. According to Philippe Blanchet:

> une langue n'est pas qu'un outil de communication, elle est également une façon d'être au monde. Toute langue a deux fonctions essentielles, une fonction communicative qui contribue à relier les personnes et les communautés entre elles, une fonction existentielle qui contribue à les différencier [123].
>
> a language is not only a communication tool; it is also a way of being in the

world. Each language has two essential functions: a communicative function that contributes to linking people and communities and an existential function that contributes to differentiating them.

Language is a paradox itself. Thanks to the diverse views that they offer of the world, languages are a source not only of humanity's richness, but also, as is the case for African languages, in particular, of cultural history. The authenticity of both oral civilization and the quality of African lives finds its roots in languages. As we will see in depth in the next chapter, the *griot/griotte* incarnates the spirit of oral cultural communication. S/he is a transmitter of traditions and history, a veritable intellectual library and keeper of the most intimate secrets, and as such is the object of deep respect within his community because, as Cheikh Hamidou Kane says, "orality is the symbol of life."[21]

3

Francophone African Poetry in the Modern World

> "To have any sense of evolving African poetics, one must be aware of the sociopolitical significance of literary expression and the ideological character of literary theory."—*Thomas Knipp* (117)

This chapter conducts both an examination of the macroculture of poetry on the continent of Africa as well as an examination of the microculture of poetry originating from Francophone Africa. One of the main points that I underscore repeatedly throughout the course of this book is the interconnectedness of the continent of Africa. Not wishing to disregard the unique characteristics of each nation, however, I must cite examples of social, cultural, and political interconnectivity. Bringing to mind two of the leading figures of post-independence Africa, Léopold Sédar Senghor (Senegal) and Nelson Mandela (South Africa), it would be a mistake to claim that neither of these two national leaders impacted nations outside of their own. With the death of Nelson Mandela on December 5, 2013, in particular, some scholars and journalists have labeled the former President of South Africa as the "Most Influential Person of the 20th Century." Although engaging in dialogue on such matters extends beyond the scope of the present study, the impact of both Senghor and Mandela is most assuredly reflected in the cultural and poetic products of their respective eras. Let us consider as evidence two poems referring to the leaders' impact ("Poem for Senghor" by M'Bana Diop and "Poem for Mandela" by Zolani Mkiva). M'Bana Diop's "Poem for Senghor" presents a recounting of the Senegalese leader's contribution to his nation and to the world community[1]:

> You appealed to the people to have patience and to pray.
> The course of destiny cannot be stopped
> …Each region received its fair share.
> You brought back peace and harmony.

> Oh! Leopold, oh! Independence is pleasant!
> You are not a man of war.
> Not a shot fired, not a sword drawn.²

"Poem for Mandela":

> The umbilical cord has snapped!...
> The anchors of hatred and oppression have snapped...
> That is then, Mandela,
> The nations of the world reacted and applauded vociferously.
> ...
> That is Mandela
> The rest of the world cried with us
> Nations wept...
> And the struggle continues...³

A reading of each of the two poems evidences two important details. Firstly, it shows that the content of these particular poems cannot be separated from the sociocultural and historic events that led to their compositions. Secondly, it shows the role that the international community played in the independence of both Senegal and South Africa. In both poems, it is obvious that the two national leaders are also "world" leaders. The hordes of international spectators who attended the funerals of both Senghor—in 2001—and Mandela—in 2013—validate their individual contributions to the international community. Diop's poem was performed at the annual convention of the *Union Progressive Sénégalaise* (Senegalese Progressive Union), which was Senghor's political party. Mkiva's poem was performed in 1950 during Mandela's inauguration as the first president of the *African National Congress* (ANC).⁴

These poems are thus part and parcel of the overall sociocultural and sociopolitical systems of their respective ages reflecting, in part, the continued vital role that the *griot* plays in African society.⁵ In Senegal, since 1980, in particular, the *griot*, as seen in Mkiva's poem, has become increasingly more visible on the world political scene, appearing regularly on behalf of the government. There is no attempt to hide this reality from view. The most significant example is that of El Hadj Mansour Mbaye, current *Président des communicateurs traditionnels du Sénégal* (President of traditional communicators of Senegal). As Cornelia Panzacchi wrote in "The Livelihoods of Traditional Griots in Modern Senegal,"

> The prototype of the "new griot" in politics is El Hadj Mansour Mbaye, known as "le griot de la Présidence." Lacking higher education, and a poor speaker of French, he has nonetheless become a journalist ... and a high-ranking political counsellor. El Hadj Mansour [Mbaye] is the most famous, but not the only griot who has made his way in the political scene [197].

During the presidency of Abdou Diouf, President of Senegal from 1981 to 2000, Mbaye performed for him as well. The function of *griots* in the current era as socio-political storytellers remains arguably unchanged. It is evident that those individuals who hold power, the *griot*s who serve as commenters on current events, and the general populous who continue to work to make democracy a continued possibility throughout parts of Africa, will continue to guide and shape the tradition of oral poetry. Let us now explore this particular poetic tradition.

African Poetry: A Continental History

Modern African poetry, like any other poetry created throughout the world, has served to express various emotions and themes ranging from love, death of a loved one, hope and faith, to the praise of nature. However, cultural and political themes have tended to dominate. Modern African poetry thus has been used to express the concerns of the peoples of Africa regarding the "playing out" of politics in the African world in both the 20th century and in the New Millennium. Politics in contemporary Africa maintains deep roots into the colonial period that was assured by the redistribution of Africa by Europeans in the Council of Berlin of 1884–1885. The current neocolonial age maintains a colonial institutional (administrative and educative) presence throughout the independent African nation-states. Colonial cultural politics transformed the largely independent African ethnic groups and brought the latter together into large units irrespective of cultural, linguistic, or religious histories. Although the ushering in of a "new democracy" in the form of modern political systems of governance came about from the onset of independence in 1960, colonial power was turned over in short shrift to the new African political elite. The latter group often perpetuated the colonial structures with which they were already very familiar. Though seemingly independent African nation-states emerged across the continent, what many saw also emerge were political thugs, tribal genocide, corruption, civil wars, coups, and political assassinations throughout Africa that continue to propagate today. As Claude Wauthier explains:

> The year of African independence was 1960 marking the end of European tutelage in seventeen colonial territories. Some fifteen years later, the number of coups d'état, mostly military, occurring in Africa was in the region of thirty, not counting the plots that were uncovered. The two richest and most populous countries in black Africa, Congo-Kinshasa (later Zaïre) and Nigeria were torn by appalling civil wars triggered off by attempts at secession on the part of Katanga and Biafra respectively. In Ethiopia, the overthrow of the oldest monarchy in the

world has not resolved the problem of Eritrea, where the guerrilla forces have continued their struggle to free their country from the tutelage of Addis Ababa. Three presidents, Jean Bedel Bokassa of the Central African Empire, Marcias N'guema of Equatorial Guinea and Idi Amin Dada of Uganda, have filled the columns of the international press with stories of bloodshed and buffoonery [289].

The modern African poet thus emerged from the backdrop of his or her sociocultural setting. Misery and the bitterness were the result of the betrayal of their hopes and dreams. In view of this situation, the contemporary African poet is, by definition, *engagé* ("socially or politically committed"). Their energies have been dedicated to the depiction of the prominent problems within their society. Therefore, contemporary African poetry has largely been the poetry of commitment: commitment to the political configuration of the African world with a view to bringing about desired change. In other words, cultural politics is the substance while poetry is the form *par excellence* of its portrayal.

There remains much to be understood and related with regard to the history of poetry on the continent of Africa. If we are looking for a "red letter date" in the history of the study of African poetry, we might place it between 1962 and 1963 during the time that modern African literature (including poetry) gained traction as a subject of academic enquiry set in motion by the conferences that took place at Makerere, Dakar and Freetown. Edited by Gerald Moore, the published proceedings of the conferences entitled *African Literature and the Universities* (1965) poured the foundation for the study of African literature from the colonial period. The main goals of both the papers that were presented there and the literature that was composed were to examine the question of African literary identity and the challenges associated with bringing this writing to the surface. Although no academic conference could fully map the African literary tradition, it was a solid beginning. While there are certainly many commonalities that tie the diverse peoples of Africa together, how to conduct an evaluation of these diverse cultures was inherently problematic. In order to truly begin to evaluate African literature, scholars needed to better understanding how they perceived the literature in question. Were 20th century forms of literary evaluation relevant in the study of African literatures? The conflicting critical standpoints with regard to the possibilities of understanding African literatures represent critical positions that have attracted numerous scholars and reflect changing perspectives on African literature. In "Emerging Definitions of African Literature," Sandra Barkan states that "changes in definitions of African literature reflect and respond to political and social realities, trends in literary criticism, and changes within the texts themselves" (27). As literary scholars, our natural inclination is to apply the same tools that we use to evaluate European literary forms to the study of African literatures. Thus, we define our critical principles in relation to European literary traditions that obviously have different sociocultural origins and histories. Although proposing new tools of evaluation remain difficult, at minimum we must admit that the glasses through which many scholars view the production and distribution of African literatures are myopic.

Consequently, we remain critical of looking at African literature from a European perspective. Nonetheless, bringing a European point of view to the exploration of African literature is exactly what many of the early African literary scholars did. Pioneering critics of African poetry, however, created anthologies such as *Modern Poetry from Africa* co-edited by Gerald Moore and Ulli Beier (1963) and *A Book of African Verse* by John Reed and Clive Wake (1969) that function in a mindset that is brazen in claiming African identity for literary works that did not fully show diverse African experiences. Whereas most of these anthologies form nothing but a catalog of the poetic compositions springing from sub–Saharan Africa, the claim that these texts represent a unique and authentic perspective on African identity are wide sweeping. Romanus Egudu's *Modern African Poetry and the African Predicament* (1978) and Ken Goodwin's *Understanding African Poetry* (1982) provide a widely-distorted picture of African poetry. Goodwin is the type of scholar who tries to create an encyclopedic understanding of African writing by suggesting a theory that explains the transformation of African poetry over time. Rather than arguing for an organic genesis of Africa poetry, Goodwin states that most modern African poets simply imitated European models so that the poetry of the former is largely an interpretation of the latter. Although we certainly must acknowledge that African poets did receive inspiration from Europe and beyond, to discount their work to a simple "cutting and pasting" of a European template overwhelmingly undervalues the contribution of African poetry both at home and abroad.

Despite the early preponderance of anthologies and articles suggesting a European foundation for the production of African poetry, there remain excellent examples of works that cite the various parts of Africa herself as the originators of African literary traditions. Tanure Ojaide's *Poetic Imagination in Black Africa* (1996) is the first text to accurately trace a course for African poetic history by underscoring the uniqueness of the African poetic space. Central to Ojaide's argument, he states that,

> ...the assumption that the Black poetic imagination must be differentiated from the Western tradition of poetry so long as the artistic philosophy of African writers is rooted in traditional African poetic traditions: the artistic principles and

practices shared by various Black African societies which also provide the common base for modern African poets and poets of African descent [cited in Okunoye 771].

Although I resist the temptation to put his work in a box, his book is the first real attempt to create a theory for African poetry by looking at both form and function as having the same point of origin. According to Ojaide,

> Modern African poetic aesthetics are unique in possessing a repertory of authentic African features. This authenticity manifests itself in the use of concrete images derived from the fauna and flora, proverbs, indigenous rhythms, verbal tropes, and concepts of space and time to establish a poetic form. Besides (and unlike in the West), content is more important than form and images do not aim to reflect the senses. Content is not perceived by poet and audience as extraliterary. The mere fact that foreign languages are used could occasionally create discord in discourse but modern African poetry attempts to reflect indigenous rhythms. In fact, an authentic African world forms the backdrop of modern African poetry [30].

Ojaide's perspective focuses on the notion of an organic form of black aesthetics that emerged from the shared cultural and artistic principles of sub–Saharan Africa and spread throughout the world by means of the Diaspora through the Négritude movement. His work constructs a black literary tradition based on its own cultural and historic cornerstones. If the earliest approaches to the study of African poetry from the 1960s tended to construct an African poetic tradition centered on both uniformity and "buying into" a European model, the paradigm that Ojaide proposes highlights the significant role that regional cultural traditions have played in the development of modern poetic production throughout the continent of Africa. African writing thus emerges from these unique, yet shared, natural foundations that takes into account in its appraisal the particular cultural and historical developments occurring in the various regions. Ojaide's framework makes it possible to recognize shared beliefs and techniques of poetic composition. Thus, the fact that different regions of the continent experienced varied forms of colonialism—British, French, etc.—remains significant, for it draws together the four corners of Africa to such an extent that the apartheid era of South Africa is no longer "foreign" to other parts of the continent. Though I will certainly acknowledge that regional discourse dominates poetic creation within Africa, it goes without saying that there is a continental discourse that has emerged since independence that truly merits closer investigation. This said, we must continue to be careful to not marginalize African poets by pigeonholing their work as speaking only at the microcultural level.

In *West African Poetry* (1986), Robert Fraser questions Goodwin's notions that the latter illustrated in *Understanding African Poetry*. In response to Goodwin's assumptions, Fraser seeks to underscore the debt that modern West African poets owe to their indigenous poetic traditions. Though his work represents a noteworthy attempt at defining the character of a regional poetic tradition, it still suffers from the same weakness identified with all such studies in that it tries to define each region as a homogeneous cultural formation thereby ignoring said region's ethic and cultural diversities. Dorothy Blair's *African Literature in French* (1976) had already shed light on the danger of rendering a particular region homogeneous. The case for regional poetic traditions in Africa is always problematic. Any examination of recent anthologies of African poetry, notable among which include Tanure Ojaide and Tijan Sallah's *The New African Poetry* (1999) will confirm the fact that classifying the microcultural as a homogeneous group is a game of "splitting hairs" that the scholar cannot win. Researchers such as Abiola Irele acknowledge the fact that "there has been a movement in African literary studies towards the recognition of national literature in the new African states" (52). Ojaide explains this idea further:

> Unlike in the 1960s when the poets were culturally obsessed, nature-oriented and "universal," today, old and young poets are addressing their national issues more aggressively than before [...]. In their desire to effect changes, they use the nation state as their starting point. The poets are very particularized in their treatment of problems peculiar to their countries. Thus poets from The Gambia, Sierra-Leone, Ghana, Nigeria, Kenya, Malawi, Zimbabwe, and South Africa are creating national literatures, making it more plausible now to talk about an individual nation's poetry as was not the case before the mid-1970s [80–81].

It is for this very reason that the present study does not wish to enter the game of suggesting the idea that it promotes or even understands the notion of a "national literature." As Aijaz Ahmad has stated well, "(a) 'national' literature [...] has to be more than the sum of its regional constituent parts, if we are to speak of its unity theoretically" (244). It is thus difficult to consider the "nation" as a dependable category for the scholarly exploration of African poetry largely because these nations were formed from the external influence of colonialism itself thereby fundamentally denying the diverse cultural and ethnic composition of its citizens. In short, "the international boundaries that have come to be seen as defining national identities are, at best, convenient instruments of former colonial establishments to assign spheres of neocolonial influence and manipulation in Africa" (Okunoye 776). Hence, any attempt to construct a Senegalese—or Congolese, Malian, etc.—identity that emerges purely from the poetic creations of these nations is inherently flawed.

In order to avoid any sort of entanglements that might result from attempting to portray African poetry in a way that neglects the diversity and lack of homogeneity to which we have already referred, many critics have chosen to limit their evaluations of African poetry to a study of form rather than of cultural content. As Fraser stated in the Introduction to his text *West African Poetry*, "the emphasis ... is unashamedly on form" (2). For the critic who conducts assessments of literary works primarily from a "literary" perspective, an examination of the poetic form expressed in African poetry initially appears to be the safest route to follow, for it allows the critic to forsake any cultural elements of which he or she might not be fully aware. It does not, however, free the critic from the fact that he or she might then use a European literary framework to evaluate African poetry. Although this technique is a bit like driving a nail with a screwdriver, there are, in fact, Eurocentric literary (critical) approaches that seem to lend themselves toward an application within the African context. Making a case for the Marxist critical framework within the context of Africa, Emmanuel Ngara states: "There is no necessary contradiction between Marxism and Afrocentrism in literary criticism. While Marxism originated in Europe historically, it is a truly revolutionary theory which is well suited to the task of liberating African literature and criticism from Eurocentrism" (7). He further claims that "a Marxist analysis of African literature cannot but emphasize the historical and social conditions which have given rise to African literature" (7). Though obviously Eurocentric, Marxist critics sometimes exaggerate the significance of critical framework and suggest that it is not indigenous to Africa. As Thomas Knipp states well, "literary theory (as a whole) is an import into or an imposition on traditional Africa-part of the legacy of colonialism" (116). Many African scholars practice Marxist criticism on African texts without fully evaluating its relevance as a tool of examination.

The literary analysis of African poetry should be rooted in the restoration of African values and traditions that were either discarded or marginalized during colonization. And if technology makes the world smaller, African literary scholarship in the New Millennium must discuss the problems of neocolonialism and globalization as they relate to Africa itself from within Africa herself. The scholarly enquiry to date has largely disregarded the development of critical methodologies that could be used in the evaluation of African literary production in order to assure that the uniqueness of the African culture experience is conveyed in the literature that is examined. In "African Cultural Standards for African Literature and the Arts," Joseph Okpaku wrote that "Critical standards derive from aesthetics. Aesthetics are culture dependent. Therefore critical standards must derive from culture" (53). It is for this reason that throughout the course of this book I have attempted to remain focused on the cultural components at play in the literary works under consideration here. We must constantly ask ourselves how the diverse peoples scattered throughout the continent of Africa will develop their own cultural identities if we continue to subject them to a Eurocentric critical framework. As Chidi Maduka has stated so well, "[an] uncritical assimilation of foreign theories is inimical to the African's justifiable quest for cultural identity" (186). Although we should not forget the role that colonization played in the development of African nation-states, constantly foregrounding our analyses of African literary works through elitist European frameworks is both questionable and invalid for it does not take into account the far more influential sociocultural entities in contemporary Africa. Such analyses deny the role that ethnic formations play as cultural units in the African context. In the context of literary criticism, overlooking the ethnic component has had the effect of sanitizing or creating a *blanchissement* ("whitening") of the literary history of individual countries.[6] At best, we refer to the oral tradition exemplified in the *griot/griotte*, but we then quickly turn him/her into a mystical figure thereby ignoring the important role that he or she plays in contemporary Africa. Identifying and expounding on ethnic traditions in African literature constitute a primary step towards creating a practical alternative to the dominant Eurocentric discourse in the explanation of the African literary experience. As Albert Gérard underscored in his book entitled *Four African Literatures*, "African literature ought to include within the compass of its definition the ethnic literatures of Africa" (31–2). Nonetheless, the most fully-informed perspective would also juxtapose African literary traditions against the backdrop of Postcoloniality so as to simultaneously acknowledge the effects of the colonial experience on modern African poetic expression and strengthen the development of critical means of evaluating this literature. One can never sever the relationship between colonialism and contemporary African writing. As Adebayo Williams articulated well in "Literature in the Time of Tyranny: African Writers and the Crisis of Governance,"

> If colonialism changed forever the course of Africa's political and economic history, it also profoundly altered its literary destiny. To date, colonialism represents the single most disruptive factor in Africa's history. It is to this epochal intervention that Africa owes the emergence of its contemporary nation-states. Modern African literature also owes its existence to the phenomenon of colonialism [351].

William's assessment unquestionably underscores the notion that the critical reception of modern African poetry must recognize the particular sociocultural experiences of the nations under investigation before it can ever hope to express both fully and accurately the literature produced in Africa. Until this objective is met, contemporary African poetry will continue to endure the marginalization that it has always known.

Francophone African Poetry: A Study of Exile

Marginalization and self-discovery are among the most common themes of both Francophone and Postcolonial literature. Francophone African poetry is no exception. The theme of exile in contemporary Francophone African poetry is central to the understanding of its people. Francophone African poets have played an important role in helping their respective citizens to understand this reality. In his article entitled "From the Local to the Global: A Critical Survey of Exile Experience in Recent Africa Poetry," Senayon Olaoluwa has argued that the exile experience has played an important role in recent Anglophone Africa poetry. Here, in my continued attempt to bring Francophone Africa back into the fold of the entire continent, I will suggest that the exile theme is not unique to poetry created within the former British colonies, but rather is part of the greater African *malaise* to "find a place in this world." In order to reconnect Francophone Africa with the rest of Africa, I will rely on both the overarching theme of African exile and several African poets *d'expression française* whose work depicts the exile experience.

The statement that "We are seeking to find our place in this world" echoes throughout poetry. The marginalization brought about through exile—whether physical or psychological—is apparent. Physical displacement is an inalienable part of human history. Our story is one of migration, emigration, immigration, and relocation. George Lamming's assertion underscores this claim: "The exile [is] ... a universal figure ... and to be in exile is to be alive" (24). Moreover, exile itself "must be viewed as a human condition which is defined by dispersal or drift usually against the wish of an individual or community" (Olaoluwa 223). Human beings will never escape their vulnerability to "body drift." Globalization has accentuated the importance of both international trade and international labor markets. Individuals must often move in order to find work. Famine, war, and disease create instability in our world's nations often causing families to leave their native lands in search of a better life elsewhere. This is the story of the United States. There is also the on-going political instability of our modern world. It thus becomes understandable why the writers of this planet would express the exile phenomenon, as it is embedded within our cultures. In the modern era, we refer to this displacement as the "diaspora." The diaspora to which I refer here has been echoed throughout the passage of time. The diaspora has the effect of creating an "Other." One of the earliest references to a diaspora in world literature is the Exodus from the Bible. The global nature of this Exodus that literally means "road out" signifies that an ever increasing number of individuals who have fallen victim to oppression in their native lands have been forced to find alternative places to reside. This trend affects the intellectual community as well. Thus, there is a recognizable pattern of intellectual diasporic activity emanating from the former colonies towards the West. It is for this reason, among others, that we find so many African intellectuals, including many Francophone African writers, residing in countries such as France and the United States where their intellectual curiosities have "wide open spaces" in which to roam. However, the vast majority of "wanderlusters" are not *littéraires*, but rather they are common people whose initial exhilaration surrounding the idea of relocation is often quickly undermined by the realities of displacement. For many individuals, exile is a psychological condition. As Edward Said explains in *Reflections on Exile and Other Essays*, the physical displacement ultimately produces the invention of nationalism as a coping mechanism for the sorrows of exile (176). The physical displacement engenders the creation of a critical means by which scholars might evaluate the psychological state of exile. Within the Francophone literary context, the emergence of a means to critically assess the diaspora has led to a sense of empowerment for some individuals who no longer perceive their condition as one of homelessness. This brings about an evaluation of the condition from a privileged perspective that does not clearly and accurately reflect the experience of the typical (common) individual. Not surprisingly, then, as Said continues to underscore, "achievements ... are permanently undermined by the loss of something left behind" (173).

From its genesis, modern French-speaking African poetry has found a way to write about the exile phenomenon. Early Francophone African poets were neither indifferent to the issue, nor were they separated from the world dialogue. From the beginnings of the colonization of Africa in the 19th century, writers and other artists on the "Dark Continent" used their talents to shed light on the issue of displacement. According to Chinua Achebe, however, taking into account the peripheral placement of Africa in relation to the West, the African exile's situation is contrastively different with the claim about the possibility of dual, and perhaps, multiple citizenships (92). Francophone African writers who simultaneously describe themselves as "French" or "American" and "African," for example, are rather common. In a sense, the development of modern African poetry has occurred as a way to respond to an overwhelming feeling of psychological displacement centering on the concept of the African "identity." It manifested mainly in a cultural sense both as a separation forced between Africans and their own world as a result of colonialism and as a perpetuation of this reality during the neocolonial era. Directly, this manifestation was a result of the highly systematic reorganization of the African ontological space. Explaining this reorganization, Said states that it was "a cultural process" that benefited from its "massively organized rule" that was an "invigorating counterpoint to the economic and political machinery that we all concur stands at the center of imperialism" (71–2). At the beginning, African poetry felt the need to articulate the African experience both to its own constituents and beyond its externally-created political borders. Through poetic verses, African literature sought to literally "textualize" the African living space for the larger community in order to better explain the cultural, political, and religious deracination that had occurred as a result of European colonialism.

Négritude poetry became a spring from which the feelings of physical and cultural uprooting flowed. It was the opportune moment for poets, as African intellectuals, to put in perspective the paradox of embracing the colonizing culture that, although it might appear empowering, is still marginalizing. In the 20th century, Africans began to realize that although some might call themselves French cultural citizens, the larger dominant culture might not share this same opinion. The Francophone African diaspora had created a polarizing effect between races by creating in French-speaking Africans at home, as it did in Paris, a sense of "Otherness." Therefore, a cultural nationalism was formed to speak to the problem of otherness mediated through the colonial politics of marginalization. Thus, by embracing "Blackness," Africans began an ontological return from exile. This return was backed in several ways from the celebration of blackness to the valorization of African culture and society. What started essentially as a cultural phenomenon evolved into a strong sense of nationalism that resulted in the emergence of a political dimension around which narratives of independence struggle were subsequently woven throughout the continent of Africa. This return is characterized in the works of Senegalese writer and former President Léopold Sédar Senghor.

Léopold Sédar Senghor (1906–2001) was a Senegalese poet, politician, and cultural theorist who served as the first president of Senegal for two decades (1960–1980). Senghor was the first African elected as a member of the *Académie française*. Before independence, he founded the political party called the Senegalese Democratic Bloc. He is regarded by many as one of the most important African intellectuals of the 20th century. Senghor's family was a culturally-mixed group. His father belonged to the bourgeois Serer tribe. At eight years of age, Senghor began his studies in Senegal in the Ngasobil boarding school, a religious establishment. In 1922, he entered a seminary in

Dakar. After renouncing religious life, he became passionate for French literature. He was an excellent student, earning recognition in French, Latin, and Mathematics. After taking his *baccalauréat*, he earned a scholarship to continue his studies in France. In 1928, Senghor left for France where he would attend a variety of institutions of higher learning including *La Sorbonne*. He left *La Sorbonne* to attend the *École Normale Supérieure* where he rubbed elbows with several individuals who would become prominent in French society including Robert Verdier and Georges Pompidou, the latter after whom the famous ultra-modern museum, the *Centre Pompidou*, in Paris is named. Senghor graduated from the *Université de Paris* where he received the *agrégation* in French grammar. From 1935–1945, he taught at the *Université de Tours* and the *Université de Paris*. He also taught at several *lycées* in both Tours and in Paris. Eventually, he studied linguistics at the *École pratique des hautes études* under the tutelage of important scholars including Paul Rivel, director of the *Institut d'ethnologie de Paris*. From his earliest days on the *Rive Gauche* in Paris, Senghor showed himself to be an intellectual. In a cry of revolt against the racism that he saw in Paris at the time, he and his fellow African thinkers coined the term *Négritude*. This term that sought to bring power from the denigrating term "nègre," became a "call to arms" for Black intellectuals of his age both within France, throughout French colonies, and in the United States. Further, this term became a cornerstone on which Senghor built his literary and political ideology. Without any doubt, it is the concept of *Négritude* for which Senghor has earned the greatest recognition. Co-developed with Aimé Césaire (Martinique) and Léon Damas (French Guiana), this intellectual and literary movement had, among others, the purpose of bringing value to what the group defined as "distinctively African values and aesthetics." The *Négritude* movement was an outgrowth of the French colonial presence on the African continent, a response to the notion put forth first in the 19th century that the peoples of Africa did not have rich cultures like those of European countries. In an argument for the worthiness of African culture, Senghor underscored the fact that his sub–Saharan Africa and the continent of Europe were inextricably linked through Egypt forming, thus, a cultural unity stretching from Africa, "The Cradle of Mankind," to Egypt, through Greece and to the Roman Empire, then extending into Modern Europe. We should not, however, perceive the *Négritude* movement as a racist one. *Négritude* was a reaction both to colonialism and to the neocolonialism that followed independence.

During World War II, Senghor served in the French military and was imprisoned for a period of two years. After the war ended, he was chosen to serve as Dean of the Linguistics Department at the *École Nationale de la France d'Outre-Mer*. He served in this position until 1960, the year that his home country earned its independence. Senghor held a variety of political roles including as *député* of Sénégal-Mauritanie and as the first president of the Republic of Senegal (elected September 5, 1960). It is his work as a writer that is of greatest interest within the present work. In 1964, Senghor published the first volume of a series of five books entitled *Liberté* containing speeches and essays. He is also credited with being the author of the Senegalese national anthem. Senghor supported the development of *La Francophonie*, seeking to bring the public's attention to the problems plaguing these particular nations of the world. On June 2, 1983, he became the first African elected to sit on the prestigious *Académie française*. Senghor died on December 20, 2001 in a small French town called Verson where he had spent the final years of his life. As a writer, Léopold Sédar Senghor is best known for his poetry for which he received several literary prizes including the *Prix mondial Cino del Duca* in 1978. In 1948, Senghor edited a collection of Francophone poetry entitled *Anthologie de la nouvelle poésie nègre et malgache* for which Jean-Paul Sartre wrote the Introduction called "Orphée Noir." Senghor penned numerous works including: *Prière aux masques* (1935), *Chants d'ombre* (1945), *Hosties noires* (1948), *La Belle Histoire de Leuk-le-Lièvre* (1953), *Éthiopiques* (1956), *Nocturnes* (1961), *Nation et voie africaine du socialisme* (1961), *Pierre Teilhard de Chardin et la politique africaine* (1962), *Poèmes* (1964), *Lettres de d'hivernage* (1973), *Élégies majeures* (1979), *La Poésie de l'action: Conversation avec Mohamed Aziza* (1980), and *Ce que je crois* (1988).

Speaking more specifically about Négritude as a literary means to explain the significance of exile, the poetry of Senghor readily comes to mind. In "Prière aux masques"/"Prayer to Masks" from his collection entitled *Chants d'ombre* (1945), for example, Senghor invokes African gods and ancestors in order to bring about an intervention with and a protection for the lives of living Africans:

Voici que meurt l'Afrique des empires—c'est l'agonie d'une princesse pitoyable
Et aussi l'Europe à qui nous sommes liés par le nombril [29].
Now while the Africa of imperialism is dying–it is the agony of a pitiable princess,
Just like Europe to whom she is connected through the naval.

Senghor's poem expressed a loss of hope on the continent of Africa. Moving beyond the literary interpretations to which Senghor's poem naturally lent itself, we should ultimately discuss the multi-layered cultural dimension of the exile theme in the poetry of Senghor and others who write within the same cultural tradition. Approaches to recounting the effects of exile range from descriptions of colonial education in a colonial system to the psychological consequence of the colonized African that makes strong allusions to the colonized personality outlined later in the works of Frantz Fanon. But to relegate these characteristics as a unique component of Négritude poetry would form an incorrect assertion, for the evocation of exile in African poetry, whether in English or French or Portuguese, manifested themselves in similar ways because they were each rooted in analogous colonial ideologies.

Whereas we might continue to argue strongly that from a literary perspective, Francophone African poetry primarily treats the subject of alienation, from a sociocultural perspective, it is clearly a matter of speaking to the real and measurable effects of human "continental drift." Taking into consideration that the great migrations of the 20th century were largely a global trend, in her book entitled *Nomadic Identities: The Performance of Citizenship*, May Joseph states:

> Migration has become a way of life in the latter part of the twentieth century. The large scale displacement of people from the rural to the urban or across nations has heightened the precariousness of arbitrary boundaries while fuelling contemporary identifications with ossified national identities. The 1970s in particular witnessed a global reconfiguration of national citizenship. As new nations contended with older ones, new geopolitical arrangements–neocolonialism, globalization, structural adjustment–shifted relations of power in less unilateral directions, creating multiple nodes of transnational interrelatedness. In the process, peoples around the world have aspired to conception of world citizenship while also asserting their particular social identities [154].

Both positioning the second generation of Francophone African poets on the pathway poured by Senghor and understanding the migratory nature of African poetic writing, in general, it becomes necessary to explain the constant "restless movement of peoples and cultures" within Africa (Venn 18). Yet it is also for this reason that many theorists of Postcolonialism insist on the creation of new postcolonial theories for the New Millennium. Interestingly, although "nomadism" is increasingly more prevalent at both the end of the 20th century and the beginning of the 21st century, these so-called nomads flock to urban centers where life, in general, is much less migratory. Thus, the literary compositions of New Millennial Africa tend to have a rather "urban" feel. Certainly, we should underscore the fact that just as the nations and regions on the African continent are different, so also there are different impetuses that have in the past two or three decades encouraged exile, especially in the sense that the path toward a better future is often found in a the very country that stole the future from you. In "Marching to the Tune: Colonization, Globalization, Immigration, and the Ghanaian Diaspora," Martha Donkor comments on the tendency of "colonized people to turn to migration as an option to living difficult lives" (27). Donkor speculates on the circumstances that lead individuals to forsake their native lands in order to eke out a better life in an unknown country. When African poets, playwrights, novelists, and storytellers recount their experiences, these writings should not be seen as emanating exclusively from the authors' experiences, but should rather appropriately be understood to represent the much larger community of African exiles for which they speak in describing "representations of colonialism, nationhood, postcoloniality, the typology of rulers, their powers, [and]corruptions..." (Ahmad 124).

Our exploration here would be deficient if it failed to acknowledge the existence of other possible interpretations of exile, particularly as the exile theme relates to certain classes of African peoples including intellectuals, writers, artists, political dissidents, the ethnically persecuted, and the internally dispersed throughout the African continent. Martha Gimenez's "The Politics of Exile: Class, Power, and the 'Exilic'" calls for a "democratization of exile" that is entirely relevant within the present study, which she defines as:

> an experience common to millions of displaced people who are not necessarily political actors in a narrow sense, but owe their uprooted conditions to the interplay of economic and political forces beyond their control. Labor market dynamics are not politically innocent while political processes are never wholly disengaged from economic interests and constraints (Web, n. pag.).

Gimenez's suggestion of the "democratization of exile" removes exile from the exclusive reach of the privileged few (the elite), thus placing the dialogue within the mouths of those individuals who are likely the greatest recipients of the ill effects of deracination. There is certainly a strong uprooting in progress in Africa at present, particularly in Central African Republic. I will admit here that because of the fact that it focuses on poetic texts that are written, largely, by the cultural and politic actors to whom Gimenez refers, the present study simply cannot democratize alienation. This is an inherent limitation of the study's source material.

The Négritude Movement and Beyond

Léopold Sédar Senghor and David Diop were prominent among the "Négritude" poets of the period directly before and after African nations earned their independence. In the poems of these Francophone African poets, emphasis was placed both on political themes and on the cultural and philosophical condition of being a black individual living in a white man's world.

Descriptions included African images, signs, and symbols that served to vocalize the "Négritude" message. Poetic examples include Senghor's "Femme noire" and David Diop's "Les Vautours." One of the founders of the Négritude movement, in his idealization of Africa, Senghor depicts Africa allegorically as a woman. In his poem entitled "Femme noire," Senghor sees Africa both as a symbol of beauty and as the source of all life. Like the woman that Africa is, she is gentle. Her nakedness represents her purity and innocence. After examining the numerous body parts and qualities (voice, mouth, breath, skin and eyes) of his beloved woman (Africa), which the poet compares to other beautiful objects, he ends his poem with an arresting note that both describes an African ideal and relates the fate of the continent of Africa. Africa is symbolized as a woman, and the persona, her lover. Here, too, the subject-matter is the praise of the African identity. Romanced by her beauty, the poet lauds the woman. In the poem, the poet's voice employs sensuous images that create a warm ambiance that seems entirely fitting for a continent such as Africa that is dissected by the Equator.

In "Les Vautours," in contrast, David Diop recounts Africa's first encounter with colonialism. The vultures are used metaphorically to represent white European colonialists. And in the image of the vulture is indicated the violent manner that characterized the way in which Europe colonized Africa. After portraying the agonizing memories associated with colonial imposition, Diop expresses the hope of that the seeds of freedom will be sown:

> Malgré vos chants d'orgueil au milieu des charniers
> Les villages désolés l'Afrique écartelée
> L'espoir vivait en nous comme une citadelle [*Coups de Pilon* 206].
> In spite of your songs of pride in the heart of the ossuaries
> The desolate villages of Africa torn apart
> Hope lived in us as in a fortress....

Diop's verses recount the story of a Modern Africa, a continent that has been infiltrated by and subjugated to foreign invaders for more than a century. Culturally speaking, he presents the European notion of "civilisation" with great irony. Against the wave of intruders who brought both death and the resurrecting powers of the Christian cross, like a small fire struggling against the wind to remain lit, hope within Africa endures in Diop's words. Hope also endures in those of Diop's poetic descendants.

In the New Millennium, Francophone African poetry is experiencing a Renaissance both in form and in function led, in part, by expatriate writers including the Cameroonian poet Paul Dakeyo. In an effort to pay homage to Nelson Mandela, who at the time of publication in June 2013 was in the twilight of his life, Dakeyo published a collection of poems entitled *Monsieur*

Mandela praising Mandela's myriad contributions both within Africa and throughout the rest of the world. In their verses, the dozens of Francophone African writers who contributed to Dakeyo's collection echo the goodness of the former President of South Africa: "Le but du monde est bien la paix/The goal of the world is peace," writes Jean-Damien Roumieu in the Introduction to Dakeyo's anthology (9). In his Introduction, the French writer uses the metaphor of a healthy body to describe the state in which the world should seek to form itself. Here, Roumieu cites Mandela's indomitable spirit, the one that pushed him through protests and a twenty-seven-year imprisonment and a strength of soul from which we can presume that the former leader drew as he fought for life at ninety-five years of age.

Throughout *Monsieur Mandela*, neither Dakeyo nor any of his contributors paint a West or Middle Africa that is either separated from the rest of the continent or from the rest of the world. It is for this very reason that throughout the course of this book, the reader will notice that at times I refer to the continent of Africa as a whole, rather than focusing specifically on the nations that constitute Francophone Africa. As Roumieu states,

> Nelson Mandela est de ceux-là, n'hésitant à protester contre l'absurde écartèlement entre diverses couleurs d'hommes, s'enfouissant pour un long temps, tel un maudit, tel un voyant, dans les geôles infernales, pour resurgir, ami de tous, et fondateur d'un nouveau monde, plébiscité par l'intelligence des nations qui lui attribue le Prix Nobel, la plus sublime distinction [9].
>
> Nelson Mandela is one of those who does not hesitate to speak out against the absurd quartering between different colors of men, burrowing himself for a long while like a bandit or a clairvoyant in the infernal jails to resurface as a friend to all and the founder of a new world, elected by the intelligence of nations that grant him the Nobel Prize, the most sublime honor.

Many of the diverse peoples of Africa have seen Nelson Mandela as a pillar of African strength in the face of great adversity. In the winter of 1964, Nelson Mandela arrived on Robben Island where he would spend eighteen of his twenty-seven years of imprisonment. Confined to a small cell, the floor his bed, a bucket for a toilet, he performed hard labor in a quarry. As fellow prisoner Neville Alexander stated, "He [Mandela] always made the point, if they say you must run, insist on walking. If they say you must walk fast, insist on walking slowly. That was the whole point. We are going to set the terms" (*Frontline* "Mandela"). Setting the terms for the future of Africa has become the baton that Mandela has passed on to the rest of the people of this diverse continent. Given his recent death, a discussion of the life of Nelson Mandela would fill numerous anthologies. Heroism, Honor, Respect. These are three words that come to mind when talking about the former president of South Africa.

Therefore, there is arguably no figure–political or otherwise–who has embodied the struggle of Africa more visibly over the last five decades than former President of South Africa Nelson Mandela. Recently a continuous world news story as a result of his failing health and ultimate death, for some Africans, Mandela has played a messianic role. Mandela was born Rolihlahla Mandela on July 18, 1918 into the Madiba clan in Mvezo, Transkei. His father, Nkosi Mphakanyiswa Gadla Mandela, was chief advisor to the Acting King of the Thembu people (Jongintaba Dalindyebo). Following the death of his father, Rolihlahla, who was still a child, became a ward of Jongintaba at the Great Place in Mqhekezweni. Rolihlahla was deeply impacted by the stories of his ancestors that he heard told there and he dreamed of freeing his people. While attending primary school in Qunu, his teacher gave him the Christian name Nelson. Nelson completed his primary and secondary school studies and ultimately completed a Bachelor of Arts degree at the University of South Africa in 1943. Mandela was not a particularly strong student as he bounced from institution to institution (University of the Witwatersrand, University of London) without completing any additional degrees. In 1989, while in the last months of his imprisonment, he obtained an L.L.B. through the University of South Africa.

What Nelson Mandela lacked as an academic he made up for in his civic and politic-mindedness. Mandela rose through the ranks of the African National Congress Youth League (ANCYL) and through its work the African National Congress (ANC) adopted in 1949 a more radical mass-based policy, the "Programme of Action." This campaign of civil disobedience against six unjust laws was a joint program between the ANC and the South African Indian Congress. For their participation in the campaign, in 1952, Mandela and nineteen others were charged under the Suppression of Communism Act and sentenced to nine months hard labor. He was also arrested on December 5, 1955 during a countrywide police raid. Mandela retreated to the political underground. From 1962 onward, he took on the name David Motsamayi. He left South Africa secretly, traveling throughout Africa and England to gain support for the armed struggles of his people. He received military training in Morocco and Ethiopia and returned to South Africa in July 1962. On August 5, 1962, he was arrested in a police roadblock outside Howick. He was charged both with leaving South Africa illegally and for provoking workers to strike. He was tried, convicted, and sentenced to five years imprisonment which he began serving in Pretoria. In October 1963, Nelson Mandela joined nine others on trial for sabotage in what became known as the Rivonia Trial. Facing the death penalty his words to the court at the end of his famous "Speech from the Dock" on 20 April 1964 became immortalized:

I have fought against white domination, and I have fought against black domination. I have cherished the ideal of a democratic and free society in which all persons live together in harmony and with equal opportunities. It is an ideal which I hope to live for and to achieve. But if needs be, it is an ideal for which I am prepared to die [Statement in the Rivonia Trial, Pretoria Supreme Court, April 20, 1964].

On June 11, 1964 Nelson Mandela was convicted and the next day was sentenced to life imprisonment. He was released on February 11, 1990. On May 10, 1994, Mandela was inaugurated South Africa's first democratically elected President. He stepped down from the presidency in 1999. As the Nelson Mandela Foundation clearly states on the foundation's web site, "Nelson Mandela never wavered in his devotion to democracy, equality and learning. Despite terrible provocation, he never answered racism with racism. His life has been an inspiration to all who are oppressed and deprived, to all who are opposed to oppression and deprivation" (nelsonmandela.org). Francophone African writers such as the Congolese poet Pius Ngandu Nkashama[7] has claimed that many African peoples have not actually gone far enough to extend Mandela's impetus into the future:

> Dans une Afrique qui avait été prophétisée "belle," qui avait été proclamée la citadelle de toutes les splendeurs, et voilà qu'elle évoque parfois un continent à la dérive. Il [Mandela] avait pourtant permis d'insuffler l'espérance, la prudence, le courage pour continuer la lutte jusqu'à la conquête [*Monsieur Mandela* 11].
>
> In an Africa that was prophesied "beautiful," which had been proclaimed the citadel of all splendors, and here it is that it sometimes evokes a continent adrift. Yet he [Mandela] had helped to infuse hope, prudence, and the courage to continue the struggle until the conquest.

Working on the other side of the Atlantic Ocean, his works champion Mandela's contribution to the international community and underscore the reality that the problems of Africa impact the entire world.

In *Monsieur Mandela*, Paul Dakeyo dedicates several pages of his own pen to elegiac "Mandelian" poetry. Dakeyo, born in Bafoussam, Cameroon in 1948, is a sociologist by trade. In 1980, he founded the publishing company *Éditions Silex* in Paris. Dakeyo has written several volumes of "poésie engagée" and his works form a poetic battlefront against the atrocities occurring both in Africa and in Latin America. His most well-known collections include *Les barbelés du matin* (1973), *Soweto! Soleils fusilés* (1977), *Les ombres de la nuit* (1994), and *Morini, cet exil* (2002), in addition to the anthologies of African poetry on which he has collaborated with other poets. These anthologies include *L'aube d'un jour nouveau* (1981), a collection devoted to the poetry of South Africa, *Poèmes de demain* (1982), an anthology of Cameroonian poetry, and *Poésie d'un continent* (1983), a collection of African poetry. Like Pius Ngandu Nkashama, Dakeyo does not see the poetry of his native Cameroon as separated from the rest of the continent of Africa, nor is it separated from the rest of the world. In his poem entitled "J'appartiens au grand jour[8]," it becomes clear that any separation that we might try to create between Francophone Africa, the continent of Africa, and the rest of the world is completely imaginary:

> Envoyez-moi des nouvelles
> Des nouvelles de notre terre
> Sans nord sans Sud
> Envoyez-moi des nouvelles de notre terre
> De notre terre que je veux prendre
> Dans mes bras comme le vent nu [73].
>
> Send me some news
> News from our earth
> Without North without South
> Send me some news of our earth
> Of our earth that I want to take
> In my arms like the naked wind.

Dakeyo's poetic rhythm and his imagery make clear that, like Mandela, Dakeyo sees himself as a member of the world community. His use of the word "notre" suggests that he shares both a common interest in world events and a common destiny with other citizens of the world. A world without a compass ("Sans nord sans Sud"/"Without North without South") invokes a world in which we look more closely at the similarities of our life experiences rather than at the characteristics that make our lives different.

Numerous Francophone African poets lent their words to Dakeyo's anthology, including Oumar Diagne (Mauritania, Senegal), Mamadou Guèye (Senegal), and Georges Tadonki (Cameroon). Poet, essayist, and novelist Oumar Diagne (Mauritania, Senegal) expressed his sentiments regarding Nelson Mandela's contribution to humanity in a poem entitled "Mandela mon père, fils de mes ancêtres" in which he turns the former president into a Messianic figure: "L'étoile a parlé dès ta naissance.... À l'horizon, s'est dessinée une lueur" (99)/"The star spoke from the moment of your birth.... On the horizon a glimmer took form." Raised from the branches of a tree, Diagne describes Mandela as a sort of "Rolihlahla" (Mandela's real name) or "troublemaker" who had taken root in Africa in order to deliver her from oppression and to build a new Africa. In "Chants pour Mandela," in comparison, Mamadou Guèye begins his poem in the style of a traditional African "praise poem." Beginning with a Wolof chant that the *griot* would sing at the honor of dignitaries or prominent *hommes militaires*, Guèye traces the glory of Mandela throughout the continent of Africa from the shouts of the Maasai people of Kenya and northern Tanzania, to the tambourines of the Maghreb, to the drums of the Burundi, "Soit loué!"/"Be praised!" (123) is the call for Africa that Guèye endorses. In his poem that he dedicates to Mandela entitled "Sphinx nègre du Kalahari," in contrast, Cameroonian international civil service worker and university professor Georges Tadonki, in a style that brings to mind Dr. Martin Luther King, Jr.'s famous "I Have a Dream" speech, recounts Mandela's dream of bringing freedom to his people. Like Guèye, Tadonki's poem takes the reader on an African voyage from Gorée to Zanzibar and Carthage to Zimbabwe. Painting Mandela as the "Sphinx nègre" or "Black Sphinx," the poet discusses how the former president of South Africa neither abandoned, nor did he give up the fight. Forever linked to Gandhi and to Dr. Martin Luther King, Jr. "du fil d'or de la paix"/"with the golden thread of peace" (262), the struggle that Mandela fought for many decades was not his own, but rather that of the people of the world.[9]

On December 5, 2013, Nelson Mandela "transitioned." Instead of greeting the former leader's passing with sorrow, the people of South Africa rejoiced in celebration of the life that he had lived. U.S. President Barack Obama's Facebook status of that day summarized well the impact of this historic individual: "Let us pause and give thanks for the fact that Nelson Mandela lived—a man who took history in his hands and bent the arc of the moral universe toward justice" (Facebook). In a very recognizable way, I would argue that Nelson Mandela represents a modern-day mythic hero, not in the sense that his character is steeped in foolish pride or in that his actions have in any way brought about the destruction of his own people, but in the sense that the strength and resolve that Mandela has exemplified throughout the last fifty years serve as a beacon of hope to the peoples of Africa. The poetry included in Dakeyo's collection supports this assertion. In light of the recent death of Nelson Mandela, Dakeyo's anthology has taken on greater significance. Although the former South African president certainly had his detractors, the impact of his life and work on the world is undeniable. On December 10, 2013, Heads of state from ninety-one countries descended on the nation of South Africa (Johannesburg) to pay tribute to this powerful revolutionary leader. On December 15, 2013, Mandela was laid to permanent rest in a private ceremony is his boyhood village of Qunu. Of Mandela, U.S. President Barack Obama remarked: "We will not likely see the likes of Nelson Mandela ever again," the President said. "So it falls to us, as best we can, to carry forward the example that he set" (Web NBC News 5 December 2013).

4

Histories, Legends and Myths in Francophone African Theatre

> "Thus, it can be argued that though Africa is a conglomeration of multicultural societies, in the study of African paroemiography, what is true of a particular ethnicity, may also be true in other sub–Saharan African countries"
> —*(Asimeng-Boahene 123).*

Myth plays an important role in Francophone African theatre.[1] In *The Power of Myth* (1988), Joseph Campbell, the literary scholar who outlined a hero archetype from the mythology of numerous cultures, defined a hero as "someone who has given his or her life to something bigger than oneself" (151). In his seminal text entitled *The Hero with a Thousand Faces* (1949), Campbell outlined the definition of the monomyth, or the "quest of the hero" motif, a definition illuminating the development of the hero within the genre of the novel, in particular. The hero exists in many forms and the trail that he follows was one that has been blazed by numerous individuals who may not have initially appeared to be "heroic." Campbell stated:

> ...For the heroes of all time have gone before us, the labyrinth is fully known; we have only to follow the thread of the hero-path. And where we had thought to find an abomination, we shall find a god ... we shall come to the center of our own existence; where we had thought to be alone, we shall be with all the world [18].

The general format of the hero's quest begins with a physical or emotional loss leading the protagonist to depart on a journey of self-discovery on his way toward maturation and, ultimately, the acquisition of wisdom. The motif often showcases a conflict between the protagonist and contemporary traditions in which the protagonist slowly accepts the values of his society finally leading to his own acceptance within that particular civilization. In *The Hero with a*

Thousand Faces, Campbell continued his analysis by stating that "the hero ventures forth from the world of the common day into a region of supernatural wonder: fabulous forces are there encountered and a decisive victory is won: the hero comes back from this mysterious adventure with the power to restore boons on his fellow man" (30). The world to which Campbell refers is steeped in myth. Myth criticism aids the reader to understand more fully the development of the "heroic" narrator.

As a critical approach, myth criticism, associated with a Jungian textual analysis, considers literary texts as time-honored, widely shared myths such as the Creation or the "hero's quest." The myth is a traditional narrative typically involving supernatural or imaginary persons embodying popular ideas on natural or social phenomena. This particular myth structure outlines the prototypical path of the mythological hero showing his rite of passage, or monomyth, contained in three steps: 1. Separation during which the hero receives his "call to adventure"; 2. Initiation, describing the trials and tribulations of the hero; and 3. Return: the moment at which the hero reintegrates within society with a greater understanding of its values and ideals. The first stage of the hero's quest or mythological journey is the "Call to Adventure" marked by a physical separation signifying that destiny has called on the hero and "transformed his spiritual center of gravity from within the pale of his society to a zone unknown" (58). The hero may depart to complete the adventure of his own free will or an outside force may send him. The second stage of the hero's quest is his Initiation. During this second stage, the hero enters a liminal space in which he must survive a succession of assorted trials and accomplish great tasks. Liminal spaces typically appear as places of birth, rebirth, and renewal. A loss of liminality leads to a loss of strength. Campbell describes the Initiation as follows:

> Once having traversed the threshold, the hero moves in a dream landscape of curiously fluid, ambiguous forms, where he must survive a succession of trials.... The hero is covertly aided by the advice, amulets, and secret agents of the supernatural helper whom he met before his entrance into this region. Or it may be that he here discovers for the first time that there is a benign power everywhere supporting him in his superhuman passage [97].

The third and final stage of the hero's quest is his return to society. It is in this third and final stage that the hero reaches a more complete understanding of his culture and a reintegration within his own society: "When the hero-quest has been accomplished," says Campbell, "through penetration to the source, or through the grace of some male or female, human or animal, personification, the adventurer still must return with his life-transmuting trophy" (193).

As Claude Lévi-Strauss stated in *Myth and Meaning* (1978), "Mythology is static, we find the same mythical elements combined over and over again, but they are in a closed system, let us say, in contradistinction with history, which is, of course, an open system" (17). When juxtaposed with the notion of history, the study of myth takes on an even more important role. Lévi-Strauss continues:

> The open character of history is secured by the innumerable ways according to which mythical cells, or explanatory cells which were originally mythical, can be arranged and rearranged. It shows us that by using the same material, because it is a kind of common inheritance or common patrimony of all groups, of all clans, or of all lineages, one can nevertheless succeed in building up an original account for each of them [17].

When I employ the term "myth" here, I do not mean stories that are untrue, but rather stories that are deeply rooted in the psyche of the culture. These myths express the deepest values of our society and shape our everyday lives. In *The Soul of Popular Culture*, Mary Lynn Kittleton proposes that myths "operate like our own individual dreams do, through the power of imagination, as they work on and play with issues in our inner and outer lives" (7). All myths have heroes in the form of a protagonist.

These "hero myths" use symbolic language to tell stories that teach us how to overcome obstacles that we encounter either in the world or within ourselves. Carl Jung suggested that all symbolic language was rooted in patterns of human existence called "archetypes," stating that:

> From the unconscious there emanates determining influences which, independently of tradition, guarantee in every single individual a similarity and even a sameness of experience, and also of the way it is represented imaginatively [*The Archetypes* 58].

The content of the archetype is filled with personal elements, but the constructive pattern is universal. In *Tracking the Gods: The Place of Myth in Modern Life*, James Hollis underscores the importance of the individual in the collective unconscious as follows: "Whether the hero archetype manifests on a collective or an individual level, it attests to the universal human need to expand the limits of possibility" (22). In 1957, Roland Barthes defined myth as discourse; a system of communication; a message that is not confined to oral speech but is hidden in many representations such as photography, sports, shows, and cinema. For myth is

> *depoliticized speech* ... Myth does not deny things, on the contrary, its function is to talk about them; simply, it purifies them, it makes them innocent, it gives them a natural and eternal justification, it gives them a clarity which is not that of an explanation but that of a statement of fact [*Myth Today* 109].

Barthes contended that although there may be ancient myths, no particular myth can endure forever largely because human history determines both the life and death of mythic language. Today, Francophone African poetic literature has become a fertile ground for the discussion of myth, since it reflects the social *status quo*. However, the patriarchal system consistently assures that male supremacy will remain at the top of its hierarchy. This is accomplished through myth and its subtle and above suspicion qualities. In her book entitled *Her Kind: Stories of Women from Greek Mythology*, Jane Cahill appropriately reminds us that,

> The stories that we call Greek myths are men's stories.... Their substance is the stuff of men's lives and fantasies victory in war, glorious death on the battlefield, heroic enterprise, the slaying of monsters, the fathering of sons.... Female characters in myth are mothers or wives or virgins, defined always in terms of men. Most of them are bad or unusual women: there is Medea who kills her children; there is Clytemnestra who, though married to the richest king in Greece, commits both adultery and murder; there is Thetis who puts her babies on the fire; there is Jocasta who marries her own son [7].

In other words, the great myth of patriarchy inventively states that no matter how many things women have accomplished, they will always be less of a "hero" than their male counterparts.

African National Theatre and the Myth of Shaka (Shaka Zulu)

Like other so-called "national" theatres (Greek, French, German, etc.), the definition of what constitutes African theatre is often rooted almost exclusively in notions of performance and focused on the traditional theatre play called the "pièce de théâtre." Although I would certainly acknowledge the fact that there is nothing inherently wrong with including such a definition as part of the way of defining theatre, this single definition alone, however, does not show itself to be particularly useful when describing what actually takes place within the Francophone African "theatre space." It is therefore necessary to think about how theatre is actually two complementary halves of the same coin with, on one side, the "performance" aspect of theatre and on the other side, the "reception" aspect of drama. Further, this same initial definition, however, does not take into account the consequences of "scenescaping."[2] Among other factors, "scenescaping" includes developing the relationship between the performers, on one hand, and with the audience, on the other, by means of the use of scenic space. Although such characteristics, however, might seem conclusive with particular regard to Western theatre, bearing in mind its different transformations, we cannot produce the same generalization for Francophone African theatre, for the term "theatre" itself produces a number of uncertainties that emerge, in part, because of the perspective brought to bear on theatricality itself.

The New Millennium has brought about a change in perspective that necessitates the creation of a new understanding of Francophone African theatre. When discussing African theatre in general, the majority of standard texts focuses extensively on "traditional" theatrical forms and is often quite resolute in developing religious or mythical connections. These connections are not without foundation, though we have to be careful that an exploration of such traditions does not become the only cultural exploration that we undertake. Here, I am speaking specifically about the works of the 1970s such as Bakary Traoré's *The Black African Theatre and Its Social Functions* (1972) that have seemingly forged an *a posteriori* authorization of these traditional and not-fully-developed conclusions. Since 9/11, changes in how we view the world have ushered in new means of analysis of theatrical production and performance. We stand at a moment in time during which we can consider both how Francophone African theatre comes from a larger theatrical tradition at the same time as it showcases its unique characteristics. To this end, we would be remiss if we did not focus, to some extent, on understanding and exploring the social aspects of Francophone African theatre, particularly as it relates to stage development, as well as the relevant historical aspects of African theatre aesthetics. Thus, here, we will examine the African historical tragedy, the prolepses and analepses[3] of the traditional stage drama, and finally, the most well-known form of African drama within the context of African myth: the concert party. The principle goal of this chapter, then, is to proceed from the more general notion of African theatre aesthetics toward a more specific discussion of theatre within Francophone Africa.

Like theatrical features exhibited in traditional Greek theatre, one of the most important features of African aesthetics is its function of transgression. Transgression is experienced in the cathartic moment. In "Theatricality and Social Mimodrama," Pius Ngandu Nkashama writes:

> Two observations are useful in understanding the "transgressive" dimension of such a rupture. The first is that it would be better to see in what are commonly designated "customs," "mores," or "traditions," contexts by which African society preserves its cultural equilibrium and its true legitimacy. These elements are not the result of processes of imitation modeled upon gratuitous rules, but the result of a real experience of history.... The second observation is borne out in the interpretation of this same experience of the collectivity by means of concrete

esthetic practices. The reconstruction of iterative symbols that are capable of restructuring textualized mythologies remains the primordial means for maintaining the group's security and stability [177].

The term "transgression," however, has a double-meaning, for it also signals a deviation from the modalities of the established law. Resultantly, the respecting of social mores serves to legitimize one's actions within the given society. Thus, in a society in which established authorities are challenged, such confrontation is met with excessively severe punishment. The *kotéba,* a form of rhythmic dancing (in Mali), authorizes the "playing out" of challenges to patriarchal authority. Actors can "play the role of the father," which serves to underscore the paradoxes of patriarchy within that particular culture (Sahli 6–36). In certain Central African communities, for example, where the husband's authority is typically unopposed, following his death in what is considered a "socially acceptable" performance, the wife can play the role of the dead husband (analepsis) in front of his dead body during which she acts out any of the unappreciated behaviors that he exhibited during his lifetime. She dresses in his clothing and plays out their married life in front of an audience. Therapeutic in nature, the scene contains no script, so to speak. It can thus be played out over any time or space, in a sense for long as it takes for the widowed women to experience a catharsis. Undeniably, this performance is unspoken theatricality, a characteristic of a cleansing ceremony.[4] On other occasions, a sort of cleansing can emerge through the adaptation and re-telling of traditional African myths.

One of the most prevalent myths throughout the continent of Africa that has entered into Francophone African theatre is the myth of Shaka Zulu. Shaka, known most commonly in English as Shaka Zulu, was the most influential ruler of the Zulu Kingdom, an empire in Southern Africa extending along the eastern coast of Africa on the Indian Ocean from the Pongola River in the north to the Tugela River in the south. The small kingdom that grew to dominate much of what is present-day KwaZulu-Natal in Southern Africa entered into military conflict with the British Empire in the 1870s during the Anglo-Zulu War. Despite an early Zulu victory, the kingdom ultimately fell at the hands of British colonial soldiers. Shaka is generally credited both with uniting many of the Northern Nguni people (the Mtetwa Paramountcy and the Ndwandwe) into the Zulu Kingdom as well as with forging the creation of a nation that controlled southern Africa. A remarkable statesman, he was one of the greatest Zulu kings. He is both revered as a military genius and reviled for the brutality of his reign. Although cultural historians continue to debate Shaka's role as a unifier of the people, his rule has left an indelible impact on the culture of the entire continent of Africa (Hamilton 36–130). 20th century world media tended to glorify the figure of Shaka. Though certain aspects of traditional Zulu culture still revere him, we should note that Zulu sources are sometimes critical of Shaka, and numerous negative images abound in Zulu oral history (Morris 99). The figure of Shaka therefore remains an ambiguous one in African oral history which has the effect of giving the image of Shaka its continual power and influence throughout Africa. Therefore, despite the obvious fact that the myth of Shaka originated thousands of miles away and within an entirely different culture, the myth echoes in Francophone African writing. As Kahiudi Mabana states in his article entitled "La réécriture francophone du mythe de Chaka: Éloge, démystification et interrogation," "Le mythe de Chaka, tel qu'il est repris par les écrivains francophones, incarne la fascination répulsive qui caractérise de façon énigmatique les héros de la tragédie classique"/"The myth of Shaka, such that it is taken up by Francophone writers, incarnates the repulsive fascination that characterizes in an enigmatic way the hero of classical tragedy" (68). Why does the myth of Shaka have such widespread appeal?

The hero of Thomas Mofolo's novel entitled *Chaka* has influenced a number of Francophone African playwrights throughout the continent. Appearing in several forms, it is largely the 1940 French translation of this Sotho novel that served as an important source for many Francophone African dramatists who have written plays in French inspired by the Shaka theme. In 1956, Léopold Sédar Senghor penned a dramatic poem entitled "Chaka" published in *Éthiopiques*. In 1961, the Malian Seydou Badian Kouyaté wrote a play called *La Mort de Chaka*, and in 1968 *Les Amazoulous* by Abou Anta Ka of Senegal was published. The Guinean writers Nénékhaly-Camara and Djibril Tamsir Niane wrote *Amazoulou* (1970) and *Chaka* (1971), respectively. In 1975 Nestor Sénoufo Zinsou of Togo wrote about Shaka in *On joue la comédie* and Tchihcaya U Tam'si of Congo wrote *Le Zulu* in 1976. These writings represent seven significant literary works treating the theme of Shaka. This fondness for a 19th century Zulu warrior king who ruled rather savagely might seem strange for the reader of this particular study or for anyone who is not familiar with African cultural history. According to Donald Burness, Mofolo's novel, *Chaka*, is a political text, "for Mofolo is concerned with the nature of power and the destiny of African peoples, and, therefore, his novel has much in common with contemporary African literature" (14). Burness highlights, however, that Mofolo's novel written in the Sotho language describes a Shaka who is no longer relevant:

> Mofolo's Shaka belongs to an heroic age that exists no more. His Chaka is a particularly African work for not only is it written in an African language, but it celebrates African culture, pride, tradition, and dignity. Mofolo's vision of the

potential greatness of man has been reaffirmed by African writers of our time who do not share the West's sense of despair [23].

Additionally, as cited by noted Africanist Ali Mazuri in "The Resurrection of the Warrior Tradition in African Political Culture," James Fernandez has stated that "The Shaka complex is the drama of working out the impulse to power in human affairs" (83). As a result, the Shaka myth seems fully inscribable on any African culture that sees itself experiencing struggle, particularly one that leads to independence. Within African literature, Shaka has for a long while served as a symbol of the struggle against colonization and assimilation, an emblem of African solidarity against White colonial authority that has become both one of the richest and one of the most widespread myths on the continent of Africa.

Of the actual historical figure, Shaka, little specific information is known. None can agree completely on either his physical stature or the color of his skin ("La réécriture francophone du mythe de Chaka" 64). In "The Symbol of Shaka," Dan Wylie notes that "Shaka is largely a textual invention, a malleable symbol available for any ideological distortion, from the early white settlers' self-serving monsterisation to the Inkatha Freedom Party's nationalistic lionization" (cited in *Interfaces Between the Oral and the Written* 64). In 1991, Jean Sévry published *Chaka Empereur des Zoulous: Histoire, Mythes et Légendes*. For Sévry, it was possible for one to simply fashion one's own version of Shaka: "Chacun son Chaka, parce que chacun le regarde à partir de son système de représentations, en un lieu précis, a une période historiquement datée"/"To each his Shaka, for each one sees him through his own system of representation, in a specific place, and a specific place in history" (10). When individuals go through a collective struggle, oftentimes they seek a unifying "hero" that will bring them to victory.

It should thus not be surprising that a cultural/historical figure would be turned into a national hero. In Interwar France, Joan of Arc was used to create a maternal figure who would nurture the nation back to health after the scourges of World War I. Throughout the ages, African history has been written by colonial (White) historians who sought to falsify the facts. Native Africans have worked against this current by fashioning their own account of what happened during the European colonial enterprises in Africa. For two centuries, European historians and anthropologists have descended on the continent of Africa both to explore and to explain its characteristics. These explorations have functioned sometimes as news or propaganda, but also as a supposed documentary of the African experience. Over the course of nearly six decades, French filmmaker and anthropologist Jean Rouch made ethnofiction films focusing on the Dark Continent. In 1995, Malian filmmaker and

New York University professor Manthia Diawara critiqued visual anthropology in the work of Jean Rouch through a critical framework called "reverse anthropology."[5] In "reverse anthropology," the focus of study shifts from the study of tribal and "primitive" men by so-called "superior" White men to a study of any culture by anthropologists from diverse cultural backgrounds. Since cultural anthropology itself is negativity attached to colonialism in which anthropologists are equated to colonial masters, "reverse anthropology" serves to shift the *status quo*. In terms of the optics through which the study of cultures can be observed, this particular optic is a relatively new one that returns power to native Africans. Shaka Zulu plays, therefore, serve the principle need to restore Africa's past to a time of glory. Heroes such as Shaka Zulu incarnate the spirit of the people.

The Shaka myth has captivated Francophone African writers both from an ideological as well as a historical perspective. Ideologically, Shaka symbolized a great warrior capable of unifying an entire nation. Historically, Shaka represented pure military savvy. From a cultural historical perspective, the Shaka figure represents an obvious paradox: one on hand, he was messianic; on the other hand, he was an egomaniac and a tyrant. Francophone African writers focus on different elements of the Shaka myth. Mabana writes that,

> Quoiqu'ils aient écrit en français, ils sont presque tous largement tributaires des usages langagiers et des traditions orales de leurs territoires. La richesse complexe du mythe de Chaka résulte forcément de la complexité existentielle de ses retranscripteurs. D'autre part, la valorisation nationale implique une identification au peuple, tandis que la démystification relève d'un esprit libre, rebelle et iconoclaste. Le mythe de Chaka suit donc le clivage de l'histoire. À ce titre, il est politiquement subversif lorsqu'il s'acharne à ridiculiser les chefs établis, à démonter les mythologies politiques africaines [70].
>
> Although they are writing in French, they [Francophone African writers] are almost all widely coming from the language uses and oral traditions of their own territories. The complex richness of the Shaka myth results inevitably from the essential complexity of its re-transcribers. On the other hand, the national valorization suggests identification with the people, whereas the demystification comes from a spirit that is free, rebellious, and iconoclastic. The Shaka myth thus follows the cleavage of history. In this respect, it is politically subversive when it attempts to ridicule the established leaders to take down African political mythologies.

For Léopold Sédar Senghor, for example, Shaka represented a man-of-vision, a Black Messiah who used his prophecy to save his people. When the action of Senghor's play begins, Shaka is nearing death, having received several mortal wounds at the hands of his assassins. Mocking him, the White Voice says,

> Te voilà donc à ta passion. Ce fleuve de sang qui
> te baigne, qu'il soit pénitence [*Éthiopiques* 31].

> There you are thus at your passion. This river of blood that
> Bathes you, may it be penance.

It is easy to see, however, the reason for which Senghor turned Shaka into a redeemer. His response, "Oui me voilà entre deux frères, deux traîtres, deux larrons" (31)/"Yes. Here I am between two brothers, two traitors, two thieves," had Biblical significance. Ironically, perhaps, Senghor's telling of the Shaka story seems to neglect the actual historical narrative in that it largely disregards the fact that the Zulu king's so-called heroic actions took place largely before the arrival of whites. Here, our poet turns them into a commentary on the struggle between the colonizer and the colonized as most clearly indicated in the following dream sequence:

> Je voyais dans un songe tous les pays aux quatre coins de l'horizon soumis à la règle,
> à l'équerre et au compas,
> Les forêts fauchées les collines anéanties, vallons et fleuves dans les fers....
> Pouvais- je rester sourd à tant de souffrances bafouées? [39].
> I saw in a dream all the countries from the four corners of the horizon subject to
> the ruler, the square, and the compass,
> The flattened forests, the crushed hills, valleys and rivers in irons....
> Could I remain deaf to such scorned suffering?

Shaka is a warrior, fearless and strong. Like the Messiah, because of his great love, he is willing to sacrifice his own life to save his people: "Pour l'amour de mon Peuple noir"/"For the love of my black People" (36). In this same scene, the hero explains why, in fact, he seeks to gain power, for without power he will be unable to free his people: "Que le pouvoir fût bien ton but...,"/"May power indeed be your goal," says the White Voice (38). Thus, once Shaka's power is achieved, he will be able to protect his people from colonial authority. It is important to note that Senghor wrote his play several years before his homeland of Senegal achieved its own independence. Therefore, although his play might have endeavored to symbolize anti-colonial struggle, it could not possibly foresee exactly how the nation would develop after the arrival of independence. With independence came the problem of decolonization, a reality of which Martinican playwright Aimé Césaire wrote in his 1964 play entitled *La Tragédie du Roi Christophe*: "Le cadre à la fois mythique, historique et politique me paraît favorable à l'introduction du problème qui se pose à l'Afrique d'aujourd'hui: la décolonisation"/"the simultaneously mythical, historical and political framework appears favorable to me to introduce the problem that is poses itself in African today: decolonization" (Sieger 66). For Léopold Sédar Senghor, Shaka served as a model for the colonized black African, the subjugated person fighting for his freedom (Samba Diop 1995: 177).

In the case of Shaka Zulu, an individual rose to a level of great power and ultimately used that power for evil rather than for good.[6] Such is often the case in Africa. As Dorothy Dodge has stated clearly, "African leaders constantly reiterated the theme of the overriding need to provide leadership, direction and unity" (199). In his 2001 book entitled *Nationalism and African Intellectuals*, in contrast, Toyin Falola theorizes that in the case of West Africa, in particular, independence and the subsequent decolonization created a fertile ground for the rising of African intellectuals who, although they claimed a desire to sweep away remnants of the colonial state, actually used their power to expand colonial structures throughout the neocolonial period (3–55). Therefore, it is within this particular context that we consider the Francophone African "Chaka" plays of the postcolonial period.

As the light of the New Millennium began to shine, Africanists continued to consider the Shaka theme to hold a cultural significance throughout Francophone Africa. This significance is reflected in the numerous plays containing the Shaka theme. In *La mort de Chaka* (1961) by the Malian Seydou Badian Kouyaté, we find evidence of an ideological theatre at work. Like in Senghor's version, Kouyaté's play begins shortly before Shaka's death. The title character, who is absent for much of the play (not appearing until the third "tableau"), enters the drama in order to engage in a decisive battle that will serve to assure the sovereignty of his people for all time. There is dissention in the ranks, as Shaka's generals prefer to return home to their families rather than risk everything in battle. The youngest fighters who seek the glory of battle support Shaka as does Notibé, a young princess who comes to embody African women. Although the main plotline of *La mort de Chaka* suggests that the play's characters support Shaka overall, there is a small group of dissenters who plot the death of their leader: "Le peuple n'aura jamais de répit. Il faut débarrasser le pays de Chaka"/"The people will never have any rest. We must rid the country of Shaka" (192). N'Dlébé rebukes Shaka's generals for their act of betrayal: "Il faut savoir choisir; la mollesse, les plaisirs ou la grandeur"/"We must know how to choose gentleness, pleasures, or greatness" (215), to which Dingana responds, "ceux qui parlent de grandeur, d'honneur, de prestige, ne sont pas loin des fous. L'homme, il ne faut pas l'oublier, est un être de chair et de sang!"/"those who speak of greatness, honor, prestige, are not far from being crazy. Man, we must not forget, is a being of flesh and blood!" (217). It is essentially a matter of whether the sacrifice to be made is a worthy one and, if so, who would be willing to make this sacrifice. Notibé, Mapo's sister and Dingana's fiancée, is poised to make the ultimate sacrifice, for she believes that Shaka's actions are an outgrowth of his desire to bring freedom to his people. And, if as a result he makes mistakes, it is because his strong emotions sometimes cloud his otherwise skillful judgment. Shaka's fiancée, Noliwé,[7] is entirely absent from this version of the play, so Notibé plays the central female figure. The parallel between Shaka and the leaders of modern-day Mali becomes evident, which is echoed in Shaka's words to Notibé: "Sois, tranquille, ma fille. Désormais, des Chaka naîtront tout le long de l'histoire de notre people, car aucune autre catégorie d'hommes pourra commander ici. Ceux qui ne voient pas cela se trompent"/"Be calm, my daughter. Henceforth, Shakas will be born throughout the history of our people, for no other category of men will be able to command here. Those who do not see this deceive themselves" (237–8). Absolute hubris, indeed! This hubris is Shaka's tragic flaw that will ultimately lead to his downfall. Nonetheless, the assassination of Shaka does not put a definitive end to the people's problems. The people need a leader, and there is always a risk that he will be like Shaka. Success in governing becomes managing the delicate balance of sacrifice and power. Leaders cannot seek a pretense for their actions. Thus, Shaka's use of the colonial threat does not sufficiently justify the actions that he takes. In the playwright's own words, the need for balance remains unquestionable: "La construction socialiste exige que l'intérêt collectif passe avant l'intérêt individuel"/"The socialist construction requires that collective interest take place before individual interest" ("Les difficultés de la construction" 129).

Condetto Nénékhaly-Camar's (Guinea-Conakry) *Amazoulou* (1970) represents another adaptation of the traditional Shaka tale. A tragic destiny, here Nénékhaly-Camar changes the roles of the minor characters (Issanoussi, Malonga, Ndlébé). In this version, Shaka is much less sure of his own judgment, as he relies almost exclusively on the counsel of Malonga and Ndlébé. These two characters seem hell-bent on filling Shaka's mind with illusions. In contrast to the role of master that he played in Mofolo's work, here Issanoussi is a statesman and counselor to Shaka. He forms an alliance with Mohlomi, a *griot*, with whom he works to thwart the plans of Malonga and Ndlébé. Shaka has one central focus; he is preoccupied with waging war. This preoccupation inhibits his ability to enter into a deep, loving relationship. Therefore, as long as Malonga and Ndlébé succeed in building separation between Shaka and Noliwé, they will be successful in pushing him toward engaging in warfare thereby increasing the hold that the two counselors exert over Shaka. Even though the two conspire together, Malonga and Ndlébé have different perspectives on power. For Malonga, it indicates a love for one's people: "Non Ndlébé! Il y a ici un profond amour de la terre et des créatures que Oumkoulou-le-divin a répendues sur elle. Chaka est leur défenseur"/"No, Ndlébé! There is a deep love for the earth here and for the creatures that Oumkoulou-the-divine spread out on her. Shaka is their defender" (73). In contrast, Ndlébé feels that power should be used to instill fear both in one's enemies and in one's own people:

"Qui sont-ils? Des foules anonymes qui ne se connaissent pas et que seule maintient ensemble la crainte de l'épée de Chaka"/"Who are they? Anonymous crowds who do not know each other and that alone maintain together the fear of the sword of Shaka" (73). In line with what Toyin Falola suggests happens during the emergence of an African elite, Shaka's own ambitions blind him to the needs of the people. For this reason, Issanoussi must remind him that, "Le temps t'a grandi au-delà des meilleures espérances. Tu as eu la gloire, l'honneur ... et maintenant l'amour de ton peuple"/"Time raised you beyond the best of hopes. You had glory, honor ... and now the love of your people" (75). Overwhelmed by the yoke placed on his shoulders, Shaka responds, "En dehors des royaumes, il me faut songer à la condition des hommes"/"Outside of kingdoms, I must dream about the condition of men" (76). Following the deaths of Noliwé and Namdi, Shaka begins to make amends. He starts to understand the suffering of his people. In turn, in this version of the Shaka story, he does not die, but rather he cedes his power to Mosheshe who will now govern the Amazoulou. As previously mentioned, the criticism of the abuse of power within the colonial system by contemporary African leaders is worth noting. Nénékhaly-Camar's use of Shaka to represent these power abusers is evident. Nonetheless, the playwright continually keeps himself "in check" by exhibiting a system of checks and balances within the Shaka character who both lauds his accomplishments at the same time as he criticizes his own actions.

In *Chaka* (1971), fellow Guinean author Djibril Tamsir Niane forges a theatrical hero whose single objective is to obtain political power. As Shaka grows progressively more powerful, the people's misery mounts. Oppositional characters in the play work out ways to usurp Shaka's authority. What is revealed most significantly in the play is the sense of isolation and loss in the Shaka character as he becomes increasingly more aware of the fact that his people hold no esteem for him: "Me voici au sommet de la gloire, dans le désert aride de la Toute-Puissance"/"Here I am at the peak of glory, in the arid desert of All-Powerfulness" (53). But, as the adage goes, "It's lonely at the top." Niane's play, therefore, employs a common theme of the period: the notion that "absolute power corrupts absolutely." As its author stated during an interview on January 2, 1976: "...il y a derrière tout cela ce qu'on peut appeler la raison d'État. Le pouvoir a ses exigences; la création d'un empire a ses exigences"/"... behind all of that there is what we could call the reason of the State. Power has its demands. The creation of an empire has its demands" (cited in M'Baye 97). Further, Niane humanizes the hero by underscoring his physical and psychological limitations, his weaknesses and his suffering.

In *Le Zulu* (1977), Tchicaya U Tam'si (Congo-Brazzaville) poses a similar question with regard to the acquisition of power in post-independence Francophone Africa. In Tchicaya's play, the characters Ding'Iswayo and Epervier discuss different methods of governing the people. The former allows the people a lot of freedom. The people take advantage of this freedom:

> Oui, les tribus sont querelleuses, promptes à la rapine. La vue d'un corral où les bœufs sont gras et nombreux déchaïne les convoitises, et le sang de l'homme doit couler. J'arbitre quand l'excès d'insolence ne m'oblige pas à faire la guerre. Les tribus m'ont élu pour cela [*Le Zulu* 50].
> Yes, the tribes are quarrelsome, quick to plunder. The sight of a corral where the cattle are fat and plentiful unleashes greed, and the blood of man must flow. I intervene when the excess of insolence does not oblige me to make war. The tribes elected me for that.

Epervier opposes this system to that developed by Shaka himself, suggesting that Ding'Iswayo might, "Édicter d'autres règles entre les tribus"/"Enact other rules between the tribes" (50). Ding'Iswayo, for his part, seems to have his thumb on Shaka's real ambitions, which includes the sacrifice of Noliwé in order to achieve his goals. From a cultural perspective, Shaka's ambitions and his subsequent decisions reflect political events occurring in Congo during the period. Thus with each rung that he has climbed on the ladder of power, Shaka's arrogance also mounts. Following a ceremony of thunder and lightning, it is evident that Shaka has become the Zulu. The result of Shaka's increase in power is his added separation and marginalization from his own society. In Tchicaya's play, power and love are continually juxtaposed. Any move toward obtaining power is considered a failure. A successful life is one of balance, as indicated in the third scene of Act One:

> Malounga m'aidera à faire la part du rêve, de la réalité, de l'imagination.... Si mon sang ne me trahit, je triomphe de tout. Tout: le ciel et la terre unis à mon vouloir. La part égale dans chaque main, d'amour pour les hommes et pour le pouvoir. Pour être juste, je sais cela. Sans sacrifier l'un à l'autre. Est-ce danser sur une corde raide au-dessus des précipices? [30].
> Malounga will help me to consider dream, reality, and imagination.... If my blood does not betray me, I triumph over everything. Everything: heaven and earth united at my desire. Equal share in each hand: love for men and for power. To be fair, I know this. Without sacrificing one for the other. Is this dancing on a tightrope above the abyss?

Among the several affinities between Tchicaya's and Senghor's plays include the way in which Shaka seems to justify his actions: "un ciel uni, une terre unie, un peuple uni. Qu'importe si les petits seigneurs de la rapine.... Oui, le nouvel ordre, il faut qu'il advienne, le plus tôt sera le mieux"/"a heaven united, an earth united, a people united. It makes no difference if the small lords plunder.... Yes, the new order must come. The sooner, the better" (89).

Shaka's dreams of becoming all-powerful will come about with great cost: "Ton propre sang t'étouffera!"/"Your own blood will choke you" (95). Consequently, estrangement becomes the fruit of his power mongering. Following his estrangement is Shaka's assassination. Shaka ends up dying without ever having attained his stated goal, and right before his death, he questions the results of his own actions: "Et pourtant c'était de la liberté..."/"And however, it was freedom..." (130).

It is safe to say that in the majority of the Francophone Africa dramatic versions of the Shaka myth the acquisition of power forms a significant motif. Tchicaya U Tam'si's play unquestionably demonstrates the playwright's own experience living in a turbulent Congo. And although the origins of the Shaka myth come from thousands of miles away, the challenges of the Zulu people are echoed in those of post-independence peoples of Francophone Africa. For African playwrights, this question of power is hopelessly tragic. An overly tolerant ruler is quickly taken advantage of by his people. A leader who is too tyrannical risks alienating himself from the very people that he is meant to lead. The real question, then, becomes a matter of reaching a balance that works for both the leader and the people. If no such balance is reached, struggle will lead to dissention. Dissention will lead to chaos and anarchy, the ultimate result of which will be a collapse of the entire system followed by the arrival of a foreign power that will pick up the pieces and establish a new system of governing that does not respect the will of the people.

Why did these Francophone African writers choose theatre as a means to discuss the myth of Shaka? The answer is rooted in the importance that cultural history plays in the development of Francophone African states following independence in the late 1950s and the early 1960s. Theatre, with its similarities to oral history, is the greatest literary form for conveying tragedy. Thus, in these Francophone African plays, we find ourselves participating in historical theatre. African oral tradition, in general, which is theatrical, serves as a means for the dissemination of the Shaka story. Therefore, it is easy to understand how the myth of Shaka successfully left Southern Africa to reach the nations of Francophone Africa such as Senegal, Togo, Mali, Guinea, and Congo, to be quickly "translated" (*translatio studii*) into the French language for ultimate cultural exportation.

Shaka Zulu: Origin Stories

Shaka, the Zulu King, who was assassinated by his two half-brothers on September 22, 1828, is one of the most recognizable historical figures of Africa.

Born in 1787 of the Zulu king Senzangkhona, Shaka joined the army at the age of 22 and became a distinguished military commander. He succeeded his father as king in 1816. For the age and the civilization in which he lived, Shaka displayed acute military ability and he created a strong army that he used to expand his kingdom. During his twelve-year-rule, he grew his army to number more than 40,000 strong. Although Shaka's "origin story" contains scant historical data, this fact has not hampered the production of numerous filmic and literary works on his story. In fact, Shaka's story has been told numerous times over the last century, most notably, by Mosotho writer Thomas Mofolo, whose *Chaka: An Historical Romance* appeared in an English translation in 1931 and then in a French translation in 1940. Thus, Mofolo's *Chaka* is the literary origin of Shaka's cultural origin story and likely the inspiration behind the numerous reiterations of the story created throughout Francophone Africa. Many scholars have studied the Shaka theme (including Midiouhan, Blair, Spronk and N'Diaye) and have focused on varied aspects of the warrior-king's life. As Midiohouan notes, "Chaka a été diversement interprété selon les options idéologiques des auteurs"/"Shaka has been diversely interpreted depending on the ideological perspectives of its authors" (61). Given that Shaka was perceived as a unifier of his nation, it not surprising that, in the 1960s, African writers appropriated his story to symbolize the possibilities of post-independence nation-building within the continent of Africa. Thus, we can construct parallels between the Shaka Zulu cultural "movement" of the 1960s and literary "movement" such as the Négritude movement that also sought to use commonalities as a rallying point. In a sense, the historical Shaka embodied the black African: he fought off White invaders, found his inner strength, and rose up in power before bringing together diverse African societies into a unified political force with a centralized government. The historical Shaka struggled to unify the Nguni-speaking peoples. In "Cooperation and Conflict: The Zulu Kingdom and Natal," Leonard Thompson points out that Shaka's goal of unifying the kingdom had the effect of disrupting the region and creating conflict among its various citizens that ultimately led to a period called the *Difaqane* or "forced migration" (391). In accomplishing the task of unifying the people, Shaka created an army based on its own brand of nationalism, discipline, and strength.

Thomas Mofolo's version of the Shaka story is the primary point-of-access for French-speaking readers and it is, arguably, the most authentic of Shaka stories. If Mofolo's version does, in fact, represent the most genuine of early reworkings of the Shaka Zulu story, it is due to the author's visit to the land of the Zulu. Events of his day including the defeat of the Bambatha at the hands of the British echo in Mofolo's closing words:

> Even to this very day the Zulus, when they think how they were once a strong nation in the days of Chaka, and how other nations dreaded them so much that they could hardly swallow their food, and when they remember their kingdom which has fallen, tears well up in their eyes, and they say: "They ferment, they curdle! Even great pools dry away!" [168].

What remains clear in Mofolo's reworking of the Shaka story is paradoxical, for it reveals at once a man who is the hero of the Zulu, but also one who is inherently flawed. Shaka's own "origin story" takes us back to his childhood, a time in which he was treated poorly:

> "How will it be the day I become a man and I take over the kingship? How shall I take my revenge the day that sun of mine shall rise!" He saw all the affairs of his life, from the time of his childhood, and he found that they were ugly and frightening, and made a man shudder. [...] he decided that here on earth the only person who is wise and strong and beautiful and righteous, is he who knows how to fight with his stick; and he decided that, from that day on, he would do just as he pleased, and that, whether a person was guilty or not, he would simply kill him if he so wished, for that is the law of man [35].

In this part of Mofolo's narrative, the reader learns that Shaka makes a pact with the witch, Issanoussi in which he swears complete obedience to the witch. As his reward, he will become "a great king, one who is independent, to whom all lesser kinds own allegiance" (41). Shaka's selfishness and lack of consideration for the rights of others is underscored in this part of the story. A popular motif throughout poetic literature, like in Shakespeare's Macbeth, Mofolo's title character makes a "deal with the devil," so to speak, thus yielding his own humanity to serve his own selfish ambitions. The end result of Shaka's egocentrism is his own death at the hands of his two half-brothers. The creation of Issanoussi as a literary device fulfills the writer's goal of showcasing to what lengths the protagonist will go to ensure his own personal success. As readers, we gain further insight into Mofolo's corrupt character who ultimately sets out to murder his fiancée Noliwé and his mother Nandi.[8]

By acknowledging Peter Hoffer's assertion that "we should just embrace the paradox that we historians cannot know what we proclaim to know" (x) and that history is impossible yet necessary at the same time, we will have a greater understanding of both the historical and the literary importance of the Shaka story. This statement made, it is important to bear in mind that the line between fact and fiction here, at best, remains blurry. Any recounting of the Shaka story will contain its own cultural ideologies and its own brand of nationalism that will inevitably enter into conflict with other tellings of the story. To cite two examples, Mofolo's own recounting of the story might have been subjected to his own Christian views. It is for this reason that the moralizing that he does in recounting the story sometimes occurs with a very strong narrative hand. In contrast, in Ernst Ritter's *Shaka Zulu: The Rise of the Zulu Empire* (1955), the account that he gives on the life and personality traits of the Zulu king differ significantly from those described by Mofolo. In Ritter's recounting, he did not include the fiancée Noliwé. Furthermore, Ritter described Shaka's mother's death as the result of an illness, not as matricide. For Ritter, the death of Shaka's mother was the "trigger." This traumatic life event set into motion the wheels of his bloodthirstiness. Instead of creating primarily a literary or historical text, Ritter's version leads the reader down an alternate path in which psychosis, a mental break, or what we might even today call Post Traumatic Stress Disorder (PTSD), is the origin of Shaka's fall that leads the latter to order the deaths of his own people.

The appeal of the Shaka story outside of South Africa is evidenced in theatre, poetry, and television such as in the ten-part mini-series *Shaka Zulu* broadcast in 1986 by the South African Broadcasting Corporation. As a hero motif, Shaka contains a timeless quality. It is not by simple happenstance that some important Francophone African writers have drawn parallels between Shaka and Soundiata (Sundiata). Sundiata Keita, who ruled from approximately 1217 until 1255, was the founder of the Mali Empire and revered as a hero of the Mandinka people of West Africa in the semi-historical *Epic of Sundiata*. The *Epic of Sundiata* is known most commonly through the West African oral tradition and is transmitted from generation to generation by Mandinka *griots*. Uniting the continent of Africa nearly from stem to stern, the Sundiata and Shaka legacies embody the Africa of "times gone by." Individually, both stories represent African determination and dignity. Combinations of the Shaka story and the Sundiata story exist in several places in Francophone African writing, appearing most strikingly in the poetry of David Diop (France, Senegal) and in that of the Congolese Marie-Léontine Tsibinda. In Diop's poem, "Le nègre clochard," from his collection *Coups de Pilon* (1973), Diop described the downtrodden blacks living in Paris, we see the merging of the two African heroes:

> Je vois Soundiata l'oublié
> Et Chaka l'indomptable
> Enfouis au fond des mers avec les contes de soie et de feu [28].
> I see Sundiata, the forgotten one
> And Shaka the unshakeable
> [Both] buried at the bottom of the sea with tales of silk and fire.

In the mid–1980s, at approximately the same time that the South African Broadcasting Corporation was filming its made-for-television reworking of the Shaka story, the Congolese Marie-Léontine Tsibinda crafted her own telling of the Shaka/Sundiata story in a poem entitled "Voix des ancêtres" published in the collection entitled *Une Lèvre naissant d'une autre: Poèmes* (1984). In Tsibinda's version of the Shaka myth, the two African heroes (Shaka and Sundiata) shared a common heritage serving as a possible common point of origin in the development of an African identity:

> Entends-tu
> le galop de Chaka
> ou celui de Soundiata? [22].
>
> Do you hear
> Shaka's galloping
> or that of Sundiata?

Taking into account the manner in which each of these poets appropriates a historical figure that is not from his or her own nation or geographic region combined with the fact that each writer, in turn, contrasts the two African heroes provides some evidence to suggest that exploring Africa as a macroculture, rather than limiting ourselves to examinations of her numerous and varied microcultures, in fact, yields interesting results and suggests that there might be greater geographic unity and historical continuity in African than has been previously posited.

It is clear that the Shaka story became a cultural well from which Francophone African writers could draw to express the problems facing the nations that had recently gained independence. In *Théâtre et société en Afrique noire francophone,'* Ibrahim N'Diaye described how African theatre reflected both the sociocultural status of its writers and the evolution of societal demands at the emergence of independence (13–33). In a sense, this *is* the Shaka theme, so appropriation of the Shaka story was well within the scope of vision of post-independence era writers. Senghor's own poem (see above) published in *Éthiopiques* (1956) emphasized the Zulu warrior-king's resistance to white authority and foresaw the rise of apartheid in South Africa, while at the same time it centered on showing the importance of love for one's one people. The Malian Seydou Badian Kouyaté's play entitled *La Mort de Chaka* (1961) focused on the need to not let one's own selfish ambitions get in the way of doing when is best to build and defend a nation. Condetto Nenekhaly-Camara's drama *Amazoulou* (1970), in contrast, both portrayed Shaka's desire to serve the will of the people and the need to forge alliances with neighboring tribes in order to ensure peace for all peoples. In the preface to his own version of the Shaka story, the Senegalese Abdou Anta Kâ writes, "Il y a eu un Chaka d'un Poète-Président de la République; un Chaka d'un Ministre; il faut bien un Chaka d'un homme de la rue.... Chaka n'était-il pas en partie un homme de la rue, un bâtard...?"/"There has been a Poet-President of the Republic, a Minister's Shaka. We need a Shaka from the street.... Wasn't Shaka, in part, a man from the street, a bastard...?" (Preface). Kâ's Shaka was a different breed, a class of warrior-king who sought to right the inequalities present within his society. He was a leader so driven in his goal to look out for the good of the common people that he was ironically prepared to sacrifice his own fiancée in the process.

Modern Theatrical Adaptations of the Shaka Zulu Myth

If the versions of the Shaka story that emerged during the era of independence (1960s) focused on issues related to rebuilding African nations, the emphasis of those Shaka stories that appeared in the 1980s was visibly different. In the versions from the earlier period, Shaka was certainly a conflicted character who struggled to keep his own ambitions in check while he worked to bring peace to his people. In the more recent versions, however, there is a change in perspective. Now, it is Shaka himself who has become a subversive hero questioning the decisions of others. In his book entitled *Nationalism and African Intellectuals* (2001), Toyin Falola makes an astute observation regarding the rise of intellectuals during the period of African independence and nation-building. In his work, Falola notes that there is a misconception that when the current ruling power falls, it will be replaced with one that is more in touch with the needs of the people. He argues that what has happened throughout much of Africa over the course of the decades following the beginning of independence, in fact, is that a new elite emerged that governed the nations in much the same way that previous leaders had done. Although the people had hoped to see turmoil replaced with stability, this turmoil has often been replaced with yet another kind of turmoil. It is for this very reason that some of the Shaka stories of the 1980s—although they might change the names of the countries and their central figures—openly criticized fascist and totalitarian leaders of the Cold War era.

Set in a Spanish-speaking country of Africa led by a fascist ruler, through a mélange of Spanish, Portuguese, and African names, Baba Moustapha's play, *Le Commandant Chaka* (1983), forms a critique of neocolonialism on the African continent.[9] Mahamat Baba Moustapha (1952–1982) was a Chadian playwright who wrote almost exclusively in the French language. He died in an accident in 1983. Moustapha's plays included *Makarie aux Épines* (1973) and *Le Maître des Djinns* (1977). His posthumously-published play *Le Com-*

mandant Chaka, a denunciation of military dictatorships, is considered to be his finest work. Moustapha is the namesake of the *Association Artistique et Culturelle-Théâtre Vivant Baba Moustapha* (ACT-TVBM), a theatre company that still gives theatrical performances more than thirty years after Moustapha's death. *Le Commandant Chaka* is replete with symbols denouncing fascism such as the beer that the commander drinks (Felicidad) who is involved in the trafficking of arms: "On boit un verre de Felicidad/De Madrid jusqu'à Trinidad"/"They drink Felicidad/From Madrid to Trinidad" (1). The plot of the play centers around a dictator named General Dos Santos Bagoza who has been troubled for years by a Commandant Shaka who has been hatching a plan for a revolt and a revolution. After seeking the latter for an undetermined amount of time, we learn that Shaka is actually a man named Chico Samora, a commoner who has managed to marry into one of the nation's oldest and most notable families, the Muntu. The revolt that Shaka has planned is set into motion by his daughter, Argelia, who is an actress, during the course of one of her theatrical performances. Moustapha's use of the character Argelia as a catalyst of revolt suggests that he sees theatre as having a revolutionary component. In the end, both Argelia and Shaka are killed, but the brother of the former, José, who is an officer in the army and who was previously loyal to General Dos Santos Bagoza and the government that he represents, joins the rebellion and helps to bring about the overthrown of the dictator. As evidenced in the dialogue of two of Moustapha's minor characters, the choice of this particular beverage suggests the side of politics on which one stands:

> AGOSTINO: Bonsoir, José.
> JOSÉ: Salut, Agostino. D'où viens-tu?
> AGOSTINO: De la Présidence.
> JOSÉ: Je t'offre quelque chose à boire?
> AGOSTINO: Oui, un verre de Felicidad.
> JOSÉ: Un verre de Felicidad ?
> > Tu as toujours refusé de goûter à cette bière...
> AGOSTINO: Que veux-tu, on change [3].

> AGOSTINO: Good evening, José.
> JOSÉ: Hello, Agostino. Where are you coming from?
> AGOSTINO: From the Presidential residence.
> JOSÉ: Can I offer you something to drink?
> AGOSTINO: Yes. A glass of Felicidad.
> JOSÉ: A glass of Felicidad?
> > You have always refused to sample this beer...
> AGOSTINO: What do you want? People change.

Moustapha's play is fundamentally nationalistic and propagandistic with comic and satirical overtones. The beer to which José and Agostino refer plays an important role throughout the drama. It is present during a scene in which Bagoza celebrates the eighteenth anniversary of his rise to power. Its uninspiring jingle serves as a comic refrain throughout the play and ultimately becomes a metaphor for the type of national slogans that although they initially serve to unite the people actually end up dividing them.[10] Although the Felicidad beer and the image of "happiness" that the Spanish-language translation might suggest are catchy, the rebels mock the beer as the drink of the colonizers in the same way in which in *Notre fille ne se mariera pas* (1969), a play by Cameroonian writer Guillaume Oyônô-Mbia, *camembert* mocks French "cheese" culture that is sometimes "hard to swallow" (Moustapha 126).

In Moustapha's play, Shaka's personal struggles embody the struggles of his own people. Due to the fact that his wife came from one of the oldest families of the country and that she married him without the approval of her family, Shaka represents the class of traditional culture rooted in its inflexible idea(l)s and the popular rebellion that seeks to sweep away the customs of yesteryear. When José takes up the baton of rebellion after Shaka's fall, this event signals an opportunity to recruit the upper classes to join the revolution. Nevertheless, Shaka himself holds even greater significance for his people. He is a man of the people who has messianic qualities. As the Interior Minister states, "le Messie, ... monté sur on ne sait quel Pégase avec un glaive à la main pour punir les méchants"/"The Messiah, ... mounted on who knows what Pegasus, with a sword in his hand to punish the wicked" (58). If France has her Roland with his sword Durendal to save the fatherland from the infidels, Francophone Africa has her Shaka with sword in hand who will lead the people through revolution. Throughout the play, Moustapha stresses both Shaka's work with the people and the fact that the people support his endeavors to bring about a popular ("of the people") uprising. Strikingly, this uprising is largely brought about without any support from the social and intellectual elite that Argelia embodies. Shaka thus brings together a new form of nationalism that focuses on the democratic ideals of the people rather than those of the elite. The fact that both Shaka and Argelia die is significant in the play, for it underscores the deeply-rooted conflict of the populous and the African elite. In his own words and with obvious Fanonian overtones, he states that it is through continued struggle that true independence will be gained: "la possibilité de choisir lui-même la façon dont il entend vivre, à l'intérieur de ses frontières et avec le reste du monde"/"the possibility of choosing for itself [the people] the way in which it wants to live, within its own borders and with the rest of the world" (113–4). Because this choice must be the will of the people, the range of possibilities for the future of the country is vast. Shaka is very clear that the people must avoid dictatorships such as the one that he seeks to overthrow and that it must strive to fight off any future colonial invaders. The play ends without any formal resolution. The audience is left to think about the choices to be made.

It is clear in *Le Commandant Chaka* that the Shaka that Moustapha portrays is not the one from Mofolo's novel. The fact that his "Chaka le zoulou" (85) is multicultural reflects the effects of globalization on the African continent as they are relevant during the Cold War. Though recognizably linked to the Shaka literary tradition in the sense that the character is an outcast who seeks to unite the people in order to overthrow an oppressive government, Moustapha's Shaka is a synthesis of multiple African nations who continue to struggle to erase the effects of colonialism. Moustapha's Shaka inscribes itself into both the literary and the cultural tradition of the Zulu warrior-king who works from the position of a liminal character who is able to accomplish tasks that typical characters cannot accomplish. From the multinational to the global, the Shaka employed here embraces not only Africa but the rest of the planet, and he criticizes the international capitalism that has, in part, subjugated the local African markets to the global market. Nonetheless, as Anna Ridehalgh notes, "Moustapha does not use the modernization of the Shaka theme to introduce reflections on the present state of South Africa. This play is not about apartheid, but about revolutionary resistance to imperialism, wherever it may be found" (143). I disagree with the first part of Ridehalgh's evaluation of Moustapha's drama. How can his play not, at least in part, form a critique of the apartheid system that had been in places for decades?

Marouba Fall's theatrical adaptation of the Shaka myth entitled *Chaka ou le Roi visionnaire* (1984), in comparison, offers a more "historical" version of the Shaka theme. In a sense, Fall used historical foundations not to criticize decisions made in the past, but rather to develop a plan of action for the future. Like Moustapha's Shaka, Fall's Shaka is a liminal character. In his *Avertissement* to the play, Fall states that his Shaka is "comme exilé de lui-même pour venir habiter mon univers sensible et philosophique. Il est ainsi arraché au passé auquel il appartient et qu'il a marqué d'un sceau indélébile pour incarner de façon générale les idéaux de l'Afrique noire indépendante qui cherche à se dépasser"/"as if exiled from himself to come to live in my own universe of feeling and thinking. He has thus been ripped away from the past to which he belongs and on which he marked with an indelible seal, to incarnate, in general, the ideals of the independent black Africa that seeks to move forward" (n.pag.). The Shaka from *Chaka ou le Roi visionnaire* is a nation-builder seeking Bantu reconsolidation in order to resist the Whites that will, one day, encroach on the kingdoms governed by these diverse tribes and ultimately subdue the latter throughout South Africa. Shaka's desire to unite the tribes is met with resistance from the other Bantu leaders for they fear that unification will result in the lessening of their individual authorities. In addition, Fall suggests that the other Bantu leaders did not feel that there was any clear and present danger of the Whites invading their lands. Therefore, when his neighbors reject his idea of unification, Shaka uses force to bring his defensive plan to fruition. As the Zulu kingdom begins to grow, rumors start to circulate that Shaka has developed a greater interest in increasing the size of the kingdom and in forming defenses forces than in taking care of some of the domestic issues plaguing his people, including ever-mounting famine and poverty. Malhanga and Mapo, two relatively minor local characters, openly criticize him. His half-brother, Dingana, claims that Shaka has completed disregarded both the good and the will of the people, and that his leadership "s'embourbe de plus en plus dans la mystification du peuple et la tyrannie la plus odieuse"/"is getting increasingly more bogged down in mystification of the people and in the most odious tyranny" (67–8). In an effort to assure the good of the Zulu kingdom, Dingana, Malhanga, Mapo and others plot a coup. In the end, Fall invites the reader to empathize with and to reflect on the problems troubling Africa in the Cold War period: the struggle of classes, economic concerns, the need for democracy in a land of totalitarian government, and the need for the individual to not let his devotion to the nation cloud his judgment regarding how to truly bring about what is good for the people.

Fall's Shaka seeks to (re)build a nation and, in the process, to set into motion a revolution that will bring about real change in the lives of citizens. This clear goal notwithstanding, the reader still does not have an in-depth understanding of Shaka's character. We know that Shaka kills his fiancée Noliwé (Fall borrows this plot device from Mofolo's version of the story) and justifies his actions by claiming that she was too beautiful and that all of his previous suffering in life had made his heart unable to receive love. This particular character trait is never fully developed in Fall's version of the story, and as readers we can only understand that this particular Shaka character is more a man of sense than sensibility. Is this Shaka's tragic flaw? Compared to Mofolo's Shaka, Fall's Shaka does not have eyes full of bloodlust. Nonetheless, it is still not apparent whether Shaka has, in fact, sold his soul to the witch Issanoussi, or whether his actions are motivated by his own political ambitions. Fall's reworking of the Shaka theme fails to a certain extent because he attempts to combine the notion of nation-building with the idea of fatality, thus, leaving a number of discussions about politics and Shaka's personal agenda unexplained. For this reason, even the reason for Shaka's assassination remains unclear. Was it the result of political forces or was his assassination written in the stars?

Though scholars such as Anna Ridehalgh have claimed that some of these Shaka plays do not, in fact, discuss the context of modern South Africa, there are two French-language Shaka plays that clearly treat Shaka within this particular geographic area: Maoundoé Naïndouba's *L'Étudiant de Soweto* (1981) and Senouvo Agbota Zinsou's *On joue la comédie* (1975).[11] Chadian playwright and short-story writer Maoundoé Naïndouba's *L'Étudiant de Soweto* treats as its main theme the Soweto student uprising of 1976. Soweto is an urban area of the city of Johannesburg contiguous to the city's mining district in the south. The central character of the play, Mulubé, is a student leader who is killed during a confrontation with a white police officer following a student strike. In an interview printed in the play's appendix, Naïndouba explained the parallels that he had created between Mulubé and the historical Shaka:

> Tout jeune, je m'intéressais à l'histoire de Chaka, à la façon dont il a été trahi. En créant Mulubé, j'ai peut-être voulu inconsciemment non pas ressusciter Chaka, mais lui donner un continuateur dans l'époque moderne. Comme Chaka, Mulubé cherche passionnément la liberté. Comme lui, il sera finalement trahi et assassiné [84–5].
>
> When I was young, I was interested in the story of Shaka, in the way in which he was betrayed. In creating Mulubé, it is possible that I unconsciously wanted, not to bring Shaka back to life, but to give him a successor in the modern period. Like Shaka, Mulubé passionately seeks freedom. Like him, he is finally betrayed and assassinated.

Although during this interview Naïndouba suggests that he seeks to establish continuity in the South African historical narrative in which Mulubé can take up the yoke of struggle, this theme does not explicitly emerge from the play itself. Unlike the other Shaka plays, Naïndouba's play does not show Mulubé's impact outside of South Africa's borders. The sole attempt to expand beyond a purely South African context is Mulubé's criticism that the rest of Africa has not adequately pursued a path to abolish apartheid. Naïndouba's work was arguably too subtle in its approach of conveying this important international theme.

If Maoundoé Naïndouba's *L'Étudiant de Soweto* fails to expand its central theme beyond the Soweto student uprising of 1976, Togolese playwright Senouvo Agbota Zinsou's play entitled *On joue la comédie* reaches this important goal. As Tohonou Gbeasor explains in the Introduction to the play, *On joue la comédie* is based on a theatrical subgenre called the "concert party," a popular style of theatre that originated in Ghana and took strong roots in Togo following World War II. The play has clearly-defined stock characters and an improvised script. Zinsou's play presents its theme from the outset in a pantomime format designed to garner as much audience participation as possible. The cast of characters are paraded on stage, including a black preacher that the playwright calls "le Messie, Chaka, le Messager de la Justice qui vous libérera de l'oppression"/"the Messiah, Shaka, the Messenger of Justice who will free you from oppression." Zinsou's spontaneously-composed drama bears strong thematic affinities to Jean Genet's ritualistic (religious) play *Les Nègres* (1958). In a review of a 2007 performance of *Les Nègres* in London entitled "'The Blacks': Genet's contentious play returns," Elisa Bray notes,

> Using the framework of a play within a play, it exposes racial prejudice and stereotypes while exploring black identity. As a troupe of black actors re-enact the trial and ensuing murder of a white woman before a kangaroo court, the Queen and her entourage look on and comment. Five of the 13 black actors white up to play the establishment figures. The Queen (a whited-up woman) comes to a Command Performance, but the proceedings are far removed from any Royal Variety Show [n. pag.].

In Zinsou's play, the religious message is mocked by its actors, who, nonetheless, decide to create a play-within-a-play entitled "Chaka: Le Messie." At first glance, Shaka is a bit of a buffoon staggering across the stage. Quickly, he changes and becomes a strong leader capable of leading a group of resistance fighters represented by the other actors on stage. Shaka is ultimately betrayed by a black man seeking a reward for Shaka's capture. Imprisoned and sentenced to death, he escapes by proposing to create yet another play-within-a-play that centers on using his accomplices to liberate him. In *On joue la comédie*, the Shaka character is satirical and critical of apartheid in South Africa. Through a parody of white attitudes *vis-à-vis* the apartheid system, Zinsou lambasts the violence that this system perpetuates. At the end of the play, Shaka abandons his parodic tone to present a serious message:

> Ce soir, nous avons ouvert des prisons, brisé des chaînes, libéré des détenus, tout en riant, mais nos frères sont encore dans les prisons d'Afrique du Sud, parce qu'ils ont osé prononcer ce mot précieux: Liberté! Et vous, êtes-vous prêts ce soir à le réclamer avec nous, non seulement en paroles, mais aussi en actes? Si oui, criez avec nous! Liberté! Liberté! Criez-le dans toutes les langues, dans tous les lieux, jusqu'à la libération totale de notre peuple! Liberté! Liberté! [62].
>
> This evening, we have opened prisons, broken chains, freed prisoners, all while laughing about it, but our brothers are still in the prisons of South Africa because they dared to pronounce this precious word: Freedom! And you, are you ready this evening to proclaim it with us, not only in words, but also in actions? If so, shout it with us! Freedom! Freedom! Shout it in every language, in all places, until the complete freedom of our people! Freedom! Freedom!

Obliterating the invisible fourth wall of the theatrical space, Zinsou's play effectively encourages audience participation. If the playwright's audience, indeed, chooses to become a part of the drama to be carried out after the actual performance of the play ends, they will become the standard-bearers of transformation and change not only within South Africa, but in the rest of the continent, and perhaps, where cases of oppression exist, throughout the entire world. Zinsou and Naïndouba agree that the whole of Africa has not satisfactorily entered into this discussion.

Zinsou's presentation of the Shaka theme is arguably the most modern of the theatrical reworkings of the Mofolo story that we examine in this study. Instead of presenting a character that is full of bloodlust, Zinsou's Shaka is a truly popular ("of the people") hero. Though this Shaka also feels the need to take up the struggle to save his people, rather than triumphing over evil (White oppressors) by virtue of his mighty sword, Shaka defeats the encroachers through use of his wit. Here, Zinsou is clearly commenting on the African's supposed intellectual inferiority such as it is described in Fanon's *Peau noire, masques blancs* (1952):

> Aussi pénible que puisse être pour nous cette constatation, nous sommes obligés de la faire: pour le Noir, il n'y a qu'un destin. Et il est blanc.
> Avant d'ouvrir le procès, nous tenons à dire certaines choses. L'analyse que nous entreprenons est psychologique. Il demeure toutefois évident que pour nous la véritable désaliénation du Noir implique une prise de conscience abrupte des réalités économiques et sociales. S'il y a complexe d'infériorité, c'est à la suite d'un double processus:
> —économique d'abord;
> —par intériorisation ou, mieux, épidermisation de cette infériorité, ensuite [Introduction].
>
> As painful as this observation might be for us, we are obliged to do it: for the Black, there is only one destiny. And it is white.
> Before starting the process, we must say certain things. The analysis that we are beginning is psychological. However, it remains evident that for us the true desalination of the Black suggests an abrupt awareness of economic and social realities. If there is an inferiority complex, it is part of a dual process:
> —Firstly, economical;
> —Next, by internalization or, better, epidermization of this inferiority.

More specifically, in Zinsou's play, Shaka serves to bring about the unification of his people. Thus, in a sense, he closely resembles the historical Shaka figure, though he is living in a different space and time. The unification/unity that Shaka proposes is necessary to fight apartheid. The apartheid system is presented and critiqued throughout Zinsou's play. It appears in the factory owners who fire militant workers and replaced the latter with forced laborers in order to maximize profits. It is evidenced in the creation of separate developments (dwellings) for black individuals. In an interview of Zinsou conducted in 2002 that appears in Kahiudi Claver Mabana's book entitled *Des transpositions francophones du mythe de Chaka*, the playwright stated: "Le sujet principal de *On joue la comédie*, c'est bien sûr apartheid, mais c'est aussi toutes les formes de discrimination, d'oppression. Il suffit d'y prêter une attention pour savoir que la pièce reste très ouverte..."/"The main theme of *On joue la comédie*, is, of course, apartheid, but it is also all forms of discrimination and oppression. It suffices to pay attention to know that this play remains very open..." (178). Removing Shaka from the land of the Zulu and transporting him through time to a contemporary South Africa evidences the continuousness of resistance to oppression throughout South Africa. In addition, by simultaneously re-appropriating both a common theatrical form (the "concert party") and a popular African hero, Zinsou reinvents the Shaka theme for a modern French-speaking audience thereby giving his theatrical adaptation a wider appeal.

All of the Francophone "Shaka" plays that I have examined in this chapter contain potentially subversive overtones. This quality is entirely intentional on the part of the authors of these plays. From the mid–1970s until the mid–1980s, the liberation struggle against apartheid in South African grew increasingly stronger. In 1990, South African President Frederik Willem de Klerk began negotiations to end apartheid that resulted in the first multi-racial democratic elections in 1994 won by the African National Congress (AFC) under Nelson Mandela. Fall seems to be the only writer presented here who does not fully embrace the liberation struggle. The other writers advocate an active resistance on the part of their respective audiences. Certainly, at minimum, these Shaka plays question the role played by African governments from 1960 to the mid–1980s. Like Fanon, who argued in his book *Les damnés de la terre* (1961) that Blacks must embrace the struggle if they were ever going to overcome it, Zinsou's play contains a similar message. As French philosopher Jean-Paul Sartre wrote in the Preface to Fanon's 1961 work, "la vraie culture c'est la Révolution; cela veut dire qu'elle se forge à chaud"/"true culture is Revolution; that means that it is built in the heat of the moment" (21). For Fanon, the culture(s) that Sartre describes must also be willing to take up the struggle:

> Le combat que mène un peuple pour sa libération le conduit selon les circonstances soit à rejeter, soit à faire exploser les prétendues vérités installées dans sa conscience par l'administration civile coloniale, l'occupation militaire, l'exploitation économique. Et, seul, le combat peut réellement exorciser ces mensonges sur l'homme qui infériorisent et littéralement mutilent les plus conscients d'entre nous [*Les damnés de la terre* 288].
>
> The combat waged by a people for their liberation leads it, depending on the circumstances, either to reject or to explode the so-called truths sown in their consciousness by the colonial administration, military occupation, and economic

exploitation. And only the armed struggle can effectively exorcize these lies about man that subordinate and literally mutilate the more consciousminded among us.

When the colonial enterprise installs itself, it is naturally met with opposition. Oppositional leaders emerge who are willing to "fight fire with fire." Role models are sought. Heroes are made.

Without a doubt, through the various portrayals in the Francophone theatrical adaptations of the Shaka myth that we have examined here, despite his numerous flaws, Shaka emerges as a quintessential African hero. As readers, we continue to wonder how it came to be that Shaka, this rather questionable warrior-king of the Zulu, began to be represented in poetic form throughout the course of the 20th century. Though Zinsou's and Moustapha's Shakas might have little in common with Thomas Mofolo's original literary representation, they remain descriptions of a popular hero who devoted himself to his people. And although these modernized versions of the Shaka theme take the reader on a voyage to the four corners of the African continent, they share a common ideal of using the Shaka myth as a rallying point to bring about change to a troubled Africa. Among the great heroes of African history and legend, why has Shaka emerged as the most adapted and the most widespread? Is he, perhaps, the most universal of Africa's great heroes? In "Relire Chaka: Thomas Mofolo, ou les oublis de la mémoire française," Albert Gérard states that "il est bien plus facile de fabuler, d'idéaliser et de cristalliser à l'aise lorsqu'on n'est pas freiné par un savoir traditionnel semblable à celui qui, au Mali, au Sénégal ou en Guinée, véhicule le souvenir d'un Sundiata ou d'un Omar Tall"/"It is much easier to create fables, to idealize, and to crystalize as one wishes when one is not reined in by a body of traditional knowledge such as that which, in Mali, Senegal, or Guinea, passes on the memory of a Sundiata or an Omar Tell." (17) Therefore, as Gérard suggests, it would be easier for a Francophone African writer to connect to (and to relate) the Shaka story than, perhaps, to one of his own stories since the Zulu past is entirely removed both from the experience and from the traditions of Francophone African writers. Certain political considerations might also play a role here. To employ a local national hero when speaking out against neocolonialism would be overly subversive. The appropriation of an external national hero or figure creates an important buffer that still permits the playwright to decry neocolonialism in a more subtle fashion. The important question that remains to ask is why Francophone African writers suddenly ceased adapting the myth of Shaka.

5
Writing the Female Body in Francophone African Women's Poetry and Theatre

> African literature has to be understood as a literature by African men, for interest in Africa has, with very rare exceptions, excluded women writers. The women writers of Africa are other voices, unheard voices.
> —Lloyd. W. Brown 14

Until the publication of Jeanine Moulin's *Huit siècles de poésie féminine* (1975), women's poetry in the French tradition had been largely overlooked both in general and in poetic anthologies. If we could argue that being a poet was already a marginalizing distinction, being a women poet was even more marginalizing. Add the label of "Francophone" to the mixture, and it becomes very understandable why the list of well-known Francophone women poets remains short. In 1984, French critic Jacques Chevrier stated that it was too soon to begin a discussion of Francophone women's writing in Africa. His assertion was supported more by the fact that there was not yet a critical body of literature on the subject than by the reality that Francophone African women had not, in fact, written anything. His claim held little truth as there were numerous titles in publication at the time. Hindsight permits us to recognize that there were extenuating cultural factors at play in Chevrier's statement. As Barbara Christian notes, by failing to acknowledge the contribution of women's writing in Francophone Africa, critics such as Chevrier showed the extent to which these writers had yet to enter into the cultural and literary dialogue (225–37). Thankfully, in the 1990s, major critical works on Francophone Africa women's writing emerged including Irène Assiba d'Almeida's book entitled *Francophone African Women Writers: Destroying the Emptiness of Silence* (1994) and Odile Cazenave's *Femmes rebelles: Naissance d'un nouveau roman africain au féminin* (1996). Without question, the most up-to-date source available is Jean-Marie Volet's website at the University of Western Australia.[1] This website provides access to an updated bibliography and a rich holding of interviews of current Francophone African writers, including a host of contemporary Francophone African women writers.

To a certain extent, literary movements such as Négritude, while promoting both the revitalization and a new understanding of African cultural, historical, and literary thought, for the most part, have left women out of the dialogue. It is for this reason that the canon of poetic texts written by Francophone African women remains limited. In a discussion of Cameroonian female author Werewere Liking Gnepo outlined in his book entitled *Theatre and Drama in Francophone Africa: A Critical Introduction*, John Conteh-Morgan stated: "Whereas Francophone Africa can boast important female writers in the novelists Mariama Bâ, Aminata Sow Fall (both of Senegal) and Calixthne Béyala (Cameroon) and in the Ivoirian poets Véronique Tadjo and Yanella Boni, it has only produced one female dramatist of stature: the Cameroonian Werewere Liking" (211). How can it be that an attempt to create a list of Francophone women playwrights yields only one name? Do Francophone women not write plays?[2] In addition, generating a list of Francophone female poets is also no simple task. Does this imply, then, that women do not write either plays or poems, or is there another explanation for the lack of poetic literature *d'expression française féminine* in Francophone Africa? I would posit here that Francophone women, like women writers from other cultures, have preferred to use the novel as a space for self-expression. That is not to say, however, that these female writers do not participate in supposed poetic forms. At the dawn of the New Millennium, we continue to wonder how African women writing in French, thus, position themselves at the crossroads of these cultural, historical, and literary junctures. I offer the following response: by fashioning their own unique "feminine space" in which they can discover new paths toward explaining the feminine experience.

Before I launch into a discussion of "feminine space" and the contribution and impact of poetic literature *d'expression française féminine* in Africa, I wish to take a moment to explain one of the challenges that writing about Francophone African women presents in terms of putting together a collection of authors writing in the same literary tradition and geographic location. As I stated at the very outset of this book (Introduction), one of the main pitfalls that I had wished to avoid in writing about Francophone African authors was to marginalize these writers in the process. I share a parallel goal with regard to my writing about Francophone Africa women authors who risk a double marginalization due to both the color of their skin and their biological sex and gender distinctions. Therefore, by creating a separate chapter of this book wherein I write about the contribution of poetic literature *d'expression française féminine* in French-speaking Africa to the larger cultural and literary dialogue, I am fully aware of the inherent potential risk of marginalization to this particular group. This drawback taken into full consideration, in order to more fully understand the cultural history at play in Francophone Africa during the period in question, a discussion of these female writers is necessary. As Valérie Orlando says well in her article entitled "Writing New H(er) Stories for Francophone Women of Africa and the Caribbean":

> Female subjecthood as defined by current African and Caribbean francophone women authors is formed not only from new ideals of the mind but also from the conceptualization of a unique body politics, a corporeal reality that promotes a sexually differentiated structure of the speaking subject. Such a new speaking subject is no longer understood as an ahistorical object, but rather as a body linked to, and interwoven with, a plurality of systems: political, cultural, economic, and historical. The new feminine subject is a site of contestation where sociocultural and political struggles play themselves out, are heard by all, refashioned and retransmitted on a woman's own terms [41].

Nadia Saleh's perspective complements that of Orlando, stating that "African women's poetry is one of the least explored areas in the feminine poetic scene" (206). Francophone women poets employ a discourse that is distinctly less conflictual than their male counterparts. Thus, if we as readers and students of history are to acquire a more in-depth understanding of the concepts and ideas circulating within Francophone Africa from the arrival of independence until the modern era, our understanding would be incomplete without an examination of some of the women writers who contributed to the cultural and ideological dialogue. It is this new "body" politic generated from a Francophone African women's perspective that will offer greater illumination as it speaks toward the sexual politics at play within the region.

In her classic feminist text entitled *Sexual Politics* (2000), Kate Millet wrote that "one is forced to conclude that sexual politics, while connected to economics and other tangibles of social organization, is, like racism, or certain aspects of caste, primarily an ideology, a way of life, with influence over every other psychological and emotional facet of existence" (168). Millet underscored the role that patriarchy plays in sexual relations, particularly the dialectic created between the dominant male and the subjugated female.[3] By examining several important authors including D. H. Lawrence, Henry Miller, and Norman Mailer, she argued that these writers' perspectives were completely male-centered, marginalizing to women, and often misogynistic. By extension, any discussion of the contribution of *littérature d'expression française féminine* in Francophone Africa to the larger cultural and literary dialogue is mitigated through the filter of sexual politics that is brought about, in part, by the simple reality that the movement(s) of independence in Francophone Africa ushered in an age in which women began to occupy social spaces that had previously been "off limits." As sociologist Fatima Mernissi claims: "It is [with] access to public space, employment, and education that women's lives have undergone the most fundamental changes. Space, employment, and education seem to be the areas where the struggles which agitate society (especially the class struggle) show up in the life of women with the greatest clarity" (3). The public space is characterized by all that represents culture and politics, including the social, economic, and intellectual aspects of both the microculture and the macroculture. Women who enter into the public space become decision-makers, manipulators of the public sphere, who forge their own destinies. This agency, however, brings about a level of marginalization and exile that parallels those experienced within the larger culture. This is how Francophone African women connect thematically to the wider discourse. Before marginalization and exile can occur through any physical deracination, marginality and exile result from their biological marker: they are female.

Though the layperson might initially think that a discussion of sex and gender has no relevance within the context of poetic literature *d'expression française féminine* in Francophone Africa, a region of the world in which dialoguing about sex is generally considered taboo, such an assertion would be incorrect. Sex and gender are currently "hot topics" throughout the entire continent of Africa, where discussions of polygyny and female genital mutilation form headlines in major news markets both in Africa and, in particular, within the Western world. In the first volume of *The History of Sex*, Michel Foucault argues that the construct of "sex" itself must be understood, firstly, in terms of this power struggle that manifests itself in the form of a dialectic conceived of repression and domination. This dialectic parallels the one present within the colonizer/colonized relationship. Thus, "sex" can either be used to obtain power or it can be the power itself that it drains from its subject:

> The notion of sex brought about a fundamental reversal; it made it possible to invert the representation of the relationships of power to sexuality, causing the latter to appear, *not in its essential and positive relation to power*, but as being rooted in a specific and irreducible urgency which power tries as best it can to dominate [154, italics in original text].

Contemporary sociologists fundamentally maintain that gender refers to psychological and cultural constructs, rather than to biology. As Julia Kristeva explains, "the loss of gender norms would have the effect of proliferating gender configurations, destabilizing substantive identity, and depriving the naturalizing narratives of compulsory heterosexuality of their central protagonists: 'man' and 'woman'" (200). The implication here is that gender is a "performance" open to ruptures, deviations, and marked contrasts. Further, as Kate Millet states, "Indeed, so arbitrary is gender, that it may even be contrary to physiology" (30). Therefore, any shift in power results in a change to the *status quo* that ultimately creates controversy.

It is neither inherently incorrect nor is it "sexist" to claim that women write differently than men. Women write from a different perspective than the one from which men write. Women authors of Francophone Africa define a separate space that cultivates the feminine cultural and historical perspectives. Here in this narrative space, women find their voice—*la voix féminine*—as they both discover and invent new ways of relating their experiences. Writing in a new space is simultaneously liberating and frightening. As Francophone women writers become active in this newly-defined cultural and literary space, their writings treat a range of issues, the most significant being feminine civil and legal emancipation. African poetic literature *d'expression française féminine* speaks about the cultural mores of its writers' generations. Women's emancipation necessitates the rejection of traditional phallocratic/patriarchal roles that contained women within traditional sociocultural spaces. In contemporary Francophone African literature, women seek to push through sociocultural boundaries to forge their own self-image. As Judith Butler states, the construction of the "Not I" of the abject "establishes the boundaries of the body which are also the first contours of the subject" (181). Thus, the female's self-image is formed, in part, through the "Not I" of her existence. Gilles Deleuze refers to the physical sense of this phenomenon as "deterritorialization" that creates a "signifying rupture" thus shattering links to the past that ultimately permits female writers to discover new frontiers (12–22). But, before we create the idea that women can write about *everything* from *everywhere*, we must acknowledge some of the theoretical constraints surrounding women's foray into the world of writing resulting from perspective both of the female body and of the traditional roles that women have played within society.

The pursuit to understand the emergence of women into the public sphere is, in part, the search to understand the construction of the female identity itself. In an American context that is arguably much different than the cultural situation of modern Francophone Africa, one could argue that this pursuit began during the feminist movement of the 1960s. Referred to largely as the "second wave" of the Women's Movement in the United States, the movement addressed issues including both unofficial and official legal inequalities, sexuality, family, the workplace, and, reproductive rights. Published at the same time was the controversial New York Times bestseller, Betty Friedan's

The Feminine Mystique (1963), which "ignited the contemporary women's movement in 1963 and as a result permanently transformed the social fabric of the United States and countries around the world" and "is widely regarded as one of the most influential nonfiction books of the 20th century" ("Betty Friedan, Who Ignited Cause in 'Feminine Mystique,' Dies at 85"). Friedan hypothesized that American women were victims of a false belief system which required them to find identity and meaning in their lives through the domestic sphere, which caused them to lose their individual identity (332). Though many criticisms of Friedan's work remain, the study of the Francophone African literary female writer against the backdrop of this particular feminist context is relevant within the present study.[4]

From a theoretical perspective what is at work here in the construction of female representation and participation in the larger system is the concept known as the "male gaze." This theoretical framework was first introduced by film theorist Laura Mulvey in her essay entitled "Visual Pleasure and Narrative Cinema" (1975). In her work, Mulvey described "the concept of the gaze as a symptom of power asymmetry."[5] In principle, the male gaze "denies women agency, relegating them to the status of objects." Mulvey's perspective is unquestionably informed by the psychoanalytic theories of Jacques Lacan, and, of particular relevance here, is the notion that he called the "mirror stage." Lacan described his "mirror stage" as the moment that a child begins to recognize his own reflection in the mirror, which is a crucial moment in the development of the ego. This means that women are (re)presented as men would want to see them (449–55). Thus, women become an aberrant reflection of male desire. These same images are presented to women as something they should aspire to be if they want to attract men. In other words, in this self-perpetuating dichotomy, the female is entirely powerless, for it is mostly male writers and artists who develop the popular and acceptable representations of the idealized woman. In "Visual Pleasure and Narrative Cinema," Mulvey further underscores how, ultimately, "the meaning of women is sexual difference, the absence of the penis as visually ascertainable, the material evidence on which is based the castration complex essential for the organization of entrance to the symbolic order and the law of the father" (35). In what has become one of the most quoted passages in feminist film theory, Mulvey argues that "in a world ordered by sexual imbalance, pleasure in looking has been split between active/male and passive/female. The determining male gaze projects its fantasy onto the female figure, which is styled accordingly" (33). Furthermore, according to Julia Kristeva, Western culture's obsessive male gaze seems to have always outlined the female body antagonistically: "object of scopophilic desire and enigmatic vessel of life and death, sublime essence of beauty and abjectified, uncanny other against which the speaking subject can define himself" (9).[6] It is for this specific reason that women are more often the object of discussion rather than the speaking subject. This fact is particularly true in Francophone poetry.

In 1948, Léopold Sédar Senghor compiled his first collection of Francophone poetry entitled *Anthologie de la nouvelle poésie nègre et malgache de langue française*. In his anthology, Senghor included no female poets for two important reasons. Firstly, there were no poems penned by Francophone women that were already in print. Secondly, the French canon was overwhelmingly patriarchal, so no male writer of Senghor's period would have imagined adding women writers. The first Francophone woman author to receive recognition was Annette M'Baye d'Erneville of Senegal in *Who's Who in African Literature: Biographies, Works, Commentaries* in 1972. A decade later, the *Dictionnaire des œuvres littéraires négro-africaines de langue française; des origines à nos jours* (1983) mentioned several Francophone women authors, but it mentioned very few poets and playwrights. This reality is part and parcel of a larger lagging system that has limited women's access to education and the type of writing that education informs. As Irène Assiba d'Almeida rightly states in her book entitled *Francophone African Women Writers: Destroying the Emptiness of Silence*, "West African society *is* strongly patriarchal, and so, for contemporary women writers, writing becomes a crucial step in challenging those patriarchal restrictions" (11, italics in original text). Speech and silence have been a central theme used by Western literary critics to define African feminine writing within a postcolonial context. For authors such as the Senegalese Aminata Sow Fall, the importance of women's voices used to correct history and establish a place in it has been a central topic in their work. As d'Almeida continues to state, "Thus, writing becomes an extraordinarily liberating force because *what you cannot do or say, you can write*. Writing makes it possible to *dire l'interdit*—speak the forbidden" (11, italics in original text). The literary production of women authors from Sub-Saharan Francophone Africa, in particular, takes on myriad forms. Cultural restrictions determined how women literarily contributed to their respective societies. In Senegal and Cameroon, women were, and continue to be, the keepers and transmitters of oral traditions.[7] As *griottes*, women storytellers transmitted centuries of oral folk traditions. Thus, the truly "poetic" form that is poetry itself has always been held in the hands of women. Although modern literature (written in French by Africans) took root in Africa in the 1950s, African Francophone women did not begin to fully enter into writing until the 1960s. However, as scholars have shown elsewhere, women have been speaking subjects for ages. As women authors clearly show, when moved from the private space to the public space, women's speech becomes political, placing them on equal position with men. By writing in this public (shared) space, women simultaneously shatter the traditional feminized private space and create a new platform of agency in the public space, thereby re-contextualizing earlier representations of women.

Given that we have already referred to feminism as a structural framework for understanding women and women's writing in general, it is now appropriate to discuss the topic of feminism within a contemporary African context. As Molara Ogundipe-Leslie states, "African women have always been feminists in the sense that they have always been concerned with women's rights in society, their rights as people" (cited in *Francophone African Women Writers: Destroying the Emptiness of Silence* 12). The notion that African women have at their root an early form of feminism is evidenced by the fact that within African society, women have always played significant roles in all aspects of society. It is generally understood that African women, though they might have this historical "feminist" undergirding, have, nonetheless, remained skeptical over Western forms of feminism such as "French feminism" and "New Wave" American feminism. This skepticism could be explained, in part, because feminism itself seems to be based on cultural relativism. Cultural relativism, established as self-evident in anthropological research by Franz Boas at the beginning of the 20th century, uses as its defining principle the idea that an individual human's beliefs and activities should be understood by others in terms of that individual's own culture. Boas first articulated the idea in 1887 by stating that "...civilization is not something absolute, but ... is relative, and ... our ideas and conceptions are true only so far as our civilization goes" (589). As Chandra Talpade Mohanty states,

> The term feminism is itself questioned by many third world[8] women. Feminist movements have been challenged on the grounds of cultural imperialism, and of shortsightedness in defining the meaning of gender in terms of middle-class, white experiences, and in terms of internal racism, classism, and homophobia. All of these factors, as well the falsely homogeneous representation of the movement by the media, have led to a very real suspicion of "feminism" as productive ground for struggle [7].

Thus, the feminist perspective to which Mohanty refers suggests a framework from the Western world that is separated culturally from that of Africa. Resultantly, it would be much more appropriate to discuss multiple feminisms or, at least, different forms of feminism that would incorporate some of the significant elements of the African feminine experience such as race or class. When examined from a Western perspective, applying external feminisms to the continent is not without its problems, for Western feminism has difficulty dealing with certain traditional African cultural practices, the most obvious of which is, arguably, polygamy, that in a somewhat romanticized view, Buchi Emecheta calls "liberating to the woman" (178).

Without question, among the nations of Francophone Africa, Senegal has taken the lead in creating an environment in which African feminism can grow. The Senegalese feminist agenda promotes feminism at all levels. This perspective forms a striking contrast to the high-brow feminists of the United States and France, two countries that have led the way in helping women to create new pathways toward writing their own destinies in a phallocentric world. The brand of feminism imagined in Senegal does not distinguish between social classes or economic levels due to the fact that phallocentrism itself discriminates against all women despite their socioeconomic levels. Feminism in Senegal is brought about through self-education that centers on the belief that women are not just "people," but they also have the right to contribute their voices to the decision-making processes throughout the country. Therefore, one cannot deny the fact that feminism within Senegal is, in a sense, political in nature as it ties women to the cultural, economic, political, and social mechanisms of their country. For this reason, Senegalese women take part in the political struggle, which has the positive effect of not only giving them agency within their own communities and municipalities, but it also opens them up to thinking about how they might contribute to ending the plight of oppressed women in other parts of the African continent. This feminism, interestingly, though determined by the Senegalese women themselves, operates in a nation in which Islam is a significant determinant. Its success suggests that Senegalese women have found inventive ways to work within this traditional religious system. As Irène d'Almeida states, "feminism has to be recast in an African mold to fit the contours of issues faced by women on the African continent and within specific countries" (19). It is for this reason that although external feminist influences are certainly possible, an organic feminism seems to fit Francophone Africa best.

Along with this notion of an organic feminism is the idea that "all words are invented." In her song-novel entitled *Elle sera de jaspe et de corail* (1983), the Cameroonian writer Werewere Liking Gnepo, who has recently become a significant figure in the *théâtre-rituel* in Côte d'Ivoire, invented the word *misovire* to represent the "post-gender being" that recounts her story:

> Quand l'homme ne jouera plus au porc
> Quand la femme ne sera plus chienne en chaleur
> Quand je ne serai plus misovire et qu'il n'y aura
> plus de misogynes.... [153].
>
> When a man will no longer be a pig
> When a woman will no longer be a bitch in heat

When I will no longer be a misovire and when there will
no longer be any misogynists....

Like Monique Wittig's lexical coining of the term "Guérillères" in the 1969 novel entitled *Les Guérillères*, Liking Gnepo forges a term that gives women both agency and voice. Though not necessarily intended to sow enmity between man and woman, her new term certainly forces one to think about gender constructions and relationships. A "post-gender being" is, in a sense, genderless. Although the removal of biological (sex) determination is far from our discussion here, removal of gender as it is socially constructed signifies an attempt to "repartir à zero." The restart creates equality between genders that is necessary for a full appreciation of the other.

We can only hypothesize why Francophone African women's writing had been suppressed for many years. Was the quality of their writings not "up to par" with that their male counterparts? In 1988, Arlette Chemain suggested that the answer to this particular question was "No." In reference to the overall quality of Francophone African women's writing, she claimed that it was "en retrait par rapport à la littérature masculine"/"in decline in comparison to masculine literature" (60). By 1992, the publication of her article entitled "Emergence d'une littérature féminine de langue française en Afrique subsaharienne" reflected a change in her perspective (143–58), and by 2012, Chemain had made a complete "180" in her article entitled "L'image de la femme en ses métamorphoses: Écritures subsahariennes de langue française (1950–2010)." In the early 1990s, as Francophone Studies itself began to gain momentum, scholars started to recognize the literary contributions of Francophone African women.[9] I do not, however, wish to imply that the novels, plays, short stories, and poems of these women were—at that time or since—readily accepted into the French literary canon. Within the French literary tradition, written works by men has always been the industry standard. The French literary canon was formed by men. It is comprised almost exclusively of men's writings. Francophone African women are always writing "against the stream." Whether in the French, American, or British traditions, the notion of a literary canon remains questionable. World-renounced American Africanist and Harvard professor Henry Louis Gates, Jr. offers the following statement on the notion of canon formation: "We hear the voice of the critic who speaks the word 'canon' to invoke a closed set of texts written mostly by men who are Western and white; a most useful organizing concept for pedagogy becomes another mechanism for political control" (2). Using Gates' statement as a cultural "litmus test," we observe that the Francophone African female writer is noticeably neither male, Western, nor white. These are three qualities that are completely inalienable to her. It is no surprise then that French *lycéens* would be more likely to be found reading a copy of Jean-Paul Sartre's play *Huis Clos* (1944) than the Congolese woman writer Werewere Liking Gnepo's *Les mains veulent dire* (1981). The real question is whether or not Francophone African women writers will ever fully integrate into the French canon or if these writers will form a secondary and excluded canon whose literary works will be read by a small group who share the same inalienable qualities as these authors, thus continuing to "preach to the choir" so to speak. This is the type of exclusion against which Francophone African women writers have continually fought.

Within the "tradition" of poetic literature *d'expression française féminine* in Africa, there are a range of texts of varying forms, functions, styles, and aesthetic levels. Taking into account the fact that the primary goal of this book is to provide a cultural and historic framework for the poetic literature emanating from this region, there will be no attempt here to create any sort of hierarchy of literary texts. While I think that we would agree that certain poetic works produced in Africa are arguably of higher literary quality than are others, my intention here is to remove any sort of value judgments from the discussion. To this end, I endeavor to situate any texts *d'expression française féminine* within a relevant African context by applying Mineke Schipper's perspective in which the work is of "a more open critic who is not out to accept or reject a work on the basis of his own current set of values, but who considers literary texts against the backdrop of the contexts where they originated" (52). There is no one specific theoretical framework that facilitates such as goal. In fact, there are numerous theories of literary criticism that focus too closely on the structural components of a literary work to fully extract the cultural or historical contexts from which these texts originated. Russian Formalism is too concerned with "producing a theory of literature concerned with the writer's *technical* prowess and *craft* skill" (*Reader's Guide to Contemporary Literary Theory* 30, italics in original text) to be of use in this study. Reader-oriented theories are overly self-reflective for any objective assessment of these particular literary works. Although language certainly plays an important role as a vehicle for delivering the message of these writings, structuralist theories do not have the intrinsic malleability necessary to bring about an understanding of the relevant cultural underpinnings. Taking into account the inalienable qualities of Francophone African women writers to which I have already referred, the theories of literary criticism that emerge as the most useful to use to understand the cultural and historical backdrop of this literature are Feminist theories and Postcolonial theory.

Throughout its history, feminism has worked to disturb the balance of patriarchal cultural structures. "Women writers and women readers have always had to work 'against the grain'" (*Reader's Guide* 115). The notion of women embracing a literary theory at all is inherently problematic, for literary theories themselves conform to the phallocentric standard. Mary Eagleton correctly states that there has always been "a suspicion of theory ... throughout feminism because of its tendency to reinforce the hierarchical binary opposition between an 'impersonal,' 'disinterested,' 'objective,' 'public,' 'male' *theory*, and a 'personal,' 'subjective,' 'private,' 'female' *experience*" (Introduction, italics in original text). This suspicion has logical foundations. Furthermore, a "one-size-fits-all-races-socioeconomic classes-and-political ideologies" has yet to appear. From First Wave feminist criticism mediated through Virginia Woolf and Simone de Beauvoir to the Second-Wave in the work of Betty Friedan, Kate Millett, Elaine Showalter (gynocriticism), the French feminists, Julia Kristeva, Hélène Cixous, and Luce Irigaray that "emphasizes not the gender of the writer ('female') but the 'writing-effect' of the text ('feminine')—hence, l'écriture feminine[10]," (*Reader's Guide* 122), none of these variants is fully applicable within the context of African poetic literature *d'expression française féminine*.

One contextual component that we must also consider is the African woman writer's decision to express herself in the French language (see Chapter 2), which in "The Other's Others: 'Francophone' Women and Writing," Christine Makward and Odile Cazenave suggest that for these women writers was not an issue:

> The French language is neither an object of reverence nor a source of existential anxiety. It has not yet reached the luxurious status of a personal enemy in need of masterful deconstruction, but rather functions as an unfamiliar road to new forms of power. Here, the primary value of language in literary usage is that of an instrument to promote change or reveal its possibility [193].

I disagree with Makward's and Cazenave's interpretation. The argument that the French language is an uncomplicated issue for African women writers neglects the colonial legacy of which these authors are heirs. The fact that they are writing in a language other than the one that they grew up speaking reveals a dual identity on the part of these writers. As Fatoumata Diahara Traoré explains well, "This results inevitably in a Eurocentric way of interpreting their [...] world" (18). Perhaps, by denying the hegemonic function of the French language within Francophone Africa, these writers are rejecting how their male counterparts have bought into this notion. I do not think, however, that Francophone African writers who choose to use French as a linguistic vehicle for self-expression are oblivious to the role that that language plays. Nicki Hitchcott's "Entretien avec Tanella Boni" offers a perspective that shatters Makward's and Cazenave's interpretation:

5. Writing the Female Body in Poetry and Theatre

> Le problème de la langue, c'est un problème très important, et très souvent d'ailleurs on en discute. C'est d'autant plus important qu'il y en a a certains qui disent, "Moi, je ne peux pas continuer à écrire en français parce que c'est de l'aliénation." Bon, ce n'est pas ma langue. J'écris en français parce que je suis bien obligée. Peut-être que je l'utilise comme véhicule, parce que je ne peux pas faire autrement, parce que si je fais autrement, je n'aurai pas de lecteurs, ou bien je ne vais pas être lue que par mon village [6–7].
>
> The problem with the language is a very important one, and very often we discuss it elsewhere. It is of such importance that some say, "I cannot continue to write in French because it is alienating." Ok, it is not my language. I write in French because I have to. Perhaps I use it as a means of communication because I cannot do otherwise, because if I did do otherwise, I would have no readers, or I am only going to be read by people in my village.

Boni's response to her interviewer's question certainly reveals the "double-edged sword" of using the French language as a means of self-expression. But, instead of yielding to the controlling power of the French language, Boni proposes that African women writers find a way to make the language serve their own purposes. If African women writers are not naturally a part of the mainstream, then it stands to reason that they could, in fact, use the French language in a subversive way. And although the novel remains the most common genre for communicating female identity, there are still several prominent female writers of poetry and drama. At the dawn of the New Millennium, it is the time to reinvigorate the study of African women writers *d'expression française*.

If we are going to better situate female identity and subjectivity within the context of African women writers who use the French language as a vehicle for self-expression, we need a critical approach that blends the critical theories most appropriate to the study of this particular marginalized group. Sex, gender, and race all come to bear here. Any study of feminine writing—no matter the geographic location—that does not take into account the cultural and historical contexts of its production is not ideologically acceptable. The writer is undeniably a product of her cultural and historical *milieux*. As Roland Barthes states well in "The Death of the Author":

> Once the Author is removed, the claim to decipher a text becomes quite futile. To give a text an Author is to impose a limit on that text, to furnish it with a final signified, to close the writing. Such a conception suits criticism very well, the latter then allotting itself the important task of discovering the Author (or its hypostases: society, history, psyche, liberty) beneath the work: when the Author has been found, the text is "explained"-victory to the critic [147].

Within the context of Francophone Africa, it is important to keep the reading "open." To keep the reading "open" encourages dialogue. Dialogue promotes ideas. Ideas engender actions. In addition, inasmuch as we cannot ignore the cultural and historical *milieux* in which these literary works were produced, we also cannot ignore the sex of the authors of these texts. Barbara Harlow affirms this assertion stating that women's literature, in general, is the product of "specific material historical and intellectual processes within specific societies" (182). In the case of African women's writing, the dichotomy of cultural context and literary text is evident. African women's writing in French, in particular, defines feminine subjectivity in a specific way. In his article entitled "Oralité, écriture et le problème de l'identité culturelle en Afrique," Jean Derive outlines four criteria that much be taken into account when discussing African feminine cultural identity: socio-political; linguistic; geographic; and racial/ethnic (5-6). We should certainly add a fifth criterion to Derive's list: sex/gender. In many situations, this specific inalienable quality will become an obstacle to overcome. We should also note here that the concept of the "femme africaine" is a modern one to which many African women do not fully self-identify: "Le concept de la femme africaine est une création moderne, née de circonstances historiques. Peu de femmes, à la campagne, se définissent comme africaines (elle se pensent au niveau du village, de l'ethnie"/"The concept of the African women is a modern creation born from historical circumstances. Few women, in the countryside, define themselves as African (they think of themselves on the level of their village or at the ethnic level" (18). Given that the Council of Berlin of 1884-1885 divided and redistributed the continent of Africa without regard for the numerous ethnic groups contained within its borders combined with the fact that Africa as a continent is vast and diverse from Egypt to South Africa to Burkina Faso to Morocco, identifying one's self with the stereotypical "African" as created by White colonizers is impossible. However, instead of explicitly rejecting the label of *femme africaine*, both female writers and scholars who evaluate their works use it to explore the study of women's writing in French-speaking Africa.

If "African" women do not easily assimilate this particular cultural labeling, the African continent as a whole does not easily integrate "White" feminism either. In the United States and in France, there seems to be little difficulty for black women either to assume the feminist label or to write about it. Although it relates primarily to an American context, Joy James' and Tracy Sharpley-Whiting's edited collection entitled *The Black Feminist Reader* (2000) contains new feminist theories (or anti-theories) that could be applicable to the context of French-speaking Africa (11-4).[11] Among these theories are those that encourage women to use literature as a way to promote awareness of women's issues and to seek solidarity among each other regardless of race or ethnicity. One of the central questions that ultimately emerges is whether or not women are actually that preoccupied with notions of identity in the first place or if this is largely a subject that men seem to reflect more greatly on than their female counterparts. Furthermore, since the identity question that men seem to be asking themselves centers primarily on race/ethnicity rather than on sex/gender, it seems reasonable to assume that Francophone African women are initially preoccupied with notions of sex/gender before considering ideas on race/ethnicity identity. Even if literature *d'expression française féminine* in Africa is not explicit in its description of feminine identity within the wider cultural contexts, it is debatably implicit in the works of many contemporary women writers including those of Mariama Bâ, Ken Bugul, Aminata Sow Fall, and Werewere Liking Gnepo. Whether implicit or explicit in their descriptions of feminine identity, it is clear that Francophone women's voices *are* being heard.

Though the novel continues to be the most common genre adopted by Francophone women writers in Africa, there are a number of poetesses, most notably Annette MBaye d'Erneville (Senegal) who has published several collections including *Poèmes africains* (1965), *Kaddu* (1966), *Chansons pour Lady* (1976), and more recently, *Motte de terre et motte de beurre* (2003), and *Picc l'Oiseau et Lëpp-Lëpp le papillon* (2003). She is unquestionably the most underappreciated of the Francophone poetesses. Other female poets writing in Senegal include Kine Kirima Fall, who authored *Chants de la rivière fraîche* (1976) and Ndeye Coumba Mbengue Diakhaté, who wrote *Filles du soleil* (1980). More recently, the Cameroonian writers Félicité Mbezele and Élisabeth Éwombè Moundo, and the Beninian author Thécla Midiohouan have brought their feminine perspectives to Paul Dakeyo's anthology of poetry entitled *Monsieur Mandela* assembled to praise the former President of South Africa as a true "prince of peace." Mbezele has also published four theatre plays. Her prose poem entitled "Afrique: Ma mère" forms an interesting juxtaposition to Senghor's poem, "La femme noire." More than simply celebrating Mandela for his redemptive qualities, her poem highlights her fears about how the rest of the world views Africa: "J'ai tellement souffert que je ne souffre plus de savoir que l'on pense que l'Afrique, toi ma mère, n'enlève que des sous-hommes"/"I have suffered so much and I suffer more knowing that they think that Africa, oh my mother, only brings up sub-humans" (172). Her verses describe the colonial experience and the dream she has that one day "nous danserons et chanterons comme au bon vieux temps"/"we will sing and dance like in the good old days" (172). In her epistolary poem entitled "L'ange déchu"/"The Fallen Angel," fellow countrywoman Élisabeth Éwombè Moundo addresses her thoughts to Nelson Mandela's former wife, Winnie. In her words, Moundo portrays Winnie as "la Mère de la Nation Sud Africaine"/"The Mother of the South African Nation" (209) whose life also served to further the cause of freedom both within South Africa and abroad. Her description of Winnie could serve as a lesson for all with regard to the important role that women have played in obtaining freedom: "Quel que soit le verdict de l'Histoire, tu resteras, pour beaucoup d'entre nous, celle qui brava la loi des hommes pour que la flamme du combat ne s'éteigne pas, l'icône de la lutte anti-apartheid"/"No matter what the verdict of History might be, for many us, you will remain the one who braved the law of men so that the flame of combat might never go out. The icon of the anti–Apartheid struggle" (210). Finally, in Thécla Midiohouan's "Négritie," in a refrain that is repeated throughout the poem, the Beninian writer describes Africans as "la race des Sorciers"/"the race of Witches." Her description implies a group of people who discovered the world, decrypted it, and who can (together) reinvent it: "Nous sommes la race des Sorciers. Nous referons le monde!"/"We are the race of Witches. We will remake the world!" (192). Together, poems such as these not only recognize the contribution of individuals such as Nelson and Winnie Mandela to the "Story of Africa," but they also pose solutions as to how people throughout Africa might work together to rebuild the continent from their own perspectives.

The lion's share of poetic creation *d'expression féminine* comes from Middle Africa that includes countries such as Chad, Cameroon, Democratic Republic of the Congo, the Central African Republic, and South Sudan. Among the most well-known poetesses from this region include Clémentine-Madiya Nzuji (Democratic Republic of the Congo) and Marie-Léontine Tsibinda (Congo). Tsibinda has published several collections of poetry including *Poèmes de la terre* (1980), *Une lèvre naissant d'une autre* (1984), and *Demain, un autre jour* (1987). Though their works often blur the boundaries between the novel and poetry, Véronique Tadjo (Côte d'Ivoire) and Werewere Liking Gnepo (Cameroon) have also published well-received collections of poetry. Tadjo's *Latérite* (1983) won the *Prix Littéraire de l'ACCT* in 1983. Werewere Liking Gnepo's collection of poetry entitled *On ne raisonne pas avec le venin* appeared in 1977. Werewere Liking Gnepo is best known as a playwright and is, without question, the most important woman writer in Francophone African theatre. Her plays include *La Queue du diable* (1979) and *La Puissance de Um* (1979) with an Introduction and scene suggestions by Marie-José Hourantier, *Un Touareg s'est marié à une Pygmée* (1992), and two unedited plays, *La Veuve dilemme* (1994), and *Le Parler-Chanter* (2003). Werewere Liking Gnepo's most celebrated play, *Les mains veulent dire* (1987), not only imitates the ritual plays of its generation "but actually aspires to the condition of that ritual in its form, structure, performance style, and function" (*New Francophone and Caribbean Theatres* 10).[12] In her theatre, Liking Gnepo sought to push the marginalized elements of traditional Senegalese theatre to the center of theatrical production to such an extent that these elements would become the core of new Cameroonian theatre. In addition, beyond moving from a structural transformation of the theatre, Liking Gnepo attempted to convey the sociopolitical ethos of the age that would ultimately unleash a cultural and psychological transfiguration. If Jean Genet's theatre was a "grande purgation" of the soul in order to rid the self of the demons that torment inside the individual, Liking Gnepo's theatre functioned not only to restore the soul, but also to restore the community as a whole.[13] As Marie-José Hourantier who once collaborated with Liking Gnepo stated:

> *Les mains veulent dire* seeks to initiate all the participants by making them discover the why and how of the social ill.... By tracking down the malady, describing it, denouncing it ... the Patient takes her first steps toward lucidity and, to the rhythms of southing incantations, can dance her way to good health [85].

Thus, the focus on the spiritual dimensions of the human experience emerge as the focus that overrides the more stereotypical post-independence era focus on social or political action. In a sense, this change indicates a change of perspective. Theatre that focuses on social or political action suggests that to remove these external influences from the life of the individual will transform the individual. Theatre that centers on the spiritual dimensions of the human experience, in contrast, indicates that until the spirit is whole again, even the departure of the former oppressor will be of little consequence.

In recent years, Werewere Liking Gnepo's writings have helped Francophone women writers to "turn a corner." Although women's writing is still a long way from dethroning masculine writing, it has made significant gains. These gains have come about, in part, by an emerging African feminism that has been sprouting up throughout French-speaking Africa. By "writing themselves into being" (Dingomé 231), Francophone women writers are creating a black feminist discourse that is gaining momentum. As a suffragette, Werewere Liking Gnepo's poetic literature—especially her theatre plays—raise a sword against the phallocentric system that dictates women's lives in society. Whether in *La Queue du diable* or *La Puissance de Um*, her words reject gender-based double standards and incessant patrilinealism that are both characteristic of her society. The heroine of *La Puissance de Um* is treated poorly, for her name Ngond Libii means "daughter of a slave," thus establishing the correspondence of womanhood and servitude. Liking Gnepo's theatre that combines fiction and reality and transports the spectator (or reader) through time suggests that "woman" holds little value no matter what the realm or time reference considered. In addition, in this particular play, following the death of her husband, Ngond Libii becomes the prime suspect. Here, Liking Gnepo states very strongly the traditional notion that women cannot be trusted. In a sense, plays like *La Puissance de Um* serve to deconstruct the "self" in such a way that the woman is no longer self-indulgent of the victimization that she has suffered, but rather she casts away her anti-male anger in an effort to create a discourse that permits her to lead women through a recovery of selfhood. The "African feminism" that Werewere Liking Gnepo fashions is not rabid like the French Feminists. It does not consist of "bra burning" like popularizations of the American Feminists encouraged. It involves asking questions about gender relations in Francophone Africa that might help women acquire real cultural and literary equality such as: Why is it that modern Cameroonian (African) women who enjoy a certain amount of intellectual and economic power still cannot shake the yoke of paternalism? Are women not also, at least in part, responsible for their own fate? Thus, the modern African woman is placed in striking contrast with the traditional African woman. In spite of Liking Gnepo's obvious bias toward traditional woman, the authoress still spills plenty of ink discussing modern woman's move toward liberation. In *Les mains veulent dire*, for example, she discusses a female protagonist who is pushed to the very limits of her being leading to a loss of sanity and a drive toward suicide. Jeanne Dingomé writes that "it is through the strategic use of ritual involving the confrontation of self with self whenever a crisis arises that the Liking woman, even without arms, is seen as revolutionary" (239). If Edward Said's postcolonial theory sows the seed of identity crisis, Liking Gnepo's theory sows the seed of self-discovery and survival.

Despite Werewere Liking Gnepo's important contribution to the theatre genre, in particular, there remain relatively few women playwrights in Francophone Africa. In his groundbreaking book entitled *Theatre and Drama in Francophone Africa* (1994), in addition to Werewere Liking Gnepo, scholar John Conteh-Morgan only noted two other well-known women playwrights: Joséphine Kama-Bongo (Gabon), who published the play, *Obadi* in 1974, and Rabiatou Njoya (Gabon) who is the author of several plays including *Ange noir ange blanc* (1968), *La dernière aimée* (1974), and *Raison de Royaume* suivi de *Haute trahison* (1990).[14] Like Werewere Liking Gnepo, Njoya also directs a theatre troupe based in Yaoundé, Carmeroon, where she has published all of her theatre plays. There are several reasons why women in Francophone Africa have not entered into theatre writing in any large numbers. Firstly, as Congolese author and arguably its most famous playwright Sony La'bou Tansi has stated: "en Afrique, une femme qui fait du théâtre est immédiatement considérée comme suspecte"/"A women who participates in theatre is immediately seen as suspicious" (cited in Jaccard 161). Secondly, there is so little financial theatrical infrastructure in much of French-speaking Africa, which makes it nearly impossible for women to succeed.[15] Given the fact that poems and plays have limited readership and that publishers in Francophone Africa, in particular, do not consider poetry and drama to be solid financial investments, African women writers have tended to choose a genre in which their words will be read and their voices will be heard: the novel.[16] If we build on the notion that poetry and drama emerged from the oral tradition, then one could reasonably argue that the Francophone women writers in Africa, at minimum, could find an outlet for their poetic voices as a *griottes*, the African traditional storytellers.

Although scholars have claimed that women in French-speaking Africa have historically been kept silent, in reality, women have always played an important part in the preservation of their communities' oral traditions. Throughout French-speaking Africa, women have always lent their voices to song. Popular singers such as Angélique Kidjo from Bénin participate in the singing of lullabies that throughout Africa are typically defined as a "women's genre." Within Senegal, there are different types of songs that women sing depending on the nature of the occasion for which the song is to be performed. The *woyi njam* is performed at tattooing ceremonies; *woyi tëddëte* focus on love and sexuality and are usually performed during wedding ceremonies; *woyi céét* are performed during the bridal recession (Larrier 14–5). Each of these has an important ritual value. In Mali, in contrast, Wassoulou music is dominated by women singers and is sung throughout the country. Important singers include Sali Sidibé and Oumou Sangaré. Like their Senegalese counterparts, Malian female singers typically sing about important "rites of passage" such as marriage ceremonies, but they also treat themes that are important within contemporary society including poverty and disease (15). In view of the fact that song is poetry, creating a line separating the two remains impossible. Female poets also produce songs within French-speaking Africa. Research presented by A. Raphaël Ndiaye in *La notion de parole chez les Sereer, Sénégal* (1981) in which he suggests that Senegalese women poets composed poems for baptisms or marriages that eventually become songs supports this assertion. Thomas Hale's extensive work on *griottes* in Niger shows that women have played an important role in the ceremonial lives of that particular nation's people.[17] There is further evidence to support African women's contribution to poetry within Cameroon, specifically. In "Poésie orale traditionnelle et expression du quotidien en Afrique noire," Emmanuel Matateyou discusses a variety of "coming of age" themes present in the work created by Bamoun women poets (70). Women's voices are important in the transmission of knowledge, especially when that information that relates specifically to the education of girls.

Within Africa, throughout literature, women are celebrated and made the personification of the continent itself ("Mother Africa"). Léopold Sédar Senghor's poem "Femme noire" published in *Chants d'ombre* presents a clear example of the role of mother as the protector of the land: "J'ai grandi à ton ombre, la douceur de tes mains bandait mes yeux"/"I grew up in your shadow, the softness of your hands shielded my eyes" (270). Like the mothers found in oral literature, the mother described in Senghor's poem is protective. Here, Senghor associated the body of his *mère* (mother) with Africa (*la terre*). He also idealizes the role of mother. The Senegalese poet is not the only male poet to celebrate Africa through descriptions of women. David Diop, for example, makes connections between his own mother and Africa in "À ma mere." Unfortunately, Francophone African male poets tend to gloss over the topics that are important to African women such as pregnancy and childbirth. The wives and mothers that these male writers describe—such as in Ousmane Sembène's *Les bouts de bois de Dieu* (1960)—are often represented as one of two extremes: either passive and silent (170–1) or as a prostitute (190). Young women who are educated in the French school and who find themselves alienated from their communities are depicted similarly (like prostitutes). It is clear that when African male writers create female characters, they rarely make women the protagonists. When women do, in fact, play important roles, they are often ultimately victims of a heinous act. Francophone women in Africa write against the backdrop of silence and a lack of agency. They must use writing as a peaceful weapon.

Representations of African Women in Literature and Beyond

African women have always been the objects of others' stories. The exoticization of the black female body has a long history. Among the earliest European representations of African exoticism is an Andreas Schlüter painting titled "Africa" (circa 1700) depicting a lion hovering over a woman who is naked above the waist. The most obvious interpretation is that African women are submissive. Within the French literary tradition, writers such as Charles Baudelaire found their works inspired by women of African ancestry. Baudelaire's muse, Jeanne Duval, a Haitian-born actress and dancer of mixed French and black–African ancestry, inspired several of his poems including "Le balcon," "Parfum exotique," and "La chevelure." "La chevelure," which appeared in his collection of poetry *Les Fleurs du mal*

(1861) is among the most well-known of French poems that exoticize black women:

> Ô toison, moutonnant jusque sur l'encolure!
> Ô boucles! Ô parfum chargé de nonchaloir!
> Extase! Pour peupler ce soir l'alcôve obscure
> Des souvenirs dormant dans cette chevelure,
> Je la veux agiter dans l'air comme un mouchoir!
> La langoureuse Asie et la brûlante Afrique,
> Tout un monde lointain, absent, presque défunt,
> Vit dans tes profondeurs, forêt aromatique!
> Comme d'autres esprits voguent sur la musique,
> Le mien, ô mon amour! nage sur ton parfum [*Œuvres complètes* 56].
>
> O fleecy hair, falling in curls to the shoulders!
> O black locks! O perfume laden with nonchalance!
> Ecstasy! To people the dark alcove tonight
> With memories sleeping in that thick head of hair.
> I would like to shake it in the air like a scarf!
> Languorous Asia and sweltering Africa,
> A whole far-away world, absent, almost defunct,
> Dwells in your depths, aromatic forest!
> While other spirits glide on the wings of music,
> Mine, O my love! floats upon your perfume.

The description of the woman's hair is clearly exoticized and even eroticized. Its texture, its color, and its scent are romanticized. There is even a hint of animalization (bestialization) in the poet's choice of words: "toison" clearly referring to a sheep's fleece; "moutonnant" from the noun "sheep," which is being used here as a verb; "encolure," which although it can mean "neck," certainly suggests the French equivalent of the English word "withers." The title itself, "La chevelure," suggests that the woman has a tail. Thus, Baudelaire has created a menagerie in which the exoticized woman is "put on display" for her male viewers. As Édouard Glissant has stated so well in *Le discours antillais*, we must form a type of poetry that promotes the development of subjects instead of objects: "pour cela même qu'on nous a trop longtemps 'objectivés' ou plutôt 'objectés'"/"if only because we have been for too long 'objectified' or rather 'objected to'" (149).

There is perhaps no depiction of black exoticism in the French-speaking world that is more famous than the menagerie that was created of American singer-dancer Josephine Baker (1906–1975). During the 1920s and 1930s, Baker's body was "put on display" throughout Europe in front of hordes of spectators. Born Freda Josephine McDonald, the St. Louis, Missouri-born star packed the clubs with her own brand of performance art consisting of dancing bare-breasted while wearing a banana skirt with an African landscape draped in the background. Known as the "Vénus d'Ébène" ("Black Venus"), Baker pleased the crowds with her exotic dance show:

> When the rage was in New York of colored people
> Monsieur Siegfied of Ziegfied Follies said its getting darker and darker on old Broadway.
> Since the La Revue Nagri came to Gai Paree Ill say its getting darker and darker in Paris.
> In a little while it shall be so dark untill one shall light a match then light another to see if the first is lit or not.
> As the old saying is I may be a dark horse but you will never be a black mare.[18]

Baker's image as a primitive African was also perpetuated in her film appearances such as in the films *Zouzou* (1934) and *Princess Tam Tam* (1935). The male European voyeuristic gaze (see Mulvey) inscribed its own sexual fantasies onto Baker's nude body, as shown in Jean-Claude Baker's biography of the singer-dancer entitled *Josephine Baker: The Hungry Heart*: "'Quel cul elle a!' What an ass! Excuse the expression, but that is the cry that greeted Josephine as she exploded onstage in 'La Danse de Sauvage.' Sixty years later, her friend and sometimes lover, Maurice Bataille, would say to me, 'Ah! Ce cul ... it gave all of Paris a hard-on.'" (3).

As Baker's adoptive son Jean-Claude explains more fully in his book, female nudity was used to lure audiences to a performance called "La Revue nègre," a dance review that began in 1925 in Paris at the newly-restored Théâtre des Champs-Elysées.[19] This review played on the spectators' desires to see an exotized female body close-up like in a "peepshow." Jean-Claude Baker elaborates, "We need tits. These French people, with their fantasies of black girls, we must give them 'des nichons'" (111). In the same way in which Baudelaire had blended the human and the animal in "La chevelure," in the Paris of the 1920s and 1930s, Josephine Baker's persona fused animality and sexuality. Her dancing imbued animal energy, jungle beats, and African mysticism, and created parallels between dance and sexual promiscuity. In "Danses Nègres" (*L'Art Vivant*, February 1925), André Levinson described Baker's performance:

> Certaines poses de Miss Baker, les reins incurvés, la croupe saillante, les bras entrelacés et élevés en un simulacre phallique, ... boquent tous les prestiges de la haute statuaire nègre.... Ce n'est plus la "Dancing-Girl" cocasse que nous croyons voir: C'est la "Vénus Noire" qui hanta Baudelaire [115–6].
>
> Some of Miss Baker's poses, back arched, haunches protruding, arms entwined and uplifted in a phallic symbol, had the compelling potency of the finest examples of Negro sculpture.... It was no longer a grotesque "dancing girl" that stood before them, but the "Black Venus" that haunted Baudelaire.

In the many photographs, posters, and sketches of Baker, she is often depicted in an animalized form, crouching down with her lips protruding and her posterior in the air. Critics describe Baker as "childlike," "exotic," and "savage." As Jean-Claude noted in his biography of Baker and as the dancer herself wrote in her memoirs, she was not always happy with the ways in which the media portrayed her. In fact, she was particularly uneasy about posing nude for the publicity poster for "La Revue nègre." Becoming less willing over time to fight those who sought to display her image for publicity purposes, she, in effect, unintentionally reinforced stereotypes about African women.[20] The stereotypical representation of Baker's black body is axiomatic and presented in contrast to the Western ideal of physical beauty. Western female beauty is characterized by blondeness, purity, and fragility. The black woman's beauty is obscured, eroticized, and commodified. Through its display of clichéd images including Harlem night clubs and African jungles, "La Revue nègre" presented a *tableau* of black life both in the United States and in Africa. During the performance, Baker performed the Charleston, which was the latest "dance craze," a variety of comedy routines, and other assorted primitive dances. The highlight of the show was *La Danse sauvage* in which she and her dance partner, Joe Alex, performed an erotic dance set against a jungle-scape calling to mind Paul Gaugin's "Tahitian" paintings of the late 19th and early 20th centuries. Baker's dance itself combined her own improvised steps, those of her French choreographer (Jacques Charles) and a particular form of gyrating stomach dance. The "savagery" of her dance—gestures, faces, strange movements, shaking her hindquarters—and her semi-naked body propelled Baker from relatively obscurity to instant fame.

Interest in black cultural forms had arrived in Paris in several waves, the capstone of which was the opening of the Musée de l'Homme.[21] Brought about by Paul Rivet for the 1937 Exposition Internationale des Arts et Techniques dans la Vie Moderne, the Musée de l'Homme served to showcase non–Western cultural artifacts obtained through French colonialism.[22] From May 10–31, 1919 at the Galerie Devambez (45 boulevard Malesherbes), Paul Guillaume opened the first "Exposition d'Art Nègre et d'Art Océanien" including the launch of a "Fête nègre" at the Théâtre des Champs-Élysées led by actor-director-producer André Daven. The initial wave of interest in black culture was combined with the growing curiosity of both primitive and popular art forms. Brought about by competing "schools" of European *avant-garde* art, African masks and sculpture became an object of interest and were integrated into a state of primordial unity. Deconstructed from their original cultural roles, these forms served as a means through which an oppositional aesthetic was born that centered on an aesthetic of cultural renewal. African artifacts acquired through colonialism such as those on display currently at the Musée du Quai Branly served as inspirations for a revamping of modern art, their conventions being quickly incorporated within the formal developments of early modern art.

The primary wave of interest in black culture emerged as a result of the increasing desire to see exotic performances. Before World War I, several exotic shows had already been mounted in Paris, including Raymond Roussell's *Impressions d'Afrique* in 1911. After the war, performances of Jean Cocteau's *Le Bœuf sur le toit* (1922) and Tristan Tzara's *Le Cœur à barbe* (1923) brought together *avant-garde* artists from a variety of specializations including writers, painters, and musicians. The musical component was the aural backbone of stage productions led by the importation of jazz music and dance into Paris by black soldiers during the war (Gates and Dalton 904). Therefore, as a result of the French colonial enterprise in Africa and the arrival of American black cultural forms, the black culture of Paris in the 1920s became an aesthetic combination of which dance reviews like "La Revue nègre" sought to take full advantage. If "timing is everything," then debuting "La Revue nègre" at the same time as the Exposition Internationale des Arts Décoratifs et Industriels Modernes that took place from April to October 1925 was well intentioned. The Exposition whose promotional poster featured a dancing woman with a black gazelle in the background brought together thousands of designs from throughout Europe, Africa, and beyond. With more than 16 million visitors, its aim was to establish the preeminence of French taste and luxury goods in the post–World War I period. Although French displays dominated the exhibition with Paris itself depicted as the most fashionable of world cities, African culture had a major display at the Exposition. With the Exposition as a cultural springboard, stage managers Rolf de Maré and André Daven mounted "La Revue nègre" by combining black American jazz and African dance juxtaposed against exotic African scenes. Initial responses to "La Revue nègre" were flat, for the show was neither exotic enough nor erotic enough for contemporary Parisian audiences. By hiring French choreographer Jacques Charles, who had mounted several *spectacles* at the Moulin Rouge, de Maré and Daven reinvented the show. With her dance and her unique body, Baker rapidly became the focal point of the review. Artist Paul Colin was responsible for creating publicity ads for "La Revue nègre." In his posters entitled *Le Tumulte noire* that ultimately immortalized both the show and the image of Baker in Paris, Colin focused on the rather stereotypical elements of Black (African) physical features including the lips, eyes, and teeth that the artist vastly exaggerated. Commenting on "La Revue nègre," the critic Paul Achard stated, "...ses joies enfantines, la tristesse d'un passé de servitude, nous avons eu tout cela en entendant cette chanteuse à la voix de forêt vierge, en admirant la science trépidante

5. Writing the Female Body in Poetry and Theatre 159

de Douglass ... et ce joli gavroche café au lait qui est la célébrité de la troupe, Joséphine Baker" ("Tout en noir ou la Revue nègre" 2) / "...its childish joys, the sad bygone time of slavery, we had all that listening to the singer with the jungle voice, admiring Louis Douglas's hectic skill, ... and the pretty coffee-colored ragamuffin who is the star of the troupe, Josephine Baker." With allusions to early French and English explorers such as Bougainville and Livingston and references to African locales including Sudan and the Congo, Josephine Baker's dance played out again in the mind's eye of its spectators the colonization of Africa and foreshadowed the concept that Edward Said later identified as the "Other." Mediated through a foreign performer, stereotypes of Africa blended on stage that served to galvanize the image of the African woman. Josephine Baker's performance brought to the forefront the contradictory black female body. She was simultaneously erotic and innocent, benevolent and menacing, natural (nude) and representational (banana skirt).[23] Baker was a black Pygmalion, a living and breathing African sculpture. French popular culture both validated and concretized Baker's representational form, thus creating of her an exotic fantasy based on the French understanding of this newfound principle of "Otherness" that, even in the 1920s, had already begun to be romanticized in the Interwar Period. As critic Gérard Bauer wrote in an October 18, 1925 review of "La Revue nègre," "Or ces étranges nègres flattent en nous notre double goût de l'exotisme et du mystère.... NOUS les regardons, inquiets et charmés et nous sommes plus satisfaits quand ils mêlent un peu d'inquiétude à nos enchantements." / "These blacks feed our double taste for exoticism and mystery.... WE are charmed and upset by them, and most satisfied when they mix something upsetting in with their enchantment." Given the scourges of World War I from which French citizens were only beginning to start their recovery, the need for renewal and escape was understandable. But Bauer's words seem to gloss over the fact that race relations in post–World War I France were tenuous at best. This need for renewal and escape had deep roots. More importantly, however, Baker's performances gauged how the French viewing public felt about these racial attitudes. France (and other European nations) had repeatedly touted itself as a "superior culture." The notion of French culture as a superior one was part and parcel of the "mission civilisatrice" initially set into motion in the 19th century. Did the mounting of "La Revue nègre" that made Josephine Baker an instant star signal that the era of France's cultural hegemony was drawing to a close, or did this show review ultimately legitimize French cultural domination both domestically and internationally?

Cultural anthropologists largely agree that the paradox of cultural exploration is two-fold: 1. It is impossible to evaluate a foreign culture without, inevitably, impacting (contaminating) the foreign culture; 2. It is impossible to evaluate a foreign culture without, inevitably, being impacted (contaminated) by the foreign culture. The French civilizing mission had occurred through the contamination of true French culture by a foreign culture with which France had come into contact during its efforts to colonize the continent of Africa. "Cultural and social contamination" was already a subject of discussion in the Republic as a result of the increasing urbanization that the country had experienced since World War I. For the most zealous of French patriots with white supremacist views, race wars, indeed, were on the horizon. To show an interest in African culture was symptomatic of a regression in the evolution of mankind. Referring again to the field of anthropology, we cite along the so-called hierarchy of races present at the time that indigenous individuals were located at the low end of the evolutionary spectrum. In their primitive state, the un-evolved human being was driven by primal urges such as eating, drinking, and sex. Dancing also figured into these primal urges. Thus, to see the "black dance" both performed and cheered in front of a white audience was problematic. The "black dance" was tribal and animalistic characterized by moments of drunkenness and uninhibited sensuality. Baker's performances sent a ripple through the pond of an Interwar culture that had become increasingly more conservative following World War I.

The "Josephine Baker Factor" and Visual Representation

The "Josephine Baker Factor" provides strong evidence to the hypothesis that states that in the Western world the visual image holds an unbelievable power.[24] It has the power to create the identity of its subject, to place its subject at the very center or relegate it to the margins (Petit 149–50). In *Orientalism*, the important postcolonial theoretical text, Edward Said explained well that we should be sensitive both to how we evaluate other cultures as well as how we categorize them. For Said, the seemingly dominant French culture has exhibited the tendency to create representations of the subordinate African culture that are based almost exclusively on cultural stereotypes. He posited that these stereotypes when understood as an ensemble constituted the foundation elements of the "Orient." The "Orient," which rapidly became a Westerner creation perpetuating African stereotypes from the arrival of French colonists in the 19th century and throughout the 20th century, has continued to typecast Africans in the New Millennium. The French colonial system, in particular, took advantage of these stereotypes in order to further advance the "mission civilisatrice" as the packaging for the indea that French culture was superior to African culture. In the 20th century, in particular, this perception gained great momentum and became ubiquitous throughout mainstream French media. There is no medium that has done this more frequently than the visual medium.

Since television became mainstream media in the 1950s, the function of the visual image has increased immeasurably. Multimedia, best evidenced through television, film, video games, and the World Wide Web, continue to exert a powerful presence in our daily lives. Among the visual media, however, photography remains arguably the most powerful means of visual representation because it presents what the spectator believes to be authentic. Photography has the power to create an optical representation, but it also has the ability to falsify the same image that it had set out to create. Our worldview is formed by the images that we see. These representational images aid in the creation of our identities as well. Individuals in both traditional and in modern societies struggle to forge their own representational identities while at the same time working both in concert with and in opposition to any identities that exist on a national level. In France, for example, slogans such as "Vive la République" and "Nos ancêtres, les Gaulois" emerged at critical moments in France's history to define the essence of a people. Each citizen began to define himself not so much as an individual, but rather as an extension of the homeland, losing a bit of the individual identity each time that he began to identify to a greater extent with the nation. Slogans of national identity, in fact, often create false identities stereotypes, or forgeries of the individuals that live within what are often extremely diverse societies. To state that all French citizens share the Gaulois as ancestors, for example, would not only be blatantly incorrect, but it would also be a forgery of the true individual and collective identities of many *French* who are descendants of other tribes, those of Germanic descents, Sub-Saharan African or North African descent, Vietnamese, Eastern European, etc., which calls into question the very notion of *francité*. To make any claims that Josephine Baker accurately represented the continent of Africa was also problematic.

"La Revue nègre" immediately turned Josephine Baker into a photographic snapshot (cliché) that could be endlessly duplicated with each copy being a further counterfeit of her true identity (an African-American woman playing the role of an African woman).[25] For the spectator, this young black woman was nothing more than part of the exotic African landscape, a tree in the *pays de rêves* in which he could only dream of visiting. Her visual representation "très carte postale" corresponded precisely to the stereotypical representation of an African woman. This was the danger inherent within the neocolonial enterprise. It was the ignorance of the spectators that risked compromising Baker's identity and those of other black women. Jean Baudrillard's notion of a postmodern iconography is relevant in our discussion here. Josephine Baker personifies Jean Baudrillard's theory of simulacra and simulation in which the image has replaced the original. Baudrillard describes simulation in these terms: "It is the generation by models of a real without origin or reality: a hyperreal" (169). As a result of her performances in "La Revue nègre," Baker had become hyperreal, a model of something that never truly existed. When the simulacrum of the African woman became the truth, then it also became a mass-market commodity for packaging and distribution. African culture *is* for sale. As Baudrillard explained: "The real is produced from miniaturized units ... and with these it can be reproduced an indefinite number of times. It no longer has to be rational, since it is no longer measured against some ideal or negative instance" (170). If we follow Baudrillard's theory to its conclusion, the simulacrum is no longer a distorted image of reality, but, becomes real in itself. "Now that we've reached the phase of desperate reproduction, and where the stakes are nil, the simulacrum is maximal—exacerbated and parodied simulation at one and the same time—as interminable as psychoanalysis and for the same reasons" (187). If the real is revealed, then the illusion disappears and Baker suddenly becomes human and reality loses the intrigue that brought the American singer-dancer both recognition and fame.

In speaking of the Iconoclasts who tried to destroy the images of God, Baudrillard argued that "their metaphysical despair came from the idea that the images concealed nothing at all, and that in fact they were not images, such as the original model would have made them, but actually perfect simulacra forever radiant with their own fascination" (172). Perhaps the mask that *is* Josephine Baker is actually empty, which makes of Baker a true simulacrum in the Baudrillardian sense:

> It is no longer a question of imitation, nor of reduplication, nor even of parody. It is rather a question of substituting signs of the real for the real itself; that is, an operation to deter every real process by its operational double, a metastable, programmatic, perfect descriptive machine which provides all the signs of the real and short-circuits [of] all its vicissitudes [170].

Like a photograph, Josephine Baker's image fell subject to replication and reduplication. It became a portrait of what the African woman was supposed to resemble. Indeed, "of all the images in the world, our own photographic portrait is the most important, for it constitutes the core of our existence" (Lapidus 7).[26] When our photographs wander, they become commonplace, and thus lose their value, their essence. When this occurs, we risk the fragmentation and marginalization of our very being. To place the photograph within Baker's own hands would ultimately give her both creative power and control of her own identity/destiny. Such a gesture would unavoidably fracture the dialect that exists between the "colonizer" and the "colonized," this mutually dependent relationship of oppression that must be constantly repeated in order to eventually self-perpetuate. To place the image in the performer's hands would, in one fell swoop, destroy the oppression initiated under the "mission civilisatrice" of France that had continued in the neocolonial period. Interestingly, it is true that within certain cultures of French-speaking Africa (such as in Mali), to take a photograph is to steal the soul of the person whose image is taken.

It is worth noting here that photography and oppression bear a striking lexical relationship. In *On Photography*, Susan Sontag underscored the fact that through its terminology, photography is linked to oppression, for the medium employs a vocabulary associated with hunting: "load," "aim," "shoot" (14). Although this comparison borders on the extreme, if considered completely within a metaphorical sense, then photography and oppression are, in fact, analogous. Sontag adds: "There is an aggression implicit in every use of the camera.... To photograph people is to violate them" (7). Photography "turns people into objects that can be symbolically possessed" (14). More importantly, the photographer produces an image that can be manipulated *ad infinitum*. Copies of images can be copied as well, creating yet another abstraction. To photograph someone is to possess them metaphorically, to such an extent that the individual is deprived of any real human value. The objective lens of the camera figuratively "captures" the essence of the subject, thus robbing the latter of any realness. This notion is particularly true within the colonial context in which the conquest through the image mirrors the conquest of a people, as Nissan Perez underscores: "The extensive photographic activity in the Orient was, indeed, an act of aggression—if not a physical occupation, a spiritual appropriation of those lands" (100).[27] To certain African peoples, in particular, this is a fact that is very real. It is a fact of which we are totally unaware when we take photographs of individuals without their permission. In contrast to the moving image that trains us to look into "the depth of the shadows of history," Walter Benjamin theorizes that the photographic image encourages absorption (qtd. in Mitrano 4). Further, according to G.F. Mitrano, "photography inaugurates a new glance—one that sees the 'here and now' that sears the subject in the still image—that supersedes the narrative of the reciprocity of the gaze" (5). A simple paradox explains Baker's situation: she will be unable to create her own identity when she is continually having a marginalized one created for her which she, in fact, is able to use successfully and which ultimately makes her famous.

In the Lacanian sense, the black woman's subject formation is a process. The "mirror stage," to which Jacques Lacan often refers, functions as a dialectic in which the "I" is identified by an understanding of the "Not I" (Homer 24–5). As is the case with Baker, in Lacan's mirror stage, there is a movement from unity to fragmentation, from collective to individual. Eventually, there is an attempt to reintegrate to the collective. In short, the images of Josephine Baker, in particular, fragment her identity, representing the "Not I" of her existence. Although the visual image cannot make her "African" in any sense of the term, it functions to normalize Baker by assuring that she both represents and perpetuates the visual stereotypes that the French have created for Africans.[28] In a sense, Baker becomes "African"—in the French sense of the term—at the very moment that she is profiled, photographed, and classified according to the Western definition of what constitutes a member of this particular group. As Vincent Colapietro states,

> ...in addition to the external Other, there exists another one, the internal other "self" created by the passing of a sign into an interpretant, interpretant into sign, and the self of one moment into the self of another moment. The radical absence of the self from its other self, semiotically evidenced by shifters, creates not a stable but a restless semiosis incessantly sliding along the slope of signification [40].

For Jacques Derrida, in contrast, marginalization is due to the loss of presence that is so intrinsic to the operation of the sign, and most evident within the written sign. Derrida speaks specifically of a transcendental signified in which he appropriates Ferdinand de Saussure's term "signified," thereby suggesting that it is the indefiniteness of reference that brings the tradition of metaphysics to desire the transcendental signified so intensely, while repressing its absence so vigorously (qtd. in Colapietro 367).

Is there any way in which Baker and other African women can reject the marginalized postcolonial self (the "Other") that is created through the power of visual representation? An "African Feminism" adapted to the cultural context of French-speaking Africa could emerge that might help to refuse a postcolonial identity based on fragmentation and marginalization that has initially led many black Africans to assume an identity based exclusively on false constructions. If we believe the narrator in Michel Tournier's postcolonial novel entitled *La Goutte d'or* (1986) who claims that "l'image est douée d'une force mauvaise"/"the image is endowed with evil power" (100), then we might conclude that the only way that Francophone Africans can escape the evil power of cultural stereotyping is by making a concerted effort to continually reject the false identities cast on them by the image. Then, and only then, might they succeed in truly obtaining a free existence.

Conclusion

> "The advent of 'globalization' requires flexibility and further comparative research across continents, cultures and languages."
> —Kaschula *"Imbongi and Griot"* 56

In the Preface to this book, I stated that "literature is the lifeblood of a people." Merriam-Webster defines the word "lifeblood" as "the most important part of something; the part of something that provides its strength and energy" (n. pag.). By definition, "lifeblood" is a life-giving force that flows through the veins of a people. It includes the imprint of a civilization's past, its present, and its future. It incorporates the hopes and fears of a people. This "lifeblood" contains the cultural DNA of a civilization. As I have underscored throughout this book, culture is a dynamic and complex whole that includes language, knowledge, beliefs, morality, law, customs and all other abilities and habits exhibited by an individual member of a given society. From this point of view, culture contains the necessary ingredients to turn an individual into a social being. Consequently, cultural identity brings together all that is common to the members of a group, such as rules, norms and values that one shares with one's community. Cultural identity breaks itself down at two distinguishable levels: microculture and macroculture. In *The Cultural Experience*, David McCurdy, James P. Spradley, and Dianna J. Shandy state that a microculture denotes specialized subgroups, marked with their own languages, philosophy and system of rules that pervade differentiated societies (13). Scholars typically refer to macroculture as "Culture." We also denote intercultural identity in the case of contact that takes place between different cultures. It is from these cultural encounters that the individual's own cultural identity emerges. According to Léon Nadjo,

> Cultural identity, in this precise domain, is thus the expression of difference, but of a difference that, far from sinking into impoverishing nationalism, excludes neither dialogue nor complementarity. It is the identifying mark of fundamental

values proper to an ethnic group, which uses them to create a bond, and to which each of its members relates, a steady spring from which every member drinks continuously but which all must know, in a certain sense, how to desert in order to acquire through dialogue with other cultures the je ne sais quoi that makes one cultivated. *This*, in effect, is the difference between collective culture and individual culture [n. pag., italics in original text].

For these precise reasons, culture is always comparative and relative to such an extent that cultural anthropologists often use to the term "cultural relativism" when describing their work. In this same vein, the literatures produced within diverse cultures have their own sense of relativism by combining both the individual culture and the collective culture.

To call the final chapter of this book the "Conclusion" would be a misnomer. In reality, we should call it the "Beginning." In a very real way, the study of cultural history in French-speaking Africa is dawning. In the New Millennium, whether we are talking about cultural studies or literary studies, Francophone African studies as a whole is standing at a crossroads that began in 2007 when Le Monde published a manifesto advocating a "littérature-monde" in the French-speaking tradition. Signed by a multinational group of writers, the manifesto received mixed reactions. Commended by some for deconstructing the hierarchical separation between French and Francophone literature that had endured for decades, others criticized it for over-exoticizing literary works created outside of continental France. The notion of a "transnational" French Studies continues to fuel debate among researchers. To some scholars, "splitting hairs" over what to call texts produced outside of the Hexagon by writers who have been impacted by French colonialism creates a fodder that has no *raison d'être*. For others, the perpetuation of two separate categories of writing—"French" and "Francophone"—that were forged out of colonial and post-colonial conflict is no longer appropriate in the same way that the continuance of the term "Third World" subjugates so-called underdeveloped countries more than it accurately defines them. Politically correct labels aside, the fact remains that the French literary canon still does not include a sufficient number of texts produced outside of continental France.

Although Francophone literature has been a subject of study for the last fifty years, it is still held on the margins of literary composition. In speaking of the rise of Francophone literature in her 2003 article entitled "Unhoming Francophone Studies: A House in the Middle of the Current," Mireille Rosello stated:

> I would hope that such transnational and transdisciplinary encounters between types of Francophone studies would lead to a sort of "unhoming" of the field: it would make us perceive our discipline not as "homeless" (Francophone studies

do have a space in the institutional home) nor exiled (home is not somewhere else), but as struggling with unhomeliness, where legitimacy is a ghost that we keep conjuring up [132].

More than a decade later, Rosello's words remain ironic. Francophone Studies has always been marginalized within the Academy. Even within university French programs, the study of French literary works created outside of France is not always valued. Inasmuch as there are many Francophone literary works that discuss the theme of exile, the study of these texts is continually held on the margins and often relegated to specific places such as specialized books and academic conferences with themes such as "Crossings, Frictions, Fusions"/"Traversées, frictions, fusions," the 2012 meeting of the 20th and 21st Century French and Francophone Studies International Colloquium. Though creating special topics such as this one that bring academics together to discuss the Diaspora, we must question how far academic dialogue can take us and what good these discussions bring to the marginalized cultures that scholars gather to discuss. The conference "Call for Papers" offers clarification:

> Twentieth- and twenty-first century literatures around the globe are marked by movement, struggles and transformations, often postulated in terms of crossings of, or intersections between, concrete and imaginary borders, communities, ethnic and racial delimitations, languages, and genres. This rings particularly true in the case of Francophone Studies, whose very core assumes a host of social, cultural, political and historical encounters as well as inter-disciplinary theoretical workings. This conference aims to delineate such spaces of encounter, ephemeral or lasting, that lead to frictions, hyphenations, cross-pollinations or fragmentations. Among questions to be considered: Is the encounter bound to be informed by what Sergei Eisenstein famously dubbed a "dialectics of collision?" Are there particular cultural fusions (music, food or art for example) that might be considered "non-threatening zones of acceptance?" What is the dynamic between these zones and the socio-political realities, ethnic segregation among others, which often accompany them? Do possibilities of conciliation exist in a world that is increasingly seen as divergent, and where the rise of new nationalisms posits a threat to the practice of an inclusive multiplicity? [n. pag.].

The fact of the matter is that the French-speaking world has been "marked by movement, struggles and transformations" that have often taken place as a result of a forged migration and the transection of boundaries without regard to differences in ethnicity, language, politics, race, or religion. La Francophonie is a world that was built on a series of events that began in 1885 and set into motion a world of cultural, linguistic, and sociopolitical diversity, fragmentation, friction, and cross-pollination that ultimately gave birth to a French-speaking world that has become so complex and world-encompassing that in

2014 it still cannot decide what to call itself. Sergei Eisenstein is correct when he describes the French-speaking world as "dialectics of collision." It is, however, from its oppositional nature that its self-definition might emerge. Given the fact that if it remains impossible to see the French-speaking world as homogenous even at the microcultural level, we continue to wonder how it would ever become possible to put back together all of the pieces of the shattered French-speaking world at a macrocultural level. At minimum, academic conferences such as the one referred to above present a forum for discussion that can engender a locus of hope.

Though it remains unclear how positive its effects will be in the long run, the rise of Francophone literature has noticeably disturbed the *status quo*. Nonetheless, the concept of a "littérature-monde en français" or any other categorization such as Négritude addresses only one part of the larger question concerning how to define—both culturally and literarily—works that are created outside of France by French-speaking individuals. What is, perhaps, an even more significant concern that is often neglected is the way in which women's writing in the French and Francophone traditions is treated. Suffice it to say, few French literary anthologies include a substantial number of texts written by French women writers. Robert Leggewie's *Anthologie de la littérature française*[1] published in 1990 contains only a few examples of works written by women. Given the year of its publication, it is no small surprise that this particular anthology of French literature does not contain any works written by women outside of continental France. Until the French canon contains literary texts that reflect the diverse regions originating from the five continents that the French language has touched that resist a labeling system, our understanding of these literatures will continue to be incomplete. Furthermore, until our study of literature *d'expression française* is culturally integrative, our perception of the importance of these literary works will also remain culturally imperfect.

This view notwithstanding, we can no longer promote images of Africa that the colonial experiment created. Perceptions of world citizens with regard to Africa are largely those that were forged in the 19th century and perpetuated in the 20th century media. In the 19th century, in particular, British and French explorers and missionaries created an image of Africa as a land of unintelligent and uncivilized humanoids awaiting the "saving grace" of white Europeans. The "civilizing mission" packaged an ideology used to justify a European presence on the continent of Africa. Even if one could successfully defend the argument that the diverse peoples of 19th century Africa needed to be "saved," to argue that salvation had the right to subjugate millions of people would be difficult to support. In addition, we can no longer proliferate the 20th century misunderstanding that Africa is completely disconnected from the rest of the world. Although it is true that during the 20th century the outside world brought to Africa modern technologies that the residents of the continent were ill-prepared to use (such as automobiles, computers, and the Internet[2]), it is also true that modern-day Africa is, in some ways, every bit as "urban modern" as its European and American counterparts. Today, in the 21st century, we find ourselves in an age of increasing globalization in which Africa exhibits a state of connectedness unlike anything that it has ever known. There are hundreds of television and radio stations scattered throughout the continent's fifty-four countries broadcasting in both colonial and indigenous languages. As our examination of the myth of Shaka illustrated, Africa thus is in "full-duplex" mode as it both receives cultural information from other African nations and transmits cultural information throughout Africa and beyond.

The international news media portray the image of an Africa that is perpetually awaiting the arrival of the Western world to save her from poverty, famine, war, and disease. Within Africa, poverty, famine, war, and disease are "The Four Horsemen of the Apocalypse" that are simple to define, yet they remain impossible to combat. From 2009, the citizens of the world have heard reports of massive genocide in Darfur. Darfur, in the western part of Sudan, is home to approximately 6 million people representing nearly 100 nomadic and semi-nomadic tribes the majority of which are Muslims. In 1989, General Omar al-Bashir seized control of Sudan though a military coup that then created an opening for The National Islamic Front government to exacerbate previously-existing regional tensions. In a struggle to gain political control over the area, weapons poured into Darfur. In 2003, the Sudan Liberation Army (SLA) and the Justice and Equality Movement (JEM) took up arms against the Sudanese government, criticizing the marginalization of the area and the failure of the government to protect citizens from attacks by nomads. The government of Sudan met the rebel opposition by sending out Arab militias called Janjaweed ("devils on horseback"). In short, Sudanese forces and Janjaweed militia attacked more than four hundred villages throughout Darfur. Millions of civilians were left homeless. In the ongoing genocide that has now lasted a decade, farmers are systematically displaced and murdered at the hands of the Janjaweed. To date, genocide in Darfur has taken 400,000 lives and displaced more than 2,500,000 people (Washington Post n. pag.). In June 2005, the International Criminal Court (ICC) began to investigate human rights violations in Darfur. On March 4, 2009, Sudanese President Omar al Bashir became the first sitting president to be indicted by the ICC for ordering a campaign of mass killing, rape, and plunder against civilians in Darfur. In 2013, news stories circulated about starving people in South Sudan. According to U.S. officials, approximately 250,000 people in the region are threatened by starvation ("Humanitarian disaster unfolds in South Sudan"). On January 14, 2014, rebel forces in South Sudan attacked Malakal, the capital of the oil-rich state of Upper Nile, amid reports of a deadly ferry boat accident that took the lives of more than 200 people who were attempting to flee the fighting. As Nicholas Kulish reported:

> The humanitarian crisis only continues to grow. According to the United Nations Office of the Humanitarian Coordinator, around 413,000 people are internally displaced and 66,500 are seeking refuge at United Nations bases around the country. More than 74,300 have already fled the country, with another 4,000 to 5,000 arriving daily in neighboring Uganda alone, four out of five of them children [n pag.].

According to United Nations estimates, 2.7 million Darfuris remain in internally displaced persons camps and over 4.7 million Darfuris depend on humanitarian aid (United Human Rights Council). Resolving the Darfur conflict is critical not just for the people of Darfur, but also for the future of Sudan and the stability of the entire region. Until peace is sown in Darfur, Darfuris and those throughout Sudan will continue to suffer atrocities at the hands of an oppressive regime.

Elsewhere in Africa, war continues to plague citizens of the Democratic Republic of Congo. On January 7, 2014, approximately twenty-six people were killed during an eight-hour battle between government and rebel forces in Lubumbashi located in southernmost part of the country (BBC News Africa, n. pag.). The rebel assault was launched by the Mai Mai Kata Katanga, a secessionist group in the region, which is fighting for the independence of Katanga, the richest province in the DRC. The leader of the group was Gédéon Kyungu Mutanga who was imprisoned in 2009 for committing crimes against humanity both during and after the Second Congo War/The Great War of Africa (1998–2003). On September 7, 2011, he was freed during an armed attack on Lubumbashi's prison. As if the news originating from Sudan and the DRC was not already enough to draw our attention, fears of sectarian genocide and accounts of the "wanderings" of more than one million people living in refugee camps are springing from the Central African Republic. On January 10, 2014, the Central African Republic's interim president, Michel Djotodia, resigned under pressure from several African leaders who had gathered in neighboring Chad for an emergency summit on how to end the widespread ethnic violence within the country. These news stories pull at our heartstrings. We see the images of suffering people on HD-television screens in our living rooms telling a tale that has become commonplace on African soil. Violence and corruption reign in Africa. Acts of violence from Rwanda and Burundi in the 1990s play themselves out again in the world's mind. Africa is a global concern.

The theme of globalization naturally brings together the various parts of this study. It is a theme that forces us to think about how globalization is depicted in Francophone African poetic literature. Our reflections on globalization within this particular context elicit several interesting questions that have been touched on, in part, during the present study, but that also require future investigation: What is the role of individual nations in local, national, and international politics? Is there a struggle for economic and political power both at the local level and at the national level? Is trade a significant part of Francophone African daily life? What role does the African elite play in contributing to the geocultural, geoeconomic, and geopolitical systems? How does the notion of "culture" function within Africa? How does literature describe the ever-evolving state of cultural, political, and social identity in Africa? In doing so, do the various literatures of Africa accurately portray the nations that they have attempted to illustrate? The last and perhaps most pressing question is the following one: Where do we go from here?

If we assume that cultural events inspire the themes that appear throughout literature, we should not be surprised at all that Francophone African poets and playwrights produce literary works that hold a mirror up to the cultures of which these writers are a part. On a continent in which famine, disease, political instability, and civil war have become pandemic, these current events that impact all strata of society find their way onto the literary page. Although certain widespread themes and literary structures appear in Francophone African poetic literature as a result of the interconnectedness of the continent of Africa with the rest of the world, this study has argued throughout that this particular literature is characterized by an overall organic quality that, interestingly, is difficult to define. The "borrowings" that this literature employs in order to express itself are the result of the impact that colonialism had on Africa. More out of necessity than by design, the French language continues to be a linguistic vessel used to disseminate the cultural message of Francophone Africa to the rest of the world. Well-known Francophone African writers including Léopold Sédar Senghor, Sony Labou Tansi, Senouvo Agbota Zinsou, David Diop, Gérald-Félix Tchicaya (Tchicaya U Tam'si), Paul Dakeyo, Bernard Dadié, Werewere Liking Gnepo, Seydou Badian Kouyaté, and many others, have used their writings to cast a light on the problems affecting Africa since the arrival of independence in the 1960s. Despite the numerous foreign military interventions, governmental humanitarian aid, and private aid such as USA for Africa (United Support of Artists for Africa), in the same way in which *littérature-monde en français* remains standing at a crossroads, Africa, the "Cradle of Mankind," also stands at the intersection of the past, the present, and the future. Which road will she take?

Appendix I

Transcript of Barack Obama's Speech at Nelson Mandela's Memorial

Johannesburg, South Africa (CNN)—To Graça Machel and the Mandela family; to President Zuma and members of the government; to heads of state and government, past and present; distinguished guests—it is a singular honor to be with you today, to celebrate a life unlike any other.

To the people of South Africa—people of every race and walk of life—the world thanks you for sharing Nelson Mandela with us. His struggle was your struggle. His triumph was your triumph. Your dignity and hope found expression in his life, and your freedom, your democracy is his cherished legacy.

It is hard to eulogize any man—to capture in words not just the facts and the dates that make a life, but the essential truth of a person—their private joys and sorrows; the quiet moments and unique qualities that illuminate someone's soul. How much harder to do so for a giant of history, who moved a nation toward justice, and in the process moved billions around the world.

Born during World War I, far from the corridors of power, a boy raised herding cattle and tutored by elders of his Thembu tribe—Madiba would emerge as the last great liberator of the 20th century.

Like Gandhi, he would lead a resistance movement—a movement that at its start held little prospect of success. Like King, he would give potent voice to the claims of the oppressed, and the moral necessity of racial justice. He would endure a brutal imprisonment that began in the time of Kennedy and Khrushchev, and reached the final days of the Cold War.

Emerging from prison, without force of arms, he would—like Lincoln—hold his country together when it threatened to break apart. Like America's founding fathers, he would erect a constitutional order to preserve freedom for future generations—a commitment to democracy and rule of law ratified not only by his election, but by his willingness to step down from power.

Given the sweep of his life, and the adoration that he so rightly earned, it is tempting then to remember Nelson Mandela as an icon, smiling and serene, detached from the tawdry affairs of lesser men.

But Madiba himself strongly resisted such a lifeless portrait. Instead, he insisted on sharing with us his doubts and fears; his miscalculations along with his victories. "I'm not a saint," he said, "unless you think of a saint as a sinner who keeps on trying."

It was precisely because he could admit to imperfection, because he could be so full of good humor, even mischief, despite the heavy burdens he carrie[d], that we loved him so. He was not a bust made of marble; he was a man of flesh and blood—a son and husband, a father and a friend.

That is why we learned so much from him; that is why we can learn from him still. For nothing he achieved was inevitable. In the arc of his life, we see a man who earned his place in history through struggle and shrewdness; persistence and faith. He tells us what's possible not just in the pages of dusty history books, but in our own lives as well.

Mandela showed us the power of action; of taking risks on behalf of our ideals. Perhaps Madiba was right that he inherited, "a proud rebelliousness, a stubborn sense of fairness" from his father.

Certainly he shared with millions of black and colored South Africans the anger born of, "a thousand slights, a thousand indignities, a thousand unremembered moments … a desire to fight the system that imprisoned my people."

But like other early giants of the ANC—the Sisulus and Tambos—Madiba disciplined his anger; and channeled his desire to fight into organization, and platforms, and strategies for action, so men and women could stand up for their dignity. Moreover, he accepted the consequences of his actions, knowing that standing up to powerful interests and injustice carries a price.

"I have fought against white domination and I have fought against black domination," he said at his 1964 trial. "I've cherished the ideal of a democratic and free society in which all persons live together in harmony and with equal opportunities. It is an ideal which I hope to live for and to achieve. But if needs be, it is an ideal for which I am prepared to die."

Mandela taught us the power of action, but also ideas; the importance of reason and arguments; the need to study not only those you agree with, but those who you don't. He understood that ideas cannot be contained by prison walls, or extinguished by a sniper's bullet.

He turned his trial into an indictment of apartheid because of his eloquence and passion, but also his training as an advocate. He used decades in prison to sharpen his arguments, but also to spread his thirst for knowledge to others in the movement. And he learned the language and customs of his oppressor so that one day he might better convey to them how their own freedom depended upon his.

Mandela demonstrated that action and ideas are not enough; no matter how right, they must be chiseled into laws and institutions. He was practical, testing his beliefs against the hard surface of circumstance and history. On core principles he was unyielding, which is why he could rebuff offers of conditional release, reminding the apartheid regime that, "prisoners cannot enter into contracts."

But as he showed in painstaking negotiations to transfer power and draft new laws, he was not afraid to compromise for the sake of a larger goal. And because he was not only a leader of a movement, but a skillful politician, the constitution that emerged was worthy of this multiracial democracy; true to his vision of laws that protect minority as well as majority rights, and the precious freedoms of every South African.

Finally, Mandela understood the ties that bind the human spirit. There is a word in South Africa—Ubuntu—that describes his greatest gift: his recognition that we are all bound together in ways that can be invisible to the eye; that there is a oneness to humanity; that we achieve ourselves by sharing ourselves with others, and caring for those around us.

We can never know how much of this was innate in him, or how much of was shaped and burnished in a dark, solitary cell. But we remember the gestures, large and small—introducing his jailers as honored guests at his inauguration; taking the pitch in a springbok uniform; turning his family's heartbreak into a call to confront HIV/AIDS—that revealed the depth of his empathy and understanding.

He not only embodied Ubuntu; he taught millions to find that truth within themselves. It took a man like Madiba to free not just the prisoner, but the jailer as well; to show that you must trust others so that they may trust you; to teach that reconciliation is not a matter of ignoring a cruel past, but a means of confronting it with inclusion, generosity and truth. He changed laws, but also hearts.

For the people of South Africa, for those he inspired around the globe, Madiba's passing is rightly a time of mourning, and a time to celebrate his heroic life. But I believe it should also prompt in each of us a time for self-reflection. With honesty, regardless of our station or circumstance, we must ask: how well have I applied his lessons in my own life?

It is a question I ask myself as a man and as a President. We know that like South Africa, the United States had to overcome centuries of racial subjugation. As was true here, it took the sacrifice of countless people—known and unknown—to see the dawn of a new day. Michelle and I are the beneficiaries of that struggle.

But in America and South Africa, and countries around the globe, we cannot allow our progress to cloud the fact that our work is not done. The struggles that follow the victory of formal equality and universal franchise may not be as filled with drama and moral clarity as those that came before, but they are no less important.

For around the world today, we still see children suffering from hunger, and disease; run-down schools, and few prospects for the future. Around the world today, men and women are still imprisoned for their political beliefs; and are still persecuted for what they look like, or how they worship, or who they love.

Nelson Mandela reminds us that it always seems impossible until it is done.

We, too, must act on behalf of justice. We, too, must act on behalf of peace. There are too many of us who happily embrace Madiba's legacy of racial reconciliation, but passionately resist even modest reforms that would challenge chronic poverty and growing inequality.

There are too many leaders who claim solidarity with Madiba's struggle for freedom, but do not tolerate dissent from their own people. And there are too many of us who stand on the sidelines, comfortable in complacency or cynicism when our voices must be heard.

The questions we face today—how to promote equality and justice; to uphold freedom and human rights; to end conflict and sectarian war—do not have easy answers. But there were no easy answers in front of that child in Qunu.

Nelson Mandela reminds us that it always seems impossible until it is done. South

Africa shows us that is true. South Africa shows us we can change. We can choose to live in a world defined not by our differences, but by our common hopes. We can choose a world defined not by conflict, but by peace and justice and opportunity.

We will never see the likes of Nelson Mandela again. But let me say to the young people of Africa, and young people around the world—you can make his life's work your own. Over 30 years ago, while still a student, I learned of Mandela and the struggles in this land. It stirred something in me.

It woke me up to my responsibilities—to others, and to myself—and set me on an improbable journey that finds me here today. And while I will always fall short of Madiba's example, he makes me want to be better. He speaks to what is best inside us. After this great liberator is laid to rest; when we have returned to our cities and villages, and rejoined our daily routines, let us search then for his strength—for his largeness of spirit—somewhere inside ourselves.

And when the night grows dark, when injustice weighs heavy on our hearts, or our best laid plans seem beyond our reach—think of Madiba, and the words that brought him comfort within the four walls of a cell:

> It matters not how strait the gate,
> How charged with punishments the scroll,
> I am the master of my fate:
> I am the captain of my soul.

What a great[1] soul it was. We will miss him deeply. May God bless the memory of Nelson Mandela. May God bless the people of South Africa.

Appendix II

Recently Published Works by Francophone Women Writers[1]

2011

Philomène Atayme, *Les secrets de ma langue*
Peggy Lucie Auleley, *Les larmes du soleil*
Safi Ba, *Les chameaux de la haine ou chronique d'un vertige*
Hadja Kadidiatou Balde, "Oui mon mari! Non mon mari!"
Masséni Barry Ben Halima, *Musulmanes sous les tropiques*
Aya Cissoko, *Danbé*
Aurore Costa, *Les larmes de cristal Nika l'Africaine III*
Delphine Coulin, *Samba pour la France*
Corinne Desarens, *Un roi*
Muriel Diallo, *La femme du Blanc*
Charline Effah, *Percées et chimères*
Lauren Ekue, *Black attitude #1 Ro$e*
Joëlle Esso, *Hanibal & Pushkin*
Adélaïde Fassinou, *La Sainte ni touche*
Esther Gauber, *Burkina, rose du désert*
Khadi Hane, *Des fourmis dans la bouche*
Amina Kaïssa, *Le Chant de Yaye: Tracés d'une vie*
Sylvie Kande, *La quête infinie de l'autre rive*
Pauline Kayitare, *Tu leur diras que tu es hutue*
Hélène Kaziende, *Les fers de l'absence*
Valérie Joëlle Kouam Ngocka, *A cause d'elle*
Nacrita Lep Bibom, *Tourbillon d'émotions*
Jacqueline Q. Louison, *Le poète est un peintre*
Laure Lugon Zugravu, *Déroutes*
Rita Mensah-Amendah, *Faits divers et d'espoir*
Edna Merey-Apinda, *Ce reflet dans le miroir*

Régine Mfoumou, *Descente aux enfers au pays des Droits de l'homme*
Léonora Miano, *Ces âmes chagrines*
Gilda Moutsara, *Les papiers de maman*
Elise Nanitelamio, *Passeport pour Douala.*
Marie Gisèle Nkom, *Les passerelles célestes*
Marie Ndiaye, *Les grandes personnes*
Mariama Ndoye, *L'arbre s'est penché*
Agathe Ngo Baléba, *Peurs virales.*
Marie Julie Nguetsè, *Sans El les dieux ne voleraient pas si haut.*
Pélagie Ntsame Obame, *Tant qu'il y aura des rêves*
Michèle Rakotoson, *Passeport pour Antananarivo.*
Salimata Togora, *Deny et Dénistar, suivi de Un 31 décembre*

2012

Jeanne Marie Rosette Abou'ou, *Lettre à Tita*
Marie-Élène Amangoua-Drujon, *Tempête sur Abidjan*
Michèle Assamoua, *Le Défi: Couples mixtes en Côte d'Ivoire*
Peggy Lucie Auleley, *L'héritière du jaspe*
Rebeca Ayoko, *Quand les étoiles deviennent noires*
Sophie Françoise Bapambe Yap Libock, *Les couloirs du bonheur*
Sylvie Bocquet N'Guessan, *Côte d'Ivoire, le pays déchiré de mon grand-père*
Angeline Solange Bonono, *Marie-France l'Orpailleuse*
Maryse Condé, *La vie sans fards*
Josette Desclercs Abondio, *Le jardin d'Adalou*
Rabia Diallo, *Amours cruelles, beauté coupable*
Sokhna Diarra Bousso Ndao, *Magenta*
Stéphanie Dongmo Djuka, *Aujourd'hui, je suis mort*
Miryl Eteno, *Les doux murmures de mon enfance*
Flore Hazoumé, *Je te le devais bien...*
Marie-Françoise Ibovi, *Rue des histoires*
Isabelle Jourdan, *C'est comme ça, à Ouaga...*
Brigitte Kehrer, *Poudre d'Afrique*
Jacqueline Q. Louison, *L'ère du serpent*
Eveline Mankou, *L'instinct de survie*
Muetse-Destinée Mboga, *Muendu Murime, le voyage du cœur*
Moulou Menguiste Ab Worke and Catherine Leenhardt, *La petite fille du grazmach a disparu.*
Saga d'une famille éthiopienne
Edna Merey-Apinda, (ed.) *Les lyres de l'Ogooué*
Léonora Miano, *Ecrits pour la parole*
Hélène Millet, *Roman bambéen*
Justine Mintsa, *Larmes de cendre*
Scholastique Mukasonga, *Notre-Dame du Nil*
Ralphanie Mwana Kongo, *La boue de Saint-Pierre*

Tomaino Ndam Njoya, *L'enfer rose*
Denise Landria Ndembi, *Tu n'achèteras pas ma peau. Madame l'ambassadrice...*
Amy Niang, *La fuite dans le symbole*
Perine-Madeleine Obono, *Et puis un jour...*
Nadia Origo, *Le bal des débutants.*
Hadiza Sanoussi, *Sopam, le duc de Liptougou*
Aminata Traoré et Nathalie M'Deal-Mounier, *L'Afrique mutilée*

2013

Marie Térèse Ambassa Betoko, *Le film de ma jeunesse*
Nadine Bari, *L'Espérancière*
Noëlle Bolou, *Un souffle de vie*
Fatou Diomé, *Impossible de grandir*
Sophie Ekoue, *Aux noms de la vie*
Liss Kihindou, *Chêne de Bambou*
Léontine Longbou Fopa, *Appelez-moi Madame Oumarou*
Martine Merlin-Dhaine, *Rayé de la carte. Chantier du barrage de Mérowé sur la 4e cataracte du Nil—Nord Soudan*
Léonora Miano, *La Saison de l'ombre*
Brigitte Tsobgny, *L'Afro-Parisienne et la suite arithmétique du Saigneur de Paris*
Chimamanda Ngozi Adichie, *Autour de ton cou*
Noo Saro-Wiwa, *Transwonderland. Retour au Nigeria*

Chapter Notes

Preface

1. All translations presented within this book are mine.
2. Throughout this book, I use both the French spelling "Chaka" and the English spelling "Shaka" when referring to "Shaka" the Zulu warrior-king. In referring to the myth itself, I use the spelling "Shaka."
3. See Appendix 1 of this book for the complete transcript of President Obama's speech at Nelson Mandela's memorial service. It is presented here to offer support to the notion that Francophone Africa, the continent of Africa, and the rest of the world are more connected than most scholars will acknowledge.

Introduction

1. The total number of countries in Africa depends on the way in which that number is evaluated. There are presently fifty-four countries that are members of the African Union. There are fifty-five recognized states in Africa, if one includes Morocco (not a current AU member). There are fifty-six recognized states and *de facto* states if we include Somaliland. For the current number of countries in Africa, visit Africacheck.org.
2. A Congolese writer, Tchicaya U Tam'si's official name was Gérald-Félix Tchicaya (1931–1988). In Kikongo, his name means "small paper that speaks for a country." U Tam'si grew up in France where he worked as a journalist until he returned to Congo in 1960 during its acquisition of independence. His poetry is known for its Surrealist characteristics, vivid imagery, and its commentaries on contemporary African culture.
3. Bernard Dadié (1916–), born near Abidjan, the capital of Côte d'Ivoire, is arguably the most prolific Ivorian writer of his time. Raised in the Catholic schooling tradition, Dadié worked for the French government in Dakar, Senegal until 1947, when he returned to his native Côte d'Ivoire. Dadié's literary work reflected his colonial experience growing up as he endeavors to recount traditional African folktales to the modern world. In 1953, he collaborated with fellow Ivoirians Germain Coffi Gadeau and F. J. Amon d'Aby to create the *Cercle Culturel et Folklorique de la Côte d'Ivoire* (CCFCI). Dadié's numerous writings reflect a hope for the equality and independence of Africans. His most significant works include *Afrique debout* (1950), *Légendes africaines* (1954), *Le pagne noir* (1955), *La ronde des jours* (1956), *Climbié* (1956), *Un Nègre à Paris* (1959), *Patron de New York* (1964), *Hommes de tous les continents* (1967), *La ville où nul ne meurt* (1969), *Monsieur Thôgô-Gnini* (1970), *Les voix dans le vent* (1970), *Béatrice du Congo* (1970), *Îles de tempête* (1973), *Papassidi maître-escroc* (1975), *Mhoi cheul* (1979), *Opinions d'un nègre* (1979), *Les belles histoires de Kacou Ananzè*, *Commandant Taureault et ses nègres* (1980), *Les jambes du fils de Dieu* (1980), *Carnets de prison* (1981), and *Les contes de Koutou-as-Samala* (1982).
4. Jean Pliya (1931–) is a playwright and short story writer who was born in Dahomey, a former kingdom in present-day Benin. Educated at the Université de Dakar and then at the Université de Toulouse, Pliya taught in

Benin before accepting work in the government there. His writings center on recounting colonial history. He has also translated tales from the Fon of Southern Benin into the French language.

5. Sony Lab'ou Tansi (1947–1995), born Marcel Ntsoni, was a Congolese novelist, playwright, and poet. Tansi remains one of the most productive Francophone African writers of his age. His novel entitled *L'Antipeuple* won the *Grand Prix Littéraire d'Afrique Noire*. Before his premature death, he ran a theatre company in Brazzaville, capital of the Republic of the Congo. Tansi was born in the village of Kimwaanza in the former Belgian Congo not far from Kinshasa in the modern-day Democratic Republic of the Congo. Initially educated in Kikongo, the local language, Tansi began to learn the French language when he was twelve years old after his family relocated to Congo-Brazzaville (Republic of the Congo). At the *École Normale Supérieure d'Afrique Centrale* in Brazzaville, Tansi studied literature and he eventually became a French and English teacher in Kindauba after earning his degree in 1971. An emerging playwright, he began to write under the name "Sony La'bou Tansi" in homage to Tchicaya U Tam'si, a fellow Congolese writer whose poetry addressed the oppressive nature of the state. At the start of his career, Tansi taught at the Collège Tchicaya-Pierre in Pointe Noire while honing his writing craft. In 1979, he founded the Rocado Zulu Theatre, a theatre company that would eventually perform his plays in Africa and throughout the world. After leaving the teaching profession, Tansi worked in government, serving as an administrator in several ministries in Brazzaville. During this period, he became more politically involved and he ultimately worked with opposition leader Bernard Kolélas in the late 1980s to create the *Mouvement Congolais pour la Démocratie et le Développement Intégral*, a local political party that sought to bring resistance against the communist regime of President Denis Sassou Nguesso and his Congolese Labor Party. In 1992, Tansi became a deputy in Parliament representing the Makélékélé arrondissement of Brazzaville. During this time, he learned that he had contracted the AIDS virus. Tansi died from AIDS-related illness in May 1995. At his death, Sony Lab'ou Tansi left a corpus of plays, novels, and short stories, many of which have yet to be fully explored. Among his most celebrated works are *Conscience de tracteur* (1979), *La vie et demie: Roman* (1979), *Je soussigné cardiaque* (1981), *La parenthèse de sang* (1981), and *Francophonie: 2 pièces* (1987). Several significant works were published posthumously, including *L'autre monde: Écrits inédits*, edited by Nicolas Martin-Granel and Bruno Tilliette (1997), *L'atelier de Sony Labou Tansi*, ed. Martin-Granel and Greta Rodriguez-Antoniotti' (2005), and *Paroles inédites: La rue des mouches (comédie tragique), Entretiens, Lettres à Sony*, ed. Bernard Magnier (2005). As a collection, Tansi's writings give the reader a glimpse of his African voice, an often politically- charged and always passionate perspective on a nation in development after gaining its independence.

6. For a detailed discussion of the rise of the African elite after independence, see Toyin Falola's book entitled *Nationalism and African Intellectuals* (Rochester: University of Rochester Press, 2001.)

7. The "monomyth" is a term first used by James Joyce in *Finnegans Wake* (New York: Viking Press, Inc., 1939), 581. The monomyth is an essential designation for the myth critic, useful in describing the evolution of the hero throughout the narrative.

8. I acknowledge the paradox of applying a Western notion of time in the deconstruction of a contemporary African world perspective.

9. "...[I]t remains common to collectively mark Africa after 1960 with a 'post'—postcolonial, postindependence—although Portugal, Britain, and the White minority regime in South Africa clawed stubbornly to African territories into the 1970s and '80s" (Talton 5).

10. This quotation is attributed to former Prime Minister Margaret Thatcher of England.

11. The current number of countries in Africa is fifty-four. See above endnote 1.

12. My comment here serves to acknowledge Barack Obama's evidenced African history, since his father Barack Obama, Sr., was a Luo from Nyang'oma Kogelo, Kenya. It contains no political connotation.

Chapter 1

1. French district administrators maintained census records during this period. See

Notes—Chapter 1

the Archives Nationales, Paris, Fonds Afrique Occidentale Française, série G, sous-série 22.

2. "Neocolonialism ... is not simply a surreptitious recapture of national resources by external agents in the aftermath of flag independence. Neocolonialism is an internal state of affairs, the unmasked recolonization of human existence...." Ato Sekyi-Otu, *Fanon's Dialectic of Experience* (Cambridge: Harvard UP: 1996): 150.

3. To define the term "ethnicity" is a challenge within itself, as there is virtually no limit to the number of ethic designations that one can construct.

4. Republic of Cameroon, January 1, 1960; Republic of Senegal, April 4, 1960; Republic of Togo, April 27, 1960; Democratic Republic of Congo (Kinshasa), June 30, 1960; Republic of Benin, August 1, 1960; Republic of Niger, August 3, 1960; Popular Democratic Republic of Burkina Faso, August 5, 1960; Republic of Côte d'Ivoire, August 7, 1960; Central African Republic, August 13, 1960; Republic of Congo (Brazzaville), August 15, 1960; Republic of Gabon, August 17, 1960; Republic of Mali, September 22, 1960.

5. The notion of an authentic identity is one that poses its own philosophical questions. Is an authentic identity even a theoretical possibility? Do all human beings not, in some way, assume identities that others have created? How, then, can one forge an authentic identity? This essay acknowledges this paradox.

6. The complete list of signers included Muriel Barbery, Tahar Ben Jelloun, Alain Borer, Roland Brival, Maryse Condé, Didier Daeninckx, Ananda Devi, Alain Dugrand, Edouard Glissant, Jacques Godbout, Nancy Huston, Koffi Kwahulé, Dany Laferrière, Gilles Lapouge, Jean-Marie Laclavetine, Michel Layaz, Michel Le Bris, JMG Le Clézio, Yvon Le Men, Amin Maalouf, Alain Mabanckou, Anna Moï, Wajdi Mouawad, Nimrod, Wilfried N'Sondé, Esther Orner, Erik Orsenna, Benoît Peeters, Patrick Rambaud, Gisèle Pineau, Jean-Claude Pirotte, Grégoire Polet, Patrick Raynal, Jean-Luc V. Raharimanana, Jean Rouaud, Boualem Sansal, Dai Sitje, Brina Svit, Lyonel Trouillot, Anne Vallaeys, Jean Vautrin, André Velter, Gary Victor, and Abdourahman A. Waberi.

7. The Breton language is currently being taught at Harvard University.

8. Since 1999, UNESCO has undertaken a vast program to inventory, define and safeguard the intangible cultural heritage of humanity. The 2013 UNESCO World Heritage List includes 981 properties forming part of the cultural and natural heritage that the World Heritage Committee considers as having outstanding universal value. In 2013, the World Heritage Committee added nineteen sites to the World Heritage List. When the readers envisions world heritage sites, what most often comes to mind are natural and cultural sites such as The Grand Canyon at the cave paintings at Lascaux. Expanding our understanding of the contribution of humanity to world cultural history, it is appropriate to also consider language as a component of our cultural heritage. As the cradle of humanity, Africa has nearly half of the world's language families, yet it has been slow to take advantage of the development of this important cultural diversity. If cultural identity is the very foundation of life–and I would like to make the claim here that it is–the diverse peoples of Africa would be negligent if they forgot to show the world their contributions to the planet's linguistic heritage. Although language is internalized by the individual speaker, Wilhelm von Humboldt maintained that language functions most fully in the collective as it both expresses and shapes the spirit of a people and the soul of a nation. During a meeting of the United Nations General Assembly held on May 16, 2007, the UNGA declared 2008 to be the International Year of Languages and placed UNESCO at the head of support campaign. The United Nations General Assembly chose UNESCO for the simple fact that the latter has considered languages as an essential component of the institution's overall focus. Within the first article of UNESCO's Constitution, languages are mentioned in its efforts to counteract language-based discrimination and as a vehicle to transport both information and ideas. Within the African continent, in particular the importance of languages has become increasing more significant in recent decades. In the New Millennium, we have witnessed the meeting of the Conference of Ministers of Culture of the African Union meeting in December 2005 which, in combination with a January 2006 decision by the African Union's Executive Board in, resulted in declaring 2006 as the "Year of African Languages." United Nations' resolution 56262 (Part II) from 2007 on the preservation and protection of all languages and the proclama-

tion of 2008 as the "International Year of Languages" has brought noteworthy attention to both the desire and the need to preserve African indigenous languages. The challenges of multilingualism are numerous and also require teamwork and collaboration among African nations.

9. According to the *Robert* dictionary, in 1965 the French Ministry of Culture created the word "francité" to refer to "characteristics unique to French culture." It is not likely by coincidence that the creation of this word in the neocolonial period coincides with the independence achieved by the former French colonies.

10. The Abbaye de Thélème is the first utopia in French literature. It is described by François Rabelais in Chapter LVII of his work entitled *Gargantua* (1534/1535).

11. For more on the use of sound and silence in Samuel Beckett, see my article entitled "A Matter of Fundamentals: Sound and Silence in the Radio Drama of Samuel Beckett" (*Babilónia* 10/11 (2011): 107–21.

12. Zinsou's adaptation of the Shaka theme will be discussed in greater detail in Chapter 4.

Chapter 2

1. Quoted in Mahamadou Sangare's article entitled "Les langues locales et l'identité africaine" available on the author's own web page.

2. In 2001, UNESCO estimated the amount of illiterates at approximately 1 billion (World Literacy Foundation).

3. Although much of Shakespeare's theatre contains the use of iambic pentameter (nobles' speech), the present example is called trochaic tetrameter. It refers to a line of four trochaic feet. Shakespeare used trochaic tetrameter to contrast his usual iambic pentameter. In *A Midsummer Night's Dream*, Shakespeare often wrote the lines of his fairies in catalectic trochaic tetrameter as is evidenced by Robin's (Puck) lines noted here with which Shakespeare closes his play (Vickers 319).

4. For more on the semiotics of narration, see Keir Elam's *The Semiotics of Theatre and Drama*. London: Routledge, 2002.

5. We could argue that the African *griot* performs a similar function.

6. I will point out here that the current politically correct label for literature written in the French language is "littérature-monde en français" that emerged in 2007.

7. Ahmadou Kourouma (1927–2003), an African writer of international fame, was born in northern Ivory-Coast and grew up with the Malinke language and culture. He died in Lyon, France, in December 2003, having spent his life's work speaking out against the effects of colonization. Kourouma wrote four novels and a stage play, including *En attendant le vote des bêtes sauvages* (1998) that received the Inter Award and *Allah n'est pas obligé, histoire d'un enfant-soldat*, which won the Prix Renaudot in 2000. Although Kourouma wrote in the French language, it is clear that he sought to make the language entirely his own by integrating his native Malinke (Maninka) into the French language.

8. The Martinican writer Suzanne Dracius was born in 1951 at Fort-de-France. She studied at La Sorbonne in Paris, France, and taught the classics in France and in Martinique. The author of several novels and short stories, her first novel, *L'autre qui danse*, was published in 1989.

9. Born in Church Point, Louisiana, United States, Barry Jean Ancelet was educated in Louisiana and received his doctorate in Creole Studies in France. He has written several books on various aspects of Louisiana's Cajun and Creole cultures and languages. He was one of the first authors to attempt to give the Cajun language a written form.

10. I am indebted here to the work of Denise Egéa-Kuehne and, more specifically, to her article entitled "Writing in the Language of the Other" in the *International Journal of the Humanities* 4.3 (2007): 103–9.

11. I must acknowledge the fact that Phillipson's theory has its own wrinkles. How does he explain, for example, that there are some individuals within colonized nations who willingly use the imperial language?

12. Niger-Congo (Sudanic) languages are still spoken throughout Sub-Saharan Africa (CIA World Factbook).

13. Derrida never truly separated his work in semiology from his interest in current affairs. See Denis Hollier's *A New History of French Literature* (Cambridge: Harvard University Press, 1994): 1039–40.

14. If the reader thinks that Derrida has no relevance in the study of Francophone African poetic literature, I will point out here

that one of Derrida's most well-known works, *Dessins et portraits*, offered a commentary on the theatrical works of 20th century writer Antonin Artaud.

15. Since 2007, the French government has been working to preserve and maintain indigenous languages spoken within continental France such as Breton. Is there any similar effort to preserve and maintain indigenous languages within West Africa?

16. For information on a specific endangered language, see UNESCO's searchable database entitled "Atlas of the World's Languages in Danger." http://www.unesco.org/culture/languages-atlas/index.php

17. This idea reflects the concept of the "language island." According to Michael T. Putnam, a "language island" is "a (for the most part) moribund, isolated language/dialect that has little if any connection with the host culture/language of origin, that (likely) shows (significant) signs of attrition and assimilation (especially w.r.t. lexical borrowing) from a now dominant L2. The oldest generation has the most fluency and the youngest has a passive knowledge of the dialect/language at best."

18. I attended the film festival during which Manthia Diawara recounted this anecdote.

19. Diawara hold three degrees from American universities: Ph.D. 1985, Indiana; M.A. 1978, American; B.A. 1976, and is, therefore, very much rooted in American life.

20. The exploration of specific African languages extends well beyond the scope of the present study. For more information on African languages and identity formation, see Christiaan Swanepoel's "African Languages and the Identity Question in the 21st century." *South African Journal of African Languages* 33.1 (2013): 19–28.

21. See Eileen Julien's article entitled "Reading 'orality' in French-language novels from sub–Saharan Africa" in *Francophone Postcolonial Studies: A Critical Introduction*. Charles Forsdick and David Murphy, eds. London: Edward Arnold, (2003): 122–32.

Chapter 3

1. The examples presented here are examples of a form of African poetry called "Praise Poetry" that serves to herald an important cultural or historic figure.

2. English translation taken from Russell A. Kaschula's article entitled "Imbongi and Griot: Toward a Comparative Analysis of Oral Poetics in Southern and West Africa." *Journal of African Cultural Studies* 12.1 (1999): 55–76. The French-language version is unavailable.

3. Zolani Mkiva's poem is found in Russell A. Kaschula's article entitled "Imbongi and Griot: Toward a Comparative Analysis of Oral Poetics in Southern and West Africa." *Journal of African Cultural Studies* 12.1 (1999): 55–76.

4. Mkiva is Nelson Mandela's former official praise singer. Following Mandela's death, Mkiva stated: "There is no tomorrow without a yesterday. There is no tonight without a yesternight. The bones of our ancestors are vibrating. The waves of African oceans are reverberating." "'Go well Madiba'-Mandela funeral quotes." *Times Live* 16 Dec. 2013. Web. 2 Jan. 2014.

5. Senegalese culture makes a distinction between the *griot*, a traditional African storyteller, and the *marabout*, or Islamic leader thought to have supernatural powers. They are not "one in the same."

6. This *blanchissement* naturally recalls Fanon's *Peau noire, masques blancs*.

7. Pius Ngandu Nkashama has written several well-known novels including *Le pacte de sang* (1984), *Un jour de grand soleil sur les montagnes de l'Éthiopie* (1991), *Le doyen marri* (1994), *La rédemption de Sha Ilunga* (2007), and *En suivant le sentier sous les palmiers* (2009) that focus on the theme of pushing Africa into the future. He has also published several literary texts in his native language, Cilubà, and is the author of several critical texts including *Littératures africaines* (Silex), *Un dictionnaire des œuvres littéraires africaines*, and several theatre plays including *Bonjour monsieur le Ministre* (1983), *L'empire des ombres vivantes* (1991), and *May Britt de Santa Cruz* (2003). Nkashama has taught at universities in Congo and in France before accepting the post of Distinguished Professor of French and Francophone literature at Louisiana State University in Baton Rouge where he works at present.

8. Parts of this poem were previously published in Dakeyo's poem entitled "Envoyez-moi des nouvelles" (Éditions Saint-Germain-des-Prés, Paris, 1979).

9. The poetic writings of several female

Francophone African writers are also included in Paul Dakeyo's *Monsieur Mandela* anthology. These works will be treated in Chapter 5.

Chapter 4

1. This chapter is informed by a conference presentation that I gave in 2013 at the 66th Kentucky Foreign Languages Conference entitled "The Monomyth: Re-reading Camara Laye's *L'Enfant noir* as The Quest of the Hero."
2. The development of the performer-audience relationship is also referred to as "stagescaping."
3. As a matter of definition, the term "prolepsis" refers to the representation of a thing as existing before it actually does. "Analepsis," in contrast, refers to a "flashback" in which earlier parts of a narrative are related to others that have already been narrated.
4. See also Pius Ngandu Nkashama's *Théâtres et scènes de spectacles: Études sur les dramaturgies et les arts gestuels*. Paris: L'Harmattan, 1993.
5. "'France Noire/Black France' Film Festival," Forum des Images, Forum des Halles, Paris, France, May 2010.
6. See also Toyin Falola's and Charles Thomas' *Securing Africa: Local Crises and Foreign Intervention* (New York: Routledge, 2013).
7. Within the Francophone adaptations of the Shaka myth, Noliwé is also sometimes spelled Nolivè.
8. Does Mofolo's Chaka seek to punish his mother for the fact that he was conceived out of wedlock? What does this perspective suggest about family life in Africa?
9. The only African nation that has Spanish as an official language is Equatorial Guinea where the official languages are French, Spanish, and Portuguese. Equatorial Guinea is also a dictatorship. ("Equatorial Guinea," CIA World Factbook.) Moustapha's play earned the *Prix special du Jury* at the Onzième Concours Théâtral, Interafricain.
10. The French slogan "Nos ancêtres, les Gaulois" exhibits a similar characteristic. We can only wonder how many French could, in fact, successfully trace their genealogical roots to the Gaulois.
11. I have also discussed Senouvo Agbota Zinsou's *On joue la comédie* in my chapter entitled "The Black Man's Burden and the Struggle for Independence" by focusing on aspects on Zinsou's play that evidence its belonging to an African theatrical subgenre called the "concert party." In this chapter, I connect Zinsou's *On joue la comédie* more specifically to the Shaka theme.

Chapter 5

1. It is significant to note here that d'Almeida and Cazenave are scholars working in the United States. Volet is a scholar working in France. Much scholarship on Francophone African poets and playwrights is conducted by scholars who live outside of Africa. For a list of current works by Francophone African women writers, see Appendix I.
2. Francophone African women, do, in fact, write plays, but it seems that they are more likely to do so either if they are residing outside of French-speaking Africa or if they are the child of an expatriate of Francophone Africa. Marie NDiaye is an excellent example of the latter case. Born in France of a Senegalese father, NDiaye has written several theatrical works including *Hilda* (1999), *Papa doit manger* (2003), and *Les serpents* (2004). She has also written a screenplay entitled *White Material* (2009), co-written with world-renowned film director Claire Denis.
3. See also my article entitled "Sexual Politics: Mapping the Body in Marguerite Duras's *L'Amant*." *Romania Silesiana* 8:1 (2013): 273–83.
4. This discussion would be weakened if I did not acknowledge the French feminist writer, Simone de Beauvoir, and her influential *Le Deuxième sexe*. In her book, de Beauvoir argues that women throughout history have been defined as the "other" sex, an aberration from the "normal" male sex. She further suggests that "One is not born, but rather becomes, a woman" (331).
5. See "Gaze," *Art & Popular Culture*. http://www.artandpopularculture.com/Gaze.
6. Although Mulvey's theory represents one of the most significant feminist theories of the second wave, this study would be weakened without recognizing the fact that recent feminist theorists (including Mulvey) have

extended the notion of the "male gaze" to show that it is not exclusively male. The notion of a "female gaze" certainly exists, though it is, perhaps, not as universally accepted as its male counterpart. For more on notions of the "female gaze," see Hollows, Joanne and Rachel Moseley (eds.) *Feminism in Popular Culture*. Oxford & N.Y.: Berg, 2006, and Tasker, Yvonne and Diane Negra (eds). *Interrogating Postfeminism: Gender and the Politics of Popular Culture*. Durham: Duke University Press, 2007.

7. We could make the argument here that while written literature affords one the opportunity to relate one's own stories, oral literature, in contrast tends to serve to recount the stories of others. Therefore, it is not surprising that African women would have difficulty entering a literary form that focuses so heavily on telling one's own story.

8. As I have stated elsewhere, I openly reject the "Third World" label that scholars continue to apply to the African context. This label reinforces the dialectic between industrialized and pre-industrialized countries.

9. The majority of supporters of Francophone African women writers tend to be female scholars. Until more male scholars give Francophone African women writers their due respect, the marginalization of female writers will continue.

10. Hélène Cixous coined *écriture féminine* in her essay, "The Laugh of the Medusa" (1975).

11. See also Sharpley-Whiting's book entitled *Negritude Women*. Minneapolis: University of Minnesota Press, 2002.

12. See also Valérie Orlando's "Werewere Liking and the Development of Ritual Theatre in Cameroon: Towards a New Feminine Theatre for Africa." In *African Theatre for Development: Art for Self-Determination*. Kamal Salhi, ed. Exeter: Intellect, 1998: 155–73.

13. For more information on the social aspects of Liking's theatre, see Alice-Delphine Tang's "L'Esthétisation des tragédies sociales dans La Mémoire amputée de Were Were Liking." In *Dire le social dans le roman francophone contemporain*. Bisanswa, Justin K., ed. Paris: Honoré Champion; 2011: 333–46.

14. Rabiatou Njoya also has a collection of unedited poetry entitled *O! Nkindi* (1991).

15. For more information on the government financing of theatre in West Africa, see Chapter 2 of John Conteh-Morgan's *Theatre and Drama in Francophone Africa* (1994).

16. Since this book focuses on poetic literature produced in Francophone Africa, I will make no attempt here to outline the contribution of women writer's to the genre of the novel. It suffices to say that women have made a strong contribution.

17. Hale has published several books and articles on *griot/griottes* in French-speaking Africa including *Griots and Griottes: Masters of Words and Music. Study of Keepers of the Oral Tradition in West Africa from the 14th Century to the Present, from Bamako to New York City*. Indiana University Press (1998/2007), "The Social Functions of Griots and Griottes in the Sahel and the Savanna Regions of West Africa" in *Camel Tracks: Critical Perspectives on Sahelian Literature*, eds. Deborah Boyd-Buggs and Joyce Hope Scott. Trenton: Africa World Press (2003): 31–60, and "Islam and the Griots in West Africa: Bridging the Gap between Two Traditions," *The African Journal* 13(1982): 84–90.

18. Handwritten letter from the cahier of Paul Colin's sketches and the epistolary preface to *Le Tumulte noir*. I have reproduced it here with its original spelling and grammar mistakes.

19. Baker was recruited to the theatre by Carol Dudley, a British casting director, who had recently taking over the operations of the theatre.

20. For more information on race and representation, see bell hooks' *Black Looks: Race and Representation* (1992).

21. The Musée de l'Homme is closed for renovations until 2015.

22. The Musée du Quai Branly opened in June 2006. Many of the artifacts of the Musée de l'homme have been transferred to the Musée du Quai Branly that contains approximately 70,000 objects from the Maghreb, Sub-Saharan Africa, and Madagascar.

23. For more on the self-contradictory female body, see Catherine Breillat's controversial film entitled *Anatomie de l'enfer* (2004).

24. I have previously written about the power of visual representation in my article entitled "Beyond the Margins: Identity Fragmentation in Visual Representation in Michel Tournier's *La Goutte d'or*." *Text Matters* 2.2 (2012): 250–63.

25. Here, I point out the fact that for some time the French have been interested in photographs of the naked female body. Along the Seine in Paris, *bouquinistes* sell postcards featuring nude women.

26. Because the portrait represents the subject's soul, it is easy to see why taking a photograph without permission "dispossesses" the subject. See Alain Busaine's "A Dispossessed Text: The Writings and Photography of Michel Tournier," Trans. Roxanne Lapidus, *Sub-Stance* 58 (1989): 27.

27. It is important to understand the term "Orient" from the French perspective, as it is commonly used to refer to both Saharan and Sub-Saharan Africa. The terms "Maghreb," "Maghrébin," and "Maghrébine" are more commonly used within a North African context. See Nissan Perez's *Focus East: Early Photography in the Near East (1839–1885)* (New York: Abrams, 1988): 100–2.

28. With regard to a Lacanian analysis of Baker's performance work, several interesting questions arise. Firstly, is it theoretically possible to actually lose an identity, to have it stolen, or even to regain it? Or does such a notion function purely metaphorically here? Further, is it theoretically possible to quantify or to qualify "identity?" If so, how would one describe it or measure it? If one can neither qualify nor quantify "identity," then does it really even exist at all?

Conclusion

1. Robert Leggewie's anthology consists of two volumes. The first focuses on literature from the Middle Ages through the 18th century. The second volume treats the 19th and 20th centuries.

2. Internetworldstats.com reports current internet usage in Africa (as of June 20, 2012) at approximately 15.6 percent of the population. When compared to the usage rate of Europe (63.2 percent) and that of the United States (78.6 percent), these data imply that Africa does not have the infrastructure to support widespread internet use.

Appendix I

1. In the live reading, President Obama changed the word "great" to "magnificent."

Appendix II

1. This list includes feminine writers throughout the French-speaking world.

Works Cited

Abdi, Ali A. *Culture, Education and Development in South Africa: Historical and Contemporary Perspectives*. Westport: Bergin & Garvey, 2002. Print.

——. "Oral Societies and Colonial Experiences: Sub-Saharan Africa and the De Facto Power of the Written Word." *International Education* 37.1 (2007): 42–59. Print.

Achard, Paul. "Tout en noir ou la Revue nègre." *Paris-midi* 27 Sept. 1925: 2. Print.

Achebe, Chinua. *Home and Exile*. Oxford: Oxford University Press, 2000. Print.

Agatucci, Cora. "African Storytelling." Central Oregon Community College, 1 Jan. 2010. Web. 26 Nov. 2013.

Ahmad, Aijaz. *In Theory: Classes, Nations, Literatures*. London: Verso, 1994. Print.

d'Almeida, Irène Assiba. *Francophone African Women Writers: Destroying the Emptiness of Silence*. Gainesville: University of Florida Press, 1994. Print.

——. *A Rain of Words: A Bilingual Anthology of Women's Poetry in Francophone Africa*, ed. Trans. Janis A. Mayes. Alexandria: University of Virginia Press, 2009. Print.

Anderson, Roger. *The Power and the Word: Language, Power and Change*. Toronto: Paladin Grafton Books, 1988. Print.

Andrzejewski, Bogumil. "Somali Literature." In W. Andrzejewski, S., Pilaszewicz, & W. Tyloch (Eds.), *Literatures in African Languages: Theoretical Issues and Sample Surveys*. New York: Cambridge University Press (1985): 337–407. Print.

Arcangeli, Alessandro. *Cultural History: A Concise Introduction*. London: Routledge, 2012. Print.

Armes, Roy. *African Filmmaking: North and South of the Sahara*. Bloomington, Indiana University Press, 2006. Print.

Artaud, Antonin, Paule Thévenin, and Jacques Derrida. *Dessins et portraits*. Paris: Gallimard, 1986. Print.

Ashcroft, Bill, Gareth Griffiths, and Helen Tiffin. *The Empire Writes Back: Theory and Practice in Post-Colonial Literatures*. London: Psychology Press, 2002. Print.

Asimeng-Boahene, Lewis. "The Social Construction of Sub-Saharan Women's Status through African Proverbs." *Mediterranean Journal of Social Sciences* 4:1 (2013): 123–31. Print.

Bakary, Traoré. *The Black African Theatre and Its Social Functions*. Ibadan: Ibadan University Press, 1972. Print.

Baker, Jean-Claude. *Josephine Baker: The Hungry Heart*. Lanham: Cooper Square Press, 2001. Print.

Barkan, Sandra. "Emerging Definitions of African Literature." In *African Literature Studies: The Present State/L'État présent*. Stephen Arnold, ed. Washington D.C.: Three Continents Press: 27–46. Print.

Barthes, Roland. "Myth Today." *Cultural Theory and Popular Culture*. Ed. John

Storey. USA: Prentice Hall (1998): 109–18. Print.

———. "The Death of the Author." In *Image-Music-Text*. Ed. Stephen Heath, London: Fontana, 1977: 142–48. Print.

Baudelaire, Charles. *Œuvres complètes*. Paris: Éditions du Seuil, 1968. Print.

Baudrillard, Jean. *Selected Writings*, ed. Mark Poster. 2nd ed. Stanford: Stanford University Press, 2001. Print.

Bauer, Gérard. "La Revue nègre." *Annales* 18 Oct. 1925. Print.

Béart, Charles. "Le théâtre indigène et la culture franco-africaine." Spec. issue of *L'Education Africaine* (1937): 1–14. Print.

Beck, Alan. "Cognitive Mapping and Radio Drama," *Consciousness, Literature and the Arts* 1.2 (Jul. 2000). *Savoyhill.co.uk*. Web. 18 Nov. 2013.

"Betty Friedan, Who Ignited Cause in 'Feminine Mystique,' Dies at 85." *New York Times* 5 Feb. 2006. Print.

Bhabha, Homi K. *The Location of Culture*. New York: Routledge, 1994. Print.

"Biography." *Nelson Mandela Foundation*. Nelson Mandela Centre of Memory, n.d. Web. 24 Nov. 2013.

Blanchet, Philippe. "Langues, identités culturelles et développement: quelle dynamique pour les peuples émergents?" *Conférence, Cinquantenaire de la Revue Présence Africaine*. UNESCO, 1998. Print.

Boas, Franz. "Museums of Ethnology and Their Classification." *Science* 9 (1887): 589. Print.

Bouche, Denise. *L'enseignement dans les territoires français de l'Afrique occidentale de 1817 à 1920: Mission civilisatrice ou formation d'une élite?* 2 vols. Lille: Atelier de reproduction des thèses, 1975. Print.

Bourdain, G. S. "French Plays Find a Soho Home." *New York Times* 13 Mar. 1988. Web. 23 Mar. 2013.

Bray, Elisa. "'The Blacks': Genet's contentious play returns." *Independent* 18 Oct. 2007. Web. 16 Dec. 2013.

Brown, Gillian. *Speakers, Listeners and Communication: Explorations in Discourse Analysis*. New York: Cambridge University Press, 1995. Print.

Burguière, André. "*anthropologie historique*." *Dictionnaire des sciences historiques*. Paris: Presses universitaires de France, 1986: 52–60. Print.

Burke, Peter. *A New Kind of History from the Writings of Lefebvre*. Trans. L. Folca. London: Routledge, 1973. Print.

———. *What is Cultural History?* Cambridge: Polity Press, 2004. Print.

Burness, Donald. *Shaka, King of the Zulus, in African Literature*. Washington, D.C.: Three Continents, 1976. Print.

Busaine, Alain. "A Dispossessed Text: The Writings and Photography of Michel Tournier." Trans. Roxanne Lapidus. *Sub-Stance* 58 (1989): 25–34. Print.

Butler, Judith. *Gender Trouble*. New York: Routledge, 1990. Print.

Cahill, Jane. *Her Kind: Stories of Women from Greek Mythology*. Orchard Park: Broadview Press, 1995. Print.

Campbell, Joseph. *The Hero with a Thousand Faces*. 2nd edition. Princeton: Princeton University Press, 1968. Print.

———. *The Power of Myth*. New York: Doubleday, 1988. Print.

Cazenave, Odile and Patricia Célérier. *Contemporary Francophone African Writers and the Burden of Commitment*. Charlottesville: University of Virginia Press, 2011. Print.

Césaire, Aimé. *Discours sur le colonialisme*. Paris: Éditions Présence Africaine, 1955. Print.

Cevaer, Francoise. "African Literatures Take the Offensive. (Cameroonian Poet Paul Dakeyo) (interview)." Trans. Patricia Geesey. *Research in African Literatures* 22.1 (1991): 101–6. Print.

Chartier, Roger. "L'histoire culturelle." J. Revel and N. Wachtel, eds. *Une école pour les sciences*. Paris: Éditions du Cerf-Éditions de l'ÉHÉSS, 1996 : 73–92. Print.

Chemain, Arlette. "Emergence d'une littérature féminine de langue française en Afrique sub-saharienne." In Hawkins, Peter (ed. and introd.), Lavers, Annette (ed. and introd.), and Guillemin, Philippe (introd.). *Protée noir: Essais sur la littérature francophone de l'Afrique noire et des Antilles.* Paris: Harmattan, 1992: 143–58. Print.

———. "L'image de la femme en ses métamorphoses: Écritures subsahariennes de langue française (1950–2010)." *Caietele Echinox* 22 (2012): 113–23. Print.

———. "Quelques réflexions sur une literature féminine de langue française en Afrique sub-saharienne." *Cham* 1 (1988): 55–63. Print.

Chemain-Degrange, Arlette. *Émancipation féminine et roman africain*. Dakar: Les Nouvelles Éditions Africaines, 1980. Print.

Christian, Barbara. "The Race for Theory." Ed. Linda Kauffman. *Gender and Theory: Dialogues on Feminist Criticism*. Oxford: Blackwell (1989): 225–37. Print.

CIA World Factbook. Central Intelligence Agency. n.d. Web. 10 Oct. 2013.

Clearsky, Eileen. "Destruction of a Language and Culture: A Personal Story." *Diaspora, Indigenous, and Minority Education: Studies of Migration, Integration, Equity, and Cultural Survival* 5.4 (2011): 260–65. Print.

Cloete, M. J. and Madadzhe, R.N. "Bury My Bones but Keep My Words: The Interface between Oral Tradition and Contemporary African Writing." *Literator* 25.2 (2004): 27–44. Print.

Colapietro, Vincent Michael. *Peirce's Doctrine of Signs: Theory, Applications, and Connections*. Berlin: de Gruyter, 1996. Print.

Collins, Georgina. *Translating Francophone Senegalese Women's Literature: Issues of Change, Power, Mediation and Orality (Volume 1 of 2)*. Diss. University of Warwick, 2010. Print.

Collins, Robert O. and James McDonald Burns. *A History of Sub-Saharan Africa*. New York: Cambridge University Press, 2013. Print.

The Columbia Dictionary of Modern Literary and Cultural Criticism. Eds. Joseph Childers and Gary Hentzi. New York: Columbia University Press, 1995. Print.

Combe, Dominique. "Littératures francophones, littérature-monde en français." *Modern & Contemporary France* 18.2 (2010): 231–49. Print.

Confer, Vincent. *France and Algeria*. Syracuse: Syracuse University Press, 1966. Print.

Conteh-Morgan, John, ed. *New Francophone African and Caribbean Theatres*. Bloomington: Indiana University Press, 2010. Print.

———. *Theatre and Drama in Francophone Africa: A Critical Introduction*. Cambridge: Cambridge University Press, 1994. Print.

Cooper, Frederick. "Possibility and Constrain: African Independence in Historical Perspective." *Journal of African History* 49.2 (2008): 167–96. Print.

Cornevin, Robert. *Le Théâtre en Afrique noire et à Madagascar*. Paris: Le Livre africain, 1980. Print.

Creary, Nicholas M. *African Intellectuals and Decolonization*. Athens: Ohio University Press, 2012. Print.

Culler, Jonathan. *Structuralist Poetics*. Ithaca: Cornell University Press, 1975. Print.

Curtin, Philip D. *African History: From Earliest Times to Independence*. New York: Longman, 1995. Print.

Dakeyo, Paul. *Monsieur Mandela*. Ivry-sur-Seine: Éditions Panafrika/Silex/Nouvelles du Sud, 2013. Print.

Davidson, Basil. *Africa in Modern History*. New York: Penguin, 1985. Print.

———. *The Black Man's Burden: Africa and the Curse of the Nation-State*. New York: Times Books, 1992. Print.

de Beauvoir, Simone. *Le Deuxième Sexe*. Paris: Gallimard, 1949. Print.

Deleuze, Gilles and Felix Guattari. *Mille Plateaux*. Paris: Minuit, 1980. Print.

Derive, Jean. "Oralité, écriture et le problème de l'identité culturelle en Afrique." *Bayreuth African Studies Series* 3 (1985): 5–36. Print.

Deroo, Éric and Antoine Champeaux. *La Force noire: Gloire et infortunes d'une légende coloniale*. Paris: Tallandier, 2006. Print.

Derrida, Jacques. *Le monolinguisme*

de l'autre ou la prothèse d'origine. Paris: Éditions Galilée, 1996. Print.

───. *The Other Heading.* Trans. Pascale-Anne Brault and Michael Naas. Bloomington: Indiana University Press, 1992. Print.

de Saivre, Denyse. "Entretien avec Senouvo Agbota Zinsou." *Recherche, Pédagogie, Culture* 57 (1982): 74–5. Print.

Diawara, Manthia. "Film Screening Talk." "'France Noire/Black France' Film Festival." Forum des Images, Forum des Halles, Paris, France, 22 May 2010.

Dingomé, Jeanne N. "Isn't Woman Woman's Worst Enemy?" In *Critical Perspectives on Cameroon Writing.* Hansel Ndumbe Eyoh, Albert Azeyeh, Nalova Lyonga, eds. Bamenda: African Books Collective, 2013. Print.

Diop, David. *Coups de Pilon.* Paris: Présence Africaine, 1973. Print.

Diop, Samba. *The Oral History and Literature of the Wolof People of Waalo, Northern Senegal.* New York: The Edwin Mellen Press, 1995. Print.

───. *Des transpositions francophones du mythe de Chaka.* (Review) *Research in African Literatures* 35.4 (2004): 177–79. Print.

Dodge, Dorothy. *African Politics in Perspective.* Princeton: Van Nostrand, 1966. Print.

Donkor, Martha. "Marching to the Tune: Colonization, Globalization, Immigration, and the Ghanaian Diaspora." *Africa Today* 52.1 (2005): 27–44. Print.

Drew, Elizabeth. *T.S. Eliot: The Design of His Poetry.* New York: Charles Scribner's & Sons, 1949. Print.

Druker, Don. "Listening to the Radio." 325–36. Print.

Dumont, René. *False Start in Africa.* New York: Praeger, 1966. Print.

Eagleton, Mary. *Feminist Literary Theory: A Reader.* Oxford: Blackwell, 2011. Print.

Eco, Umberto. *La Recherche de la langue parfaite.* Paris: Éditions du Seuil, 1997. Print.

"The Economic & Social Cost of Illiteracy." World Literacy Foundation. 12 Jan. 2012. Web. 26 Nov. 2013.

Egéa-Kuehne, Denise. "Writing in the Language of the Other." *International Journal of the Humanities* 4.3 (2007): 103–9. Print.

Ellis, John. M. *The Theory of Literary Criticism: A Logical Analysis.* Berkeley: University of California Press, 1977. Print.

Emecheta, Buchi. "Feminism with a Small 'f!'." in *Criticism and Ideology: Second African Writers' Conference.* Ed. Kirsten Holst Petersen. Scandinavian Institute of African Studies (1988): 173–85. Print.

Engleton, Terry. *Sweet Violence: The Idea of the Tragic.* Malden: Blackwell, 2003. Print.

"Equatorial Guinea." CIA World Factbook. n.d. Web. 15 Dec. 2013.

Fall, Marouba. *Chaka ou le Roi visionnaire.* Dakar: Les Nouvelles Éditions Africaines, 1984. Print.

Falola, Toyin. *Nationalism and African Intellectuals.* Rochester: University of Rochester Press, 2001. Print.

───, and Charles Thomas. *Securing Africa: Local Crises and Foreign Interventions.* New York: Routledge, 2013. Print.

Fanon, Frantz. *Les damnés de la terre.* Paris: François Maspero, 1961. Print.

───. *Peau noire, masques blancs.* Paris: Éditions du Seuil, 1952. Print.

Ferrington, Gary. "Audio Design: Creating Multi-Sensory Images For The Mind." *Journal of Visual Literacy* 14.1 (1994): 61–7. Print.

Finnegan, Ruth. *Oral Literature in Africa.* Oxford: Clarendon Press, 1970. Print.

───. *Oral Poetry: Its Nature, Significance and Social Context.* Bloomington: Indiana University Press, 1992. Print.

───. *The Penguin Book of Oral Poetry.* London: Penguin Books, 1978. Print.

Fiorio, Elisa. "Orality and Cultural Identity: The Oral Tradition in Tupuri (Chad)." *Museum International* 58.1/2 (2006): 68–75. Print.

Fisher, Max. "9 Questions about South Sudan You Were Too Embarrassed to Ask." *Washington Post* 30 Dec. 2013. n. pag. Web. 14 Jan. 2014.

Foucault, Michel. *The History of Sexuality, Volume 1: An Introduction*. Trans Robert Hurley. New York: Vintage, 1980. Print.

Fraser, Robert. *West African Poetry: A Critical History*. Cambridge: Cambridge University Press, 1986. Print.

Frick, Janari. *History: Learner's Book*. Capetown: New Africa Books, 2006. Print.

Gates, Henry Louis, Jr. "Criticism in the Jungle." In *Black Literature and Literary Theory*. New York: Routledge, 1990: 1–24. Print.

_____, and Karen C.C. Dalton. "Josephine Baker and Paul Colin: African American Dance Seen through Parisian Eyes." *Critical Inquiry* 24.4 (1998): 903–34. Print.

Gauvin, Lise. *L'Écrivain francophone à la croisée des langues*. Paris: Karthala, 1997. Print.

"Gaze," *Art & Popular Culture*. Artandpopularculture.com. n.d. Web. 19 Dec. 2013.

Gbanou, Sélom Komlan. "Dramatic esthetics in the work of Senouvo Agboto Zinsou." *Research in African Literatures* 29.3 (1998): 34–57. Print.

_____. *Un théâtre au confluent des genres: L'écriture dramatique de Senouvo Zinsou*. Frankfurtam Main: IKO-Verlag für Interkulturelle Kommunikation, 2002. Print.

Gbénouga, Dossou Martin. *Le Concert Party: Analyse structurale et fonctionnelle*. Lomé-Togo: Université de Bénin, 1993. Print.

Genet, Jean. *Les Nègres*. Lyon: Décines, 1958. Print.

Genette, Gérard. *Figures III*. Paris: Seuil, 1972. Print.

_____. *Figures of Literary Discourse*. Trans. Alan Sheridan. New York: Columbia University Press, 1982. Print.

Gérard, Albert. *Four African Literatures: Xhosa, Sotho, Zulu, Amharic*. Essex: Longman, 1981. Print.

_____. "Relire Chaka: Thomas Mofolo, ou les oublis de la mémoire francaise." *Politique Africaine* 13 (1984): 8–20. Print.

Gimenez, Martha. "The Politics of Exile: Class, Power, and the 'Exilic.'" 2003. Web. 12 Dec. 2013.

Glissant, Édouard. *Le Discours antillais*. Paris, Gallimard, 1997. Print.

_____. *L'Intention poétique* (Poétique II). Paris: Éditions du Seuil, 1969. Print.

_____. *Poétique de la Relation* (Poétique III). Paris: Gallimard, 1990. Print.

_____. *Traité du Tout-Monde*. Paris, Gallimard, 1997. Print.

"'Go well Madiba'—Mandela funeral quotes." *Times Live* 16 Dec. 2013. Web. 2 Jan. 2014.

Gramsci, Antonio. *Quaderni Del Carcere*. vol. 2. Torino: Giulio Einaudi, 1975. Print.

Gray II, Richard J. "Beyond the Margins: Identity Fragmentation in Visual Representation in Michel Tournier's *La Goutte d'or*." *Text Matters* 2.2 (2012): 250–63. Print.

_____. "The Monomyth: Re-reading Camara Laye's *L'Enfant noir* as The Quest of the Hero." University of Kentucky. 66th Kentucky Foreign Languages Conference, Lexington, KY. 19 Apr. 2013. Conference Presentation.

_____. *The Performance Identities of Lady Gaga: Critical Essays*, ed. Jefferson, N.C.: McFarland, 2012. Print.

_____. "Sexual Politics: Mapping the Body in Marguerite Duras's *L'Amant*." *Romanica Silesiana* 8:1 (2013): 273–283. Print.

Gutting, Gary. *Thinking the Impossible: French Philosophy Since 1960*. Oxford: Oxford University Press, 2011. Print.

Hale, Thomas and Aïssata G Sidikou. *Women's Voices from West Africa: An Anthology of Songs from the Sahel*. Bloomington: Indiana University Press, 2012. Print.

Hamilton, Carolyn. *Terrific Majesty: The Powers of Shaka Zulu and the Limits of Historical Invention*. Cambridge: Harvard University Press, 1998. Print.

Harlow, Barbara. *Renaissance Literature*. London: Methuen, 1987. Print.

Harrison, Nicholas. *Postcolonial Criticism: History, Theory and the Work of Fiction*. Cambridge: Polity, 2003. Print.

Herder, Johann Gottfried. "Treatise on the Origin of Language." In *Herder: Philosophical Writings*. Michael Forster, ed. Cambridge University Press, 2002. Print.

Hérubel, Jean-Pierre V.M. "Observations of an Emergent Specialization: Contemporary French Cultural History." *Journal of Scholarly Publishing* 10 (2010): 216–40. Print.

Hitchcott, Nicki. "Entretien avec Tanella Boni." *ASCALF Bulletin* 10 (1995): 3–13. Print.

———. *Women Writers in Francophone Africa*. New York: Berg, 2000. Print.

Hoffer, Peter. *The Historians' Paradox: The Study of History in Our Time*. New York: New York University Press, 2008. Print.

Hollier, Denis. *A New History of French Literature*. Cambridge: Harvard University Press, 1994. Print.

Hollis, James. *Tracking the Gods: The Place of Myth in Modern Life*. Toronto: Inner City Books, 1995. Print.

hooks, bell. *Black Looks: Race and Representation*. Boston: South End Press, 1992. Print.

Hourantier, Marie-José and Werewere Liking. *Spectacles rituels*. Lomé: Éditions Haho, 1987. Print.

Hyppolite, Jean. *Genesis and Structure of Hegel's* Phenomenology of Spirit. Trans. Samuel Cherniak and John Heckman. Evanston: Northwestern University Press, 1974. Print.

Irele, Abiola. "The African Imagination." *Research in African Literatures* 21.1 (1990): 49–67. Print.

Jaccard, Anny-Claire. "Des textes novateurs." *Notre Librairie* 99 (1989): 155–61. Print.

Jacobs, Steven Leonard. "Language Death and Revival after Cultural Destruction: Reflections on a Little Discussed Aspect of Genocide." *Journal of Genocide Research* 7.3 (2005): 423–30. Print.

James, Joy, and Tracy Sharpley-Whiting, eds. *The Black Feminist Reader*. Malden: Blackwell, 2000. Print.

Jefferess, David, Julie McGonegal, and Sabine Milz. "The Politics of Postcoloniality." *Postcolonial Text* 2:1 Postcolonial.org 2006. Web. 10 Nov. 2013. Print.

Johnson, H.T. "The Black Man's Burden," *Voice of Missions*, VII (Atlanta: April 1899), 1. Rpt. in Willard B. Gatewood, Jr. *Black Americans and the White Man's Burden, 1898–1903*. Urbana: University of Illinois Press, 1975: 183–4. Print.

Johnson, Richard. *Orality and Performance Tradition in African Literature*. Harper College. n.d. Web. 10 Nov. 2013.

Johnson, John, Thomas Hale, and Stephen Belcher. *Oral Epics from Africa: Vibrant Voices from a Vast Continent*. Bloomington: Indiana University Press, 1997. Print.

Jones, Eldridge, Eustace Palmer and Marjorie Jones. *Oral and Written Poetry in African Literature Today*. Trenton: Africa World Press, 1989. Print.

Joseph, May. *Nomadic Identities: The Performance of Citizenship*. Minneapolis: University of Minnesota Press, 1999. Print.

Joyce, James. *Finnegans Wake*. New York: Viking Press, Inc., 1939. Print.

Julien, Eileen. "Reading 'orality' in French-language Novels from Sub-Saharan Africa." In *Francophone Postcolonial Studies: A Critical Introduction*. Charles Forsdick and David Murphy, eds. London: Edward Arnold, 2003: 122–32. Print.

Jung, Carl. *The Archetypes and the Collective Unconscious*. London: Routledge, 1959. Print.

Kâ, Abdou Anta. *Théâtre*. Paris: Présence Africaine, 1972. Print.

Kaschula, Russell H. "Imbongi and Griot: Toward a Comparative Analysis of Oral Poetics in Southern and West Africa." *Journal of African Cultural Studies* 12.1 (1999): 55–76. Print.

———, and Samba Diop. "Political Processes and the Role of the Imbongi and Griot in Africa." *South African Journal of African Languages/Suid-Afrikaanse Tydskrif vir Afrikatale* 20.1 (2000): 13–28. MLA International Bibliography. Web. 13 Dec. 2013.

Kear, Jon. "Vénus noire: Josephine Baker and the Parisian Music-hall." In *Parisian Fields*. Ed. Michael Sheringham. London: Reaktion Books, 1996. Print.

Keaton, Trica D., T. D. Sharpley-Whiting, and Tyler E. Stovall, eds. *Black France/France noire: The History and Politics of Blackness.* Durham: Duke University Press, 2012. Print.

Killens, John Oliver. *Black Man's Burden.* New York: Pocket Books, 1969. Print.

Kittleton, Mary Lynn. *The Soul of Popular Culture.* Chicago: Open Court, 1998. Print.

Knipp, Thomas. "Radicalism and the Search for an African Literary Theory." In *African Literature Studies: The Present State/L'état présent.* Stephen Arnold, ed. Washington, D.C.: Three Continents Press (1985): 115–22. Print.

Konkobo, Christophe. "Dark Continent, Dark Stage: Body Performance in Colonial Theatre and Cinema." *Journal of Black Studies* 40:6 (2010):1094–1106.

Kouyaté, Seydou Badian. "Les Difficultés de la construction socialiste en Afrique." In *Afrique et politique*, ed. Maurice A. Lubin. Paris: La Pensée Universelle (1974): 129–33. Print.

———. *Sous l'orage, suivi de La Mort de Chaka.* Paris: Présence Africaine, 1972. Print.

Kristeva, Julia. *Powers of Horror: An Essay on Abjection.* New York: Columbia University Press, 1982. Print.

Lacan, Jacques. "Le stade du miroir. Théorie d'un moment structurant et génétique de la constitution de la réalité, conçu en relation avec l'expérience et la doctrine psychanalytique," Communication au 14e Congrès psychanalytique international (Marienbad). International Journal of Psychoanalysis (1937). Print.

Lamming, George. *The Pleasures of Exile.* London: Joseph, 1960. Print.

Larrier, Renée. *Francophone Women Writers of Africa and the Caribbean.* Gainesville: University Press of Florida, 2000. Print.

Leconte, Fabienne. *La Famille et les langues: Une étude sociolinguistique de la deuxième génération de l'immigration africaine dans l'agglomération rouennaise.* Paris: L'Harmattan, 1997. Print.

Levinson, André. "Danses nègres." *L'art vivant.* Feb. 1925: 115–6. Print.

Lévi-Strauss, Claude. *Myth and Meaning.* London: Routledge, 1978. Print.

Lewis, Cynthia. "At Last: What's Discourse Got to Do with It?'A Meditation on Critical Discourse Analysis in Literacy." *Research in the Teaching of English* 40.3 (2006): 373–9. Print.

Lusweti, Bramwell M. *The Hyena and the Rock: A Handbook of Oral Literature for Schools.* London: MacMillan, 1984. Print.

Mabana, Kahiudi Claver. "La réécriture francophone du mythe de Chaka: Éloge, demystification et interrogation." *Matatu-Journal for African Culture and Society* 31.32 (2005): 61–72. Print.

———. *Des transpositions francophones du mythe de Chaka.* Bern: Peter Long, 2002. Print.

Maduka, Chidi. "Formalism and the Criticism of African Literature: The Case of Anglo-American New Criticism." In *African Literature Comes of Age.* Ernest N Emenyonou and C.D. Narasimhaiah, eds. Mysore: Dhvanyahkaha, 1988: 185–200. Print.

Makward, Christine, and Odile Cazenave. "The Other's Others: 'Francophone' Women and Writing." *Yale French Studies* 75 (1988): 190–207. Print.

Makward, Edris. "Two Griots of Contemporary Senegambia." In *The Oral Performance in Africa.* Ed. Isidore Okpewho. Ibadan: Spectrum Books (1990): 23–41. Print.

Mandela, Nelson. *Long Walk to Freedom: The Autobiography of Nelson Mandela.* Boston: Little Brown, 1994. Print.

———. "Statement in the Rivonia Trial, Pretoria Supreme Court," 20 Apr. 1964. Print.

Matateyou, Emmanuel. "Poésie orale traditionnelle et expression du quotidien en Afrique noire." *Francographies* (1996): 57–79. Print.

Mazuri, Ali. "The Language of 'Francophonie' and the Race of the Renaissance: A Commonwealth Perspective." *Africa Beyond the Post-Colonial: Political and Socio-Cultural Identities.* Ola Uduku and Alfred B. Zack-Williams, eds. Aldershot: Ashgate, 2004: 50–65. Print.

———. "The Resurrection of the Warrior Tradition in African Political Culture." *The Journal of Modern African Studies*. 13.1 (1975): 67–84. Print.

———, and Mazrui, Almin. *The Power of Babel: Language and Governance in the African Experience*. Chicago: University of Chicago Press, 1998. Print.

M'Baye, Alioune. "La Réhabilitation des héros noirs dans le theâtre négro-africain d'espression française." Ma thesis. Université Cheikh Anta Diop, 1976. Print.

M'Bokolo, Elikia. "Le panafricanisme au 21ème siècle." *La diaspora africaine*. Spec. Issue of *Tribune culturelle panafricaine* 13 (printemps 2006): 7. Print.

Mernissi, Fatima. *Doing Daily Battle: Interviews with Moroccan Women*. New Brunswick: Rutgers University Press, 1989. Print.

Midiohouan, Guy. "Le Théâtre négro-africain d'expression française." *Peuples Noirs/Peuples Africains* 6.31 (1983): 54–78. Print.

Millet, Kate. *Sexual Politics*. Urbana-Champaign: University of Illinois Press, 2000. Print.

Mitrano, G.F. "The Photographic Imagination: Sontag and Benjamin." *Post Script* 26.2 (2007): 117–36. Print.

Mkiva, Zolani. "Poem for Mandela." In "Imbongi and Griot: Toward a Comparative Analysis of Oral Poetics in Southern and West Africa." Russell A. Kaschula. *Journal of African Cultural Studies* 12.1 (1999): 55–76. Print.

Mofolo, Thomas. *Chaka*. Trans. Daniel Kunene. London: Heinemann, 1987. Print.

Mohanty, Chandra Talpade, Ann Russo, and Lourdes Torres. *Third World Women and the Politics of Feminism*. Bloomington: Indiana University Press, 1991. Print.

Mongo-Mboussa, Boniface. *Désir d'Afrique*. Paris: Gallimard, 2002. Print.

Morel, Edmund D. *The Black Man's Burden: The White Man in Africa from the Fifteenth Century to World War I*. New York: Monthly Review Press, 1969. Print.

Morris, Donald R. *The Rise and Fall of the Zulu Nation*. New York: Simon and Schuster, 1965. Print.

Morrison, Donald, R. Mitchell, and J. Paden. *Black Africa: A Comparative Handbook*. New York: Paragon House, 1989. Print.

Mouralis, Bernard. *Littérature et développement: Essai sur le statut, la fonction et la représentation de la littérature négro-africaine d'expression française*. Paris: Éditions Silex, 1984. Print.

Moustapha, Baba. *Le Commandant Chaka*. Paris: Hatier, 1983. Print.

Mulvey, Laura. *Visual and Other Pleasures*. London: Macmillan, 1989. Print.

———. "Visual Pleasure and Narrative Cinema." *Screen* 16.3 (1975): 6–18. Rpt. in *Issues in Feminist Film Criticism*. Ed. Patricia Erens. Bloomington: Indiana University Press, 1990. Print.

Murphy, David. "Birth of a Nation? The Origins of Senegalese Literature in French." *Research in African Literatures* 39.1 (2008): 48–69. Print.

Nadjo, Léon. "Langue française et identité culturelle en Afrique francophone: Le cas de quelques écrivains." *Éthiopiques* 40–41.1/2 (1985): n. pag. Print.

Naïndouba, Maoundoé. *L'Étudiant de Soweto*. Paris: Hatier, 1981. Print.

Ndiaye, A. Raphaël. "La notion de parole chez les Sereer, Sénégal." Diss. Université de Paris, 1981. Print.

N'Diaye, Ibrahim. *Théâtre et société en Afrique noire 'francophone.'* Diss. Université Cheikh Anta Diop, 1979. Print.

Ndulo, Muna. "The Democratization Process and Structural Adjustment in Africa." *Indiana Journal of Global Legal Studies* 10:1 (2003): 315–68. Print.

"Nelson Mandela Memorial: President Barack Obama's Speech in Full." CNN.com. *CNN* 10 Dec. 2013. Web. 10 Dec. 2013.

Nénékhaly-Camar, Condetto. *Continent-Afrique, suivi de Amazoulou*. Paris: P.-J. Oswald, 1970. Print.

"New Documentary Tells The Story Of J.D. Salinger's Life." *NPR*. 9 Sept. 2013. Web. 9 Sept. 2013.

Ngara, Emmanuel. *Ideology and Form in African Poetry: Implication for Commu-

nication. London: James Currey, 1990. Print.
Niane, Djibril Tamsir. *Sikasso ou la Dernière citadelle, suivi de Chaka*. Paris: P.-J. Oswald, 1971. Print.
Nkashama, Pius Ngandu. *Ruptures et écritures de violence*. Paris: L'Harmattan, 1997. Print.
———. *Théâtres et scènes de spectacles: Études sur les dramaturgies et les arts gestuels*. Paris: L'Harmattan, 1993. Print.
———. "Theatricality and Social Mimodrama." *Research in African Literatures* 30.4 (1999): 176–85. Print.
Nyatetu-Waigwa, Wangari wa. *The Liminal Novel: Studies in the Francophone African Novel as Bildungsroman*. New York, Peter Lang, 1996. Print.
Obama, Barack. "Let us pause and give thanks for the fact that Nelson Mandela lived—a man who took history in his hands and bent the arc of the moral universe toward justice." Facebook.com. 5 Dec. 2013. [5 Dec. 2013].
O'Brien, Michael. "Obama on Mandela: 'He no longer belongs to us; he belongs to the ages.'" *NBC News*. 5 Dec. 2013. Web. 9 Dec. 2013.
O'Byrne, Anne. "Learning a Strange Native Language." *Social Identities* 13.3 (2007): 307–23. Print.
Office of the Press Secretary. "Remarks by the President to the Ghanaian Parliament." *White House*, Whitehouse.gov. 11 Jul. 2009. Web. 10 Oct. 2013.
Offiong, Daniel A. "The Cheerful School and the Myth of the Civilizing Mission of Colonial Imperialism." *Pan-African Journal* 9.1 (1976): 35–54. Print.
Ojaide, Tanure. *Poetic Imagination in Black Africa*. Durham: Carolina Academic Press, 1996. Print.
Okon, Friday A. "Politics and the Development of Modern African Poetry." *English Language and Literature Studies* 3.1(2013): 94–110. Print.
Okpaku, Joseph. "African Cultural Standards for African Literature and the Arts." In *New African Literature and the Arts*. New York: T. Cromwell (1967): 52–63. Print.
Okpewho, Isidore. "African Poetry: The Modern Writer and the Oral Tradition." In Jones, D.J., Palmer, E. and Jones, M. *Oral and Written Poetry in African Literature Today*. London: Currey, 1989: 1–15. Print.
Okunoye, Oyeniyi. "The Critical Reception of Modern African Poetry (La réception critique de la poésie africaine moderne)." *Cahiers d'Études Africaines* 44.176 (2004): 769–91. Print.
Olaoluwa, Senayon S. "From the Local to the Global: A Critical Survey of Exile Experience in Recent African Poetry." *Nebula* 4.2 (2007): 223–52. Print.
Ong, Walter. *Orality and Literacy: The Technologizing of the Word*. New York: Methuen Press, 1985. Print.
Orlando, Valérie. "Writing New H(er)stories for Francophone Women of Africa and the Carribean." *World Literature Today* 75.1 (2001): 40–50. Print.
Palmeirim, Manuela. "Masks, Myths, Novels, and Symbolic Ambiguity." *African Arts* 41.3 (2008): 74–7. Print.
Panzacchi, Cornelia. "The Livelihoods of Traditional Griots in Modern Senegal." *Africa* 64.2 (1994): 190–210. Print.
Peacock, Alan. "Signs of Telling: Narrative Voice and the Interactive." Copenhagen: Copenhagen Business School, 2004. Print.
Pellowski, Anne. *The World of Storytelling*. New York: R.R. Bowker, 1977. Print.
Pennycook, Alastair and Sinfree Makoni. "The Modern Mission: The Language Effects of Christianity." *Journal of Language, Identity, and Education* 4.2 (2005): 137–55. Print.
Perez, Nissan. *Focus East: Early Photography in the Near East (1839–1885)*. New York: Abrams, 1988. Print.
Petit, Susan. *Michel Tournier's Metaphysical Fiction*. Philadelphia: Benjamins, 1991. Print.
Phillipson, Robert. *Linguistic Imperialism*. Oxford: Oxford University Press, 1992. Print.
———. *Linguistic Imperialism Continued*. New York: Routledge, 2010. Print.
"Pour une 'littérature-monde' en français." *Le Monde des livres, Le Monde*. Mar. 15, 2007. Web. 10 Sept. 2013.
"The Prisoner." *Frontline*. WGBH educa-

tional foundation. n.d. Web. 21 Nov. 2013.
Putnam, Michael T. "language island." Message to Richard J. Gray II. 3 Dec. 2013. E-mail.
Ricard, Alain. *Littérature d'Afrique noire*. Paris: CNRS/Karthala, 1995. Print.
———. *Naissance du roman africain; Félix Couchoro, 1900–1968*. Paris: Présence Africaine, 1987. Print.
"Richard-Toll." *Encyclopedia Britannica*. Web. 13 Dec. 2013.
Ridehalgh, Anna. "Some Recent Francophone Versions of the Shaka Story." *Research in African Literatures* 2.2 (1991): 135–52. Print.
Ritter. Ernst A. *Shaka Zulu: The Rise of the Zulu Empire*. London: Longmans, 1955. Print.
Rodney, Walter. *How Europe Underdeveloped Africa*. London: Bogle-L'Ouverture Publications, 1972. Print.
Rosello, Mireille. "Unhoming Francophone Studies: A House in the Middle of the Current." *Yale French Studies* 103 (2003): 123–32. Print.
Rosi, Mauro. "UNESCO and Languages: A Commitment to Culture and Development." *Museum International* 60.3 (2008): 8–13. Print.
Sahli, Kamal. *African Theatre for Development: Art for Self-Determination*. Exeter:Intellect, 1998. Print.
Said, Edward. *Orientalism*. New York: Vintage Books, 2005. Print.
———. *The Pen and the Sword, Conversations with David Barsamian*. Monroe: Common Courage Press, 1994. Print.
———. *Reflections on Exile and Other Essays*. Cambridge: Harvard University Press, 2000. Print.
———. "Yeats and Decolonization." *Nationalism, Colonialism and Literature*. Minneapolis: University of Minnesota Press, 1990. Print.
Saleh, Nadia. "Introduction: Subversive and Plural Perspectives in Re-Reading French and Francophone Women's Poetry." *Symposium: A Quarterly Journal in Modern Literatures* 53.4 (2000): 204–8. Print.
Sangare, Mahamadou. "Les langues locales et l'identité africaine." *L'identité culturelle* 2004. Web. 4 Dec. 2013.
Sauvage, Marcel. *Les mémoires de Joséphine Baker*. Paris: Dilecta, 2006. Print.
Schechner, Richard. *Between Theater and Anthropology*. Philadelphia: University of Pennsylvania Press, 1985. Print.
Schipper, Mineke. *Unheard Words: Women and Literature in Africa, the Arab World, Asia, the Caribbean, and Latin America*. New York: Allison & Busby, 1984. Print.
Sekyi-Otu, Ato. *Fanon's Dialectic of Experience*. Cambridge: Harvard University Press, 1996. Print.
Selden, Raman, Peter Widdowson, and Peter Booker, eds. *A Reader's Guide to Contemporary Literary Theory*. Harlow: Pearson Longman, 2005. Print.
Sembène, Ousmane. *Les bouts de bois de Dieu*. Paris: Présence Africaine, 1960. Print.
Senghor, Léopold Sédar. "Avant-Propos ou Comment être nègre en français?" *Le Sénégal écrit: Anthologie de la littérature sénégalaise d'expression française*. Ed. Gisela Bonn. Dakar: NEA, 1977. 7–10. Print.
———. *Éthiopiques*. Paris: Éditions du Seuil, 1956. Print.
———. *On African Socialism*. New York: Praeger Publishers, 1964. Print.
———. "Prière aux masques." *Chants d'ombre*. Paris: Éditions du Seuil, 1945. Print.
Serequeberhan, Tsenay. "Africa in a Changing World." *Monthly Review* 61.8 (2000): 26–38. Print.
Sévry, Jean. *Chaka Empereur des Zoulous: Histoire, Mythes et Légendes*. Paris: Éditions l'Harmattan, 1991. Print.
Shakespeare, William. *The Works of Shakespeare: Midsummer Night's Dream*. Ed. Henry Cunningham. London: Methuen and Co., 1905. Print.
Sieger, Jacqueline. "Entretien avec Aimé Césaire." *Afrique* 5 (1961): 64–7. Print.
Simpson, Andrew. *Language and National Identity in Africa*. Oxford: Oxford University Press, 2008. eBook.
Sontag, Susan. *On Photography*. London: Penguin, 1977. Print.
Spleth, Janice. "Narrating Ethnic Conflict in Zairian Literature." *Research in*

African Literatures. 29.1 (1998): 103–23. Print.

Spronk, Johannes M. "Chaka and the Problem of Power in the French Theater of Black Africa." *The French Review* 57.5 (1984): 634–40. Print.

Sultan, Yaëlle. *Le théâtre de Zinsou ou: Les voies de la comédie*. Bordeaux: Université Michel de Montaigne, 2000. Print.

Swanepoel, Christiaan. "African Languages and the Identity Question in the 21st century." *South African Journal of African Languages* 33.1 (2013): 19–28. Print.

_____. *African Literature: Approaches and Applications*. Pretoria: Kagiso, 1990. Print.

Talton, Benjamin. "1960s Africa in Historical Perspective: An Introduction." *Journal of Black Studies* 43.1 (2012): 3–10. Print.

Tchindjang, Mesmin, Athanase Bopda, and Louise Angéline Ngamgne. "Languages and Cultural Identities in Africa." *Museum International* 60.3 (2008): 37–50. Print.

Tempels, Placide. *Bantu Philosophy*. Paris: Présence Africaine, 1969. Print.

Thiher, Allen. "Jacques Derrida's Reading of Artaud: 'La Parole soufflée' and 'La Clôture de la représentation.'" *The French Review* 57.4 (1984): 503–8. Print.

Thomas, Dominic. "One Cultural Trauma and Ritual Re-membering: Werewere Liking's *Les mains veulent dire*." *New Francophone African and Caribbean Theatres*. John Conteh-Morgan, ed. Bloomington: Indiana University Press, 2010: 60–74. Print.

Thompson, Chantal P. and Elaine M. Phillips. *Mais Oui!* 4th ed. Boston: Cengage, 2010. Print.

Thompson, Leonard. "Cooperation and Conflict: The Zulu Kingdom and Natal." *The Oxford History of South Africa*. Vol 1. Monica Wilson and Leonard Thompson, eds. Oxford, Oxford University Press, 1975. Print.

Tournier, Michel. *La Goutte d'or*. Paris: Gallimard, 1986. Print.

Traoré, Fatoumata Diahara. "'Mother and I, We are Muslim Women': Islam and Postcolonialism in Mariama Ndoye's *Comme le bon pain* and Ken Bugul's *Cendres et braises*." Ma thesis. McGill University, 2005. Print.

Tsibinda, Marie-Léontine. *Une Lèvre naissant d'une autre: Poèmes*. Brazzaville: Heidelberg, 1984. Print.

Turner, Victor. *From Ritual to Theatre: The Human Seriousness of Play*. New York: PAJ Publications, 2001. Print.

Uduku, Ola and Alfred B. Zack-Williams, eds. *Africa Beyond the Post-Colonial: Political and Socio-Cultural Identities*. Aldershot: Ashgate, 2004. Print.

UNESCO. *Culture and Development: A Symbiotic Relationship*. Paris: UNESCO, 1994. Print.

U Tam'si, Tchicaya U. *Le Zulu, suivi de Vwene le fondateur*. Paris: Nubia, 1977. Print.

Veit-Wild, Flora and Alain Ricard. *Interfaces Between the Oral and the Written/Interfaces entre l'écrit et l'oral*. New York: Rodopi, 2005. Print.

Venn, Couze. *The Postcolonial Challenge: Towards Alternative Worlds*: London: SAGE Publications, 2006. Print.

Verhelst, Thierry. *No Life Without Roots: Culture and Development*. London: Zed, 1990. Print.

Vickers, Brian. *The Collected Critical Heritage I: William Shakespeare: The Critical Heritage Volume 3 1733–1752*, ed. London: Routledge, 1975. Print.

Volet, Jean-Marie. *L'Afrique écrite au féminin*. The University of Western Australia, 24 Dec. 1995. Web. 20 Dec. 2013.

wa Thiong'o, Ngũgĩ. *Decolonizing the Mind: The Politics of Language in African Literature*. London: Heinemann, 1986. Print.

_____. *Moving the Centre: The Struggle for Cultural Freedoms*. London: James Curry, 1993. Print.

Wauthier, Claude. *The Literature and Thought of Modern Africa: A Survey*. Trans. Shirley Kay. London: Pall Mall Press, 1966. Print.

Williams, Adebayo. "Literature in the Time of Tyranny: African Writers and the Crisis of Governance." *Third World Quarterly* 17.2 (1996): 349–62. Print.

Ysern-Borras, Eduardo. *The Colonized Personality: Frantz Fanon's Concept of the Psychology of People Living under Socio-Political Conditions of Colonialism.* Berkeley: Wright Institute, 1984. Print.

Zinsou, Senouvo Agbota. *On joue la comédie.* Lomé: In De Knipscher, 1975. Print.

Zongo, Opportune. "Nation-Building, Propaganda, and Literature in Francophone Africa." *Journal of Asian and African Studies* 40.1/2 (2005): 153–6. Print.

Zuberi, Tukufu. "A Perspective on Africa and the World." *Annals* 632 (2010): 1–5. Print.

Index

Abbaye de Thélème 50, 184
Abidjan 181
Académie Française 9, 44, 95, 97
aesthetics 12, 15, 43, 51–2, 57, 89, 91, 96, 110, 145, 157–8
African National Congress 85, 102, 133
africanité 11
Afrocentrism 91
al-Bashir, Omar 169
Algeria 35, 74–5
alliteration 66
Alsatian (language) 47
Amazoulou (play) 112, 117–8, 124
Les Amazoulous (play) 112
"L'ange déchu" (poem) 149–50
Anthologie de la nouvelle poésie nègre et malgache 97
anthropology 17, 19, 21, 32, 54, 62, 68, 113–4, 142, 159–60, 166
apartheid 55–7, 89, 124, 128, 130–3, 150, 174
Arab Peninsula 28
assassination 13, 86, 114, 117, 120, 129–30
assimilation 11, 48–9, 74, 113, 148, 185
assonance 66
audience 3, 10, 12, 19, 52–3, 55–6, 65–6, 68–9, 73, 81, 89, 109, 111, 128, 131, 133, 156, 158, 160, 186

Bâ, Mariama 136, 149
Baker, Josephine 3, 14, 155–64, 187–8
Bantu (people) 128–9
Barthes, Roland 108–9, 147
Baudelaire, Charles 154–6
Baudrillard, Jean 162
Beckett, Samuel 52, 184
Belgium 33, 38–9, 182
Benin 6, 31, 42, 62, 149–50, 153, 181–3
Beyala, Calixthne 136
Bhabha, Homi 10, 48

Black Comedy 50–2, 56
Black Man's Burden 8, 31, 38–40, 186
The Black Man's Burden 40
blanchissement 92, 185
bloodlust 129, 132
Bobo-Bioulasso 32
Boni, Yanella 136
Les bouts de bois de Dieu 154
Brazzaville 118, 182–3
Brecht, Bertolt 56
Breton (language) 47, 76, 183
Bugul, Ken 149
Burke, Peter 20–1
Burkina Faso 6, 9, 32, 148, 183
Burundi 51, 105, 170
Butler, Judith 139

Cameroon 3, 6, 8, 11, 31, 49, 63, 100, 103–5, 127, 136, 141, 143, 149–53, 183, 187
Campbell, Joseph 12, 106–7
capitalism 16, 19, 25, 29, 40, 128
Caribbean 10, 137
castration complex 140
The Catcher in the Rye 43
Central African Republic 99, 150, 170, 183
Centre Pompidou 96
Césaire, Aimé 11, 44, 50, 56, 96, 115
Chad 31, 59, 125, 130, 150, 170
Chaka (1940) 112–3, 121–2, 186
Chaka (1971) 112, 118
"Chaka" (poem) 112–5
Chaka ou le roi visionnaire
Chants d'ombre 97, 154
Chartier, Roger 21–2
"Le chevelure" (poem) 154–6
Christianity 34, 37, 42, 100, 102, 123
civil war 5, 25, 86, 171
civilization 1, 8–9, 12, 16, 20, 22–3, 34, 36, 38–9, 74, 82–3, 106, 121, 142

Cixous, Hélène 146, 187
Le club 50–1
Cold War 26, 125, 128–9, 173
colonialism 6–11, 15, 22–6, 28–9, 32–5, 37–8, 42, 44, 48, 50, 61, 63, 76–7, 82, 89–92, 94–6, 98–100, 113–4, 128, 157, 159, 166, 171, 184
colonized individual 5, 8, 10, 23–5, 28, 33, 35–7, 40, 46–50, 58, 61, 75, 81, 97–100, 115, 138, 163, 184
colonizer 5, 10, 23, 36–7, 45, 48–9, 61, 75, 78, 81, 115, 127, 138, 148, 163
Le Commandant Chaka (play) 125–8
commitment 43–5, 87, 103, 173
commodification 33, 78, 157, 162
Conakry 32, 117
concert party 51–4, 56, 60, 110, 130, 133, 186
Condé, Maryse 44, 178, 183
corruption 8, 28, 40, 86, 99, 118, 122, 170
Côte d'Ivoire 6, 31–2, 42, 73, 143, 150, 181, 183
Council of Berlin 9, 14, 25, 33, 37, 86, 148
Coups de Pillon 100, 123
Cours de linguistique générale 59
"Cradle of Mankind" 5, 23, 69, 76, 96, 171
cultural history 2, 4, 15, 18–22, 25, 46, 49, 61, 69, 75, 83, 112, 120, 137, 166, 183
cultural object 18–9, 58–9, 137, 163, 187

Dadié, Bernard 6, 171, 181
Dahomey 42, 181
Dakar 32, 87, 96, 181
Dakeyo, Paul 3, 6, 11, 100–1, 103–5, 149, 171, 185–6
Damas, Léon 96
Les damnés de la terre 24, 33, 133
dance 3, 43, 51–2, 149, 151, 154–60, 162
Darfur 26, 169–70
"Dark Continent" 5, 7, 9, 23, 38–9, 42, 94, 113
"The Death of the Author" 147
de Beauvoir, Simone 146, 186
Déclaration des Droits de l'Homme et du Citoyen 34
decolonization 33, 115–6; *see also* independence
Decolonizing the Mind (1986) 16, 61
Deconstruction 74–5, 146
Deleuze, Gilles 139
Democratic Republic of the Congo 150, 182
Derrida, Jacques 10, 47, 73–8, 80–1, 164, 184–5
Diagne, Oumar 104
dialectic 7, 10, 36–7, 137–8, 164, 187

diaspora 16, 28, 89, 93–5, 98, 167
Diawara, Manthia 10, 81, 114, 185
Diderot, Denis 34
diegesis 67
diglossia 79–80
Diop, David 6, 11, 99–100, 123, 154, 171
Diop, Samba 71, 115
Dioula (language) 9, 32
Discours sur le colonialism 50
discourse 3, 16, 41, 43, 48, 50, 53, 59, 62, 69, 75, 89, 92, 108, 137–8, 151–2
disease 5, 25–6, 39, 93, 153, 169, 171, 175
displacement 93–4, 98; *see also* diaspora
diversity 15, 28, 32, 70, 82, 91, 167, 183
Djibouti 37
Duval, Jeanne 154

economics 15, 137
education 9, 14, 37, 48, 61–3, 65, 85, 97, 138, 141, 143, 153
Egypt 7, 26, 96, 148
elite 8, 45, 48, 64, 80, 86, 99, 118, 125, 127, 171, 182
England 102, 182; *see also* Great Britain
Enlightenment 8–9, 22, 34, 38
Epic of Sundiata 123
essence 11, 16, 34, 43, 55, 63, 77–8, 140, 161–3
Ethiopia 37, 86, 102
Éthiopiques 97, 112, 114–5, 124
ethnicity 1, 8–9, 16, 32, 34–8, 50, 86, 90, 92, 99, 106, 148–9, 166–7, 170, 183
ethnography 11, 20, 70, 82
L'Étudiant de Soweto 130
Ewe 52–3
exoticism 41, 45, 154–9, 161, 166

Faidherbe, Louis Léon César 31
Fall, Aminata Sow 136, 141, 149
Fall, Marouba 128
famine 5, 15, 25–6, 28, 93, 129, 169, 171
Fanon, Frantz 10, 24, 33, 35–6, 44, 64, 98, 127, 132–3, 185
female body 13, 100, 139–40, 154–9, 187
The Feminine Mystique 140
"feminine space" 14, 136
feminine writing 141, 146–7, 187
"femme noire" (poem) 100, 149, 154
feudal system 25, 43
"First World" 27
Les Fleurs du Mal 154–5
"focalisation zéro" 68
folktales 43, 53, 58, 71, 117, 123, 141, 181–2
fourth wall 52–3, 56, 131
France 3, 6, 9, 11, 13, 18, 23, 28, 33–4,

Index

37, 40, 42, 44, 47–9, 51, 76, 81, 94, 96, 113, 127, 143, 148, 159–61, 163, 166–8, 184–6
francité 48, 161, 184
Franco-Prussian War 35, 37
Francophonie 17, 44–5, 97, 167
French (language) 1, 2, 4–10, 17, 20, 40, 44–8, 61, 63, 74–6, 79–81, 85, 114, 120, 125, 136, 146–7, 171, 182, 184, 186
French settlers 9, 32, 39, 41, 113
Friedan, Betty 139–40, 146

Gabon 152, 183
Gandhi, Mahatma 4
Garden of Eden 23, 50
Gaugin, Paul 157
Gbehanzin (King) 42
gender 6, 13–4, 19, 34, 71–2, 76, 137–9, 142–4, 146–9, 151–2, 168
Genet, Jean 131
genocide 15, 26, 28, 86, 169–70
geoculture 15, 29
geoeconomics 15
geopolitics 15
Germany 33
Ghana 25, 27, 31, 90, 98, 130
Glissant, Édouard 10, 44, 78–81, 155, 183
globalization 6, 14–6, 53, 91, 93, 98, 128, 165, 169, 171
Gorée Island 105
Great Britain 33, 38, 182
Great War of Africa 170
griot 11, 61, 65, 70–3, 82–3, 85–6, 92, 104, 117, 123, 141, 153, 184–5, 187
griotte 71–2, 83, 92, 141, 153, 187
Les Guérillères 144
Guèye, Mamadou 104
Guinea 6, 32–2, 40, 64, 87, 112, 117–8, 120, 134, 186
gynocriticism 146

Hegel, Georg Wilhelm Friedrich 27, 36
hegemony 11, 61, 159
hero 12–3, 51, 66, 70–3, 101, 105–9, 112–5, 118, 122–5, 132–4, 151, 175, 182
The Hero with a Thousand Faces 12, 106–7
hero's quest 12, 106–7
HIV/AIDS 175, 182
homophobia 142
hubris 13, 105, 117
Huis clos 145
humanitarianism 26, 34, 170–1
hybridity 10–1, 47–50
hyperreal 162
Hyppolite, Jean 65

ibota 62
identity 1, 10–1, 15, 19, 23, 41, 43–4, 46–50, 54, 58–9, 64, 73, 75, 78, 81–2, 87–8, 90, 92, 94, 100, 124, 131, 138–40, 146–9, 152, 160–5, 171, 183, 185, 188
ideology 23–4, 34–5, 38, 42, 57, 82, 84, 96, 98, 113–4, 116, 121–2, 137, 146–7, 168
imbongi 70
imperialism 8, 27, 42, 64, 95, 97, 128, 142, 184; *see also* colonialism
improvisational theatre 51–3, 55–6, 130
independence 2, 5–9, 13–4, 16–7, 22, 25, 28–9, 31, 33, 37, 40–1, 43, 46–7, 50, 73, 77–8, 81, 84–6, 89, 95–7, 99, 113, 115–6, 118, 120–1, 124–5, 127, 137–8, 151, 170–1, 181–4
intervention (United States) 26, 171
Irigaray, Luce 146
Islam 32, 34, 143, 169, 185

Joan of Arc 113
Jung, Carl 107–8

Ka, Abou Anta 112
kantata 51–2
Kennedy, John F. 173
Kenya 16, 37, 46–7, 63, 90, 105, 182
Kidjo, Angélique 153
Kierkegaard, Søren 27
Kikuyu (language) 47, 64
King, Martin Luther, Jr. 4, 105, 173
Kipling, Rudyard 8, 38
Kondo le requin 7
Kotéba 111
Kouyaté, Seydou Badian 7, 58, 112, 116, 124, 171
Kristeva, Julia 138–40, 146

Lacan, Jacques 140, 164, 188
Lagos 51
"langage" 79
"language torment" 80
"langue" 79–80
Le Clézio, Jean-Marie Gustave 44, 183
Leopold II (King) 39
Lévi-Strauss, Claude 12, 21, 108
Une Lèvre naissant d'une autre: Poèmes 124, 150
Libya 26
lifeblood 1, 5, 165
Liking Gnepo, Werewere 6–7, 14, 136, 143–5, 149–52, 171
liminality 10, 17, 107, 128
"linguistic imperialism" 73–4
literary canon 14–5, 45–7, 50, 60, 75, 136, 141, 144–5, 166, 168

littérature-monde en français 44–5, 168, 171, 184
The Location of Culture 10
London 55, 102, 131
Le Louvre 19

"Ma mère" (poem)
Machel, Graça 173
macroculture 84, 124, 138, 165
Madagascar 7, 187
Madiba 102, 173–6; *see also* Mandela, Nelson
Maghreb 6, 28, 105, 187–8
Les mains veulent dire 145, 150–2
"male gaze" 14, 140, 187
Mali 6, 10, 31–2, 37, 64, 81, 90, 111–3, 116–7, 120, 123–4, 134, 153, 163, 183
Mandela, Nelson 3–4, 71, 73, 84–5, 100–5, 133, 149–50, 173–6, 181, 185
Mandela, Nkosi Mphakanyiswa Gadla 102
Mandela, Winnie 149–50
Manifest Destiny 23
marabout 185
marginalization 2, 6, 8, 14, 27, 41, 44–5, 47, 89, 91, 93, 95, 119, 135–8, 147, 150, 160, 162–4, 166–7, 169, 187
marriage 153
Martinique 44, 73, 96, 184
Marxist criticism 91
master-slave dialectic 36
Mauritania 31, 104
M'Bana Diop, Haja 10–1, 71, 84–5
M'Baye d'Erneville 141, 149
Mbezele, Félicité 149
media 18–9, 41, 112, 142, 157, 161, 168–9
microculture 84, 124, 138, 165
Midiohouan, Thécla 149–50
A Midsummer Night's Dream 65–6, 184
migration 93, 98, 121, 167; *see also* diaspora
Millet, Kate 137, 139, 146
mirror stage 140, 164
misogynism 137, 143–4
"mission civilisatrice" (civilizing mission) 22–3, 34–8, 42, 159–60, 168
Mkiva, Zolani 84, 185
modernization 40, 128
Mofolo, Thomas 112, 117, 121–3, 128–9, 132, 134, 186
Le Monde 44, 166
Le monolingualisme de l'autre ou la prothèse d'origine 47, 73, 75–8, 80
monomyth 12, 106–7, 182
Monsieur Mandela 101, 102, 103, 149, 186
Mooré (language) 9
morality 3, 20, 42, 65, 105, 123, 165, 173, 175

Morel, Edmund Dene 38–9
Morocco 181
La Mort de Chaka 7, 112, 116, 124
Moundo, Élisabeth Éwombè 149
Moustapha, Mahamat Baba 125–8, 134, 186
Mouvement de libération des femmes 13
multiculturalism 106, 128
Mulvey, Laura 140, 156, 186
Musée de l'Homme 157, 187
Musée du Quai Branly 4, 19, 158, 187
music 11, 18–9, 43, 51–2, 65–6, 153, 155, 158, 167
Mutanga, Gédéon Kyungu 170
myth 7, 11–3, 58, 105–15, 120, 124, 128, 134, 169, 181–2, 186
Myth and Meaning 12, 108
myth criticism 11–2, 107
"Myth of Shaka" 2, 3, 11–3, 109, 111–2, 120, 134, 169

Naïndouba, Maoundoé 130, 132
national literature 46–8, 90
nationalism 33–5, 44, 46, 49, 51, 75, 78, 94–5, 121–2, 127, 165, 167
native language 5, 16, 59, 63–4, 80, 185
N'Diaye, Ibrahim 121, 124
Les Nègres 131
"Négritie" (poem) 150
Négritude 11, 14, 16, 24, 43, 45, 48, 89, 95–100, 121, 136, 168
Nénékhaly.Camar, Condetto 112, 117–8, 124
neocolonialism 11, 14, 16, 37, 77, 86, 90–1, 95–6, 98, 116, 125, 134, 163, 183–4
New York 55, 59, 156
Niane, Djibril Tamsir 112, 118
Niger 153, 183
Nigeria 51, 62, 69, 86, 90
9/11 15, 45, 110
Nkashama, Pius Ngandu 103–4, 110–1, 185–6
Nobel Prize 44, 101
Notre fille ne se mariera pas 49, 127
novel 1, 6, 12, 43–5, 47, 69, 99, 104, 106, 112, 128, 136, 143–4, 147, 149–50, 153, 164, 182, 184, 187

Obama, Barack 3, 25, 27, 105, 173, 181–2, 188
Obama, Michelle 175
objectification 41, 160, 163
On joue la comédie 50–1, 54–7, 112, 130–1, 133, 186
ontology 78, 95
oppression 10, 33–4, 36, 85, 94, 103–4,

128, 131–3, 143, 151, 163, 170, 173–4, 182; *see also* subjugation
oral literature 5, 7, 46, 60–1, 66, 69–70, 73, 154, 187
orality 58–61, 72, 82–3, 165
organic literature 16, 55, 70, 73, 88–9, 143, 171
"Orientalism" 10, 41, 160
"Other" 10, 41, 64, 73, 94–5, 159–60, 164
Oyônô-Mbia, Guillaume 8, 49, 127

Pan-Africanism 43–4
Paris 3–4, 19, 51, 55, 81, 95–6, 103, 123, 156–8, 163, 183–4, 186–7
parody 56, 131, 162
patriarchy 109, 111, 137, 139, 141, 145
Peau noire, masques blancs 35, 64, 132, 185
performance 12, 17, 51–3, 55–6, 61, 65, 67, 70–3, 98, 109–11, 126, 131–2, 139, 150, 155–60, 162, 188
personification 107, 154, 162
phoneme 65
photography 108, 156, 161–4, 187–8
Picard (language) 47
Pliya, Jean 7, 181–2
poetic literature 1–3, 5–9, 11, 14, 16–8, 20, 22, 44, 60, 65, 67, 69, 76, 109, 122, 136–9, 145–6, 151, 171, 184, 187
Poétique de la relation 78–9
polygamy 13, 143
postcolonial studies 10, 16, 41, 152, 160
postcolonialism 16, 22, 24, 50, 55, 57, 63, 76, 98, 116, 164, 166
postmodernism 74, 162
poverty 26, 129, 153, 169, 175
The Power of Myth 12, 106
praise poetry 104, 185
"prior-to-first language" 76–8
propaganda 34–5, 49, 113, 126
psyche 10, 24, 34, 108, 147
Pulaar (language) 47
Pygmalion 82, 159

Rabelais, François 50, 184
race 1, 10, 24, 35, 95, 142, 146–50, 159–60, 167, 173, 187
racism 35, 40, 96, 103, 137, 142
reception 12, 46, 61, 92, 109
religion 32, 37, 56, 110, 167
representation 14, 41–3, 45, 48, 55, 67, 71, 99, 109, 113, 134, 138, 140, 142, 154, 157, 159–61, 164, 186–7
Republic of Congo 6–7, 170, 183
reverse anthropology 114
"La Revue nègre" 156–9, 161–2
rhyme 6, 65–6

Ritter, Ernst 123
ritual 51–2, 131, 150, 152–3
Robben Island 101
Rolihlahla 102, 104
Romanticism 143, 155, 159
Rouch, Jean 113–4
Rouch in Reverse (1995) 81
Rousseau, Jean-Jacques 34
Rwanda 26, 170

Sahara Desert 31–2, 64, 188
Sahel 31
Said, Edward 10, 22–4, 27, 41, 64, 94–5, 152, 159–60
Saint-Louis (Senegal) 32
Salinger, J.D. 43
Samory Touré (King) 42
Sangaré, Oumou 153
Sareer (language) 47
Sartre, Jean-Paul 97, 133, 145
satire 56
Saussure, Ferdinand de 59, 74, 164
scenic space 12, 109
Schérer, Jean 51
"Scramble for Africa" 9, 33
Sembène, Ousmane 154
semiotics 59, 67, 74, 164, 184
Senegal 1, 6–8, 10–1, 31–2, 42, 47–8, 63, 65, 70–2, 84–5, 90, 95, 97, 104, 112, 115, 120, 123–4, 134, 136, 141, 143, 149–50, 153–4, 181, 183, 185–6
Senghor, Léopold Sédar 1, 6–8, 11, 24–5, 48, 71, 84–5, 95–100, 112, 114–16, 119, 124, 141, 149, 154, 171
Senzangkhona (King) 121
sexual politics 14, 137–8
sexuality 19, 36, 137–40, 153, 156
Shaka Zulu (King of the Zulu) 2, 71, 109, 111, 114–6, 120–2
Shaka Zulu (mini-series) 123
Shaka Zulu: The Rise of the Zulu Empire 123
Shakespeare, William 17, 65–6, 122, 184
Showalter, Elaine 146
Sidibé, Sali 153
"signified" 59, 147, 164
"signifier" 59
simulacra 156, 162
slavery 5, 25, 32–3, 38–9, 64, 82, 159
social media 3, 19, 105
society 6, 9, 12–3, 18–20, 32, 34–6, 39, 41, 50, 52, 54–5, 59, 61, 66, 70, 85, 87, 95–6, 103, 106–8, 110–1, 119, 125, 138–9, 141–2, 147, 151, 153, 165, 171, 174
sociology 19, 21
Somalia 26, 37
Somaliland 181

sound 11, 52, 65–7
South Africa 3, 28, 55–6, 65, 84–5, 89–90, 101–3, 105, 123–4, 128, 130–3, 148–50, 173–6, 182
"space of narration" 67, 139
spectacle 18, 52, 158; *see also* performance
spirituality 18, 41, 63, 107, 151, 163
stereotypes 27, 35, 41, 43, 131, 157, 159–61, 164
storytelling 61–2
structuralism 21, 74–5, 145
subjugation 8–10, 13, 22–4, 35, 37, 39, 41, 45, 63, 100, 115, 128, 137, 161, 166, 168, 175
sub–Saharan Africa 1, 8, 28, 34, 40, 61, 63, 88–9, 96, 106, 161, 184, 187–8
Sudan 26, 150, 159, 169–70, 194
Sundiata 123–4, 134

Tadjo, Véronique 136, 150
Tansi, Sony Labou 6–7, 152, 171, 182
Tchicaya, Gérald-Félix (Tchicaya U Tam'si) 6, 118–20, 171, 181–2
technology 49, 59, 91
television 18, 66, 123, 161, 169–70
terrorism 55–6
Théâtre des Champs Elysées 19, 156–7
Thiam, Anchou 10, 71
"Third World" 26–7, 142, 166, 187
tirailleurs sénégalais 42
Togo 6–8, 51–3, 56–7, 112, 120, 130, 183
La tortue qui chante suivie de La femme du blanchisseur et de Yévi au pays des montres 50–1, 53
Touré, Ahmed Sékou 64
trade 9, 32–3, 37, 39, 78, 93, 171
tradition 6, 9, 11–4, 16, 19–21, 23–5, 37–8, 46, 51–3, 56–64, 68–72, 74–7, 82–3, 85–92, 97, 104, 106–14, 120, 123, 127–8, 134–6, 139, 141–5, 150, 152–4, 161, 164, 166, 168, 181, 185
La tragédie du Roi Christophe 56, 115
tragic flaw 13, 35, 117, 129
translatio studii 58, 69, 120

tribal societies 9, 24, 38, 61–2, 82, 86, 114, 160
Troupe Nationale du Togo 51
Tsibinda, Marie-Léontine 123–4, 150

Ubuntu 175
Uganda 87, 170
UNESCO 183–5
unification 26, 37, 76, 111, 113–4, 121, 129, 132
Union Progressive Sénégalaise 85
United States 5, 20, 23, 25–7, 38, 81, 93–4, 96, 139–40, 143, 148, 157, 175, 184, 186, 188
Université de Paris 51, 96

"Les vautours" (poem) 100
verse 5, 66, 95, 100–1, 149
violence 10, 22–3, 33, 76, 100, 131, 170
Voltaire 27–8, 34

wa Thiong'o, Ngũgĩ 16, 46–7, 61, 63–4
war 5, 15, 25–6, 40, 44, 85–6, 90, 93, 109, 117, 119, 169–71, 175
Washington, D.C. 25
Wasoulou 42
Weep Not, Child 47
"White Man's Burden" 8–9, 34, 38
Wittig, Monique 144
Wolof (language) 47, 71, 104
world literature in French 8, 44–5; *see also* *littérature-monde en français*
World War I 113, 158–60, 173
World War II 13, 26, 39–40, 96, 130
woyi céét 153
woyi njam 153
woyi tëddëte 153

Zimbabwe 90, 105
Zinsou, Nstor Sénoufo 112
Zinsou, Senouvo Agbota 6–8, 50–7, 130–4, 171, 184, 186
Le Zulu (play) 112, 118–9
Zulu Kingdom 111, 118, 121–2, 128–9

www.ingramcontent.com/pod-product-compliance
Ingram Content Group UK Ltd.
Pitfield, Milton Keynes, MK11 3LW, UK
UKHW042004140426
5217IPUK00015B/966